Don Juan O'Brien

Don Juan O'Brien

An Irish adventurer in nineteenth-century South America

TIM FANNING

CORK UNIVERSITY PRESS

First published in 2020 by Cork University Press
Boole Library
University College Cork
Cork T12 ND89
Ireland

Library of Congress Control Number: 2019955526

British Library Cataloguing in Publication Data

A CIP catalogue record for this book is available from the British Library

ISBN: 978-1-78205-382-8

Typeset by Dominic Carroll, Ardfield, County Cork
Printed by BZ Graf, Poland

Cover image: *General O'Brien: Consul General of the Oriental del Uruguay.* Lithograph by Thomas Herbert Maguire, 1848. Courtesy of the National Library of Ireland.

www.corkuniversitypress.com

To Conor McEnroy, another Wicklow man in South America, with thanks

Contents

Acknowledgements

Many friends and acquaintances have contributed to this book, but none more so than Conor McEnroy, whose generous financial assistance enabled me to once again visit archives in South America. Over the course of many years Conor has shown a resolute commitment to strengthening the relationship between Ireland and Latin America by funding projects that deepen our understanding of its history.

Michael Lillis is another enthusiastic supporter of this project, and he gave me every encouragement during my research. I would also like to thank Ambassador Jackie O'Halloran in Buenos Aires and Justin Harman for their help, advice and support.

John O'Brien was a wanderer who spent his life travelling between Ireland and South America, and there are many historians, archivists, genealogists and relatives of O'Brien on both sides of the Atlantic who helped me with my research.

I am particularly grateful to Paul Gorry, who showed me some of the places in Baltinglass associated with O'Brien, and helped me trace family connections in the archives. His work on O'Brien's early life in west Wicklow has been invaluable. Dr Paul Caffrey, Susan Chadwick, John Cunningham, Paul Fanning and Chris Lawlor helped me track down information about O'Brien's Irish family and acquaintances. I would also like to thank the staff of the National Library of Ireland, the National Archives of Ireland, the library of Trinity College, Dublin, and the British National Archives in Kew.

In Chile I wish to thank Sergio García Valdés, a proud descendant of John O'Brien. He has a long-held interest in his ancestor and was exceedingly helpful when it came to answering my questions about his family. Fergal Morrin has carried out his own research into O'Brien's Chilean family; he supplied me with valuable material for the book. I also wish to thank the staff of the Archivo Nacional, Santiago, especially Pedro Gonzalez Cancino and Luis Martínez Tapia, and the Biblioteca Nacional de Chile.

In Argentina the staff of the Archivo General de la Nación and the Museo

Mitre gave me every assistance. I also wish to thank Jorge Fondebrider and Tomás Hudson for their most helpful advice.

In Peru I would like to thank the staff of the Archivo General de la Nación and the Biblioteca Nacional del Perú, and Percy Graham, who helped steer me through the archives in the Centro de Estudios Histórico Militares.

In Uruguay I wish to acknowledge the assistance of Laszlo Erdelyi and Gerardo Menéndez, who helped me with research in the archives in Montevideo.

As always I am deeply grateful to Jonathan Williams for his enthusiastic support for this project. I am also grateful to my copy-editor, Dominic Carroll, for his invaluable contribution to the book, and to Mike Collins and Maria O'Donovan of Cork University Press.

Finally, I would like to thank Annalisa and Chiara for their love, support and good humour.

Note About Translations

Translations of quotations from Spanish into English by the author are marked [*a.t.*] – i.e. author translation. The original Spanish quotations are included in the notes.

'Conocemos láminas i efijies del jeneral O'Brien que le representan en su sobrio traje de coronel, de uniforme de jeneral i a caballo, de pié en gran uniforme, tallado en mármol, grabado en láminas de batallas. En todas partes le encontramos, como *copia*, suspendido a algun hospitalario muro; pero al *orijinal*, vagando siempre por el ancho mundo, es casi imposible darle alcance.'

['We know engravings and portraits of General O'Brien in which he is depicted in his sober colonel's uniform, in his general's uniform on horseback, standing in a splendid uniform, worked in marble, captured in an engraving in battle. We find him everywhere, as a *copy*, suspended on some friendly wall; but the *original*, always wandering through the wide world, is almost beyond reach.' [*a.t.*]]

Benjamín Vicuña Mackenna, *El Jeneral O'Brien*
(Santiago, 1902)

Introduction: Revolutionary, entrepreneur, self-publicist

On 23 January 2017 the remains of John Thomond O'Brien were reinterred in the Argentine city of Mendoza during the commemorations of the bicentenary of General José de San Martín's crossing of the Andes, which led to the liberation of Chile from Spanish rule. Six members of the Argentine army, wearing the dark-blue uniforms and green-trimmed shakos of the *granaderos a caballo* (mounted grenadiers), escorted the bronze urn containing O'Brien's remains to its resting place at El Plumerillo on the outskirts of the city. The 240-kilogram urn, forged from melted-down cannons, was draped in Argentina's national flag.

The ceremony recognised O'Brien's contribution to the establishment of the republics of Argentina, Chile, Peru and Uruguay. O'Brien is one of the most significant Irish soldiers to have fought in the wars of independence in South America in the early nineteenth century.[1] He was certainly celebrated as such during his lifetime, in Ireland, the wider United Kingdom, continental Europe, and the South American republics for whose independence he fought. Not only did he serve as San Martín's principal aide-de-camp in Chile and Peru, he also made vital military interventions at Chacabuco and Maipú, the most important battles of the Chilean war.

While his involvement in the wars of independence is of undoubted interest, and was pivotal in determining the course of his later fortunes, O'Brien's multifaceted postwar career also offers revealing insights into post-independence South America, including the following: trade between Ireland and South America in the early years of the nineteenth century; the British merchant community in Chile and Peru in the early nineteenth century; the Irish community in Buenos Aires in the 1820s; efforts to introduce Irish immigrants to Argentina and Chile; scientific and commercial exploration in the Amazon and the Andes; foreign diplomacy in the River Plate in the 1840s and 1850s; and nation-building in the newly independent republics.

O'Brien's career also demonstrates the social, political and geographical mobility of a confident Irish Catholic middle class at the beginning of the nineteenth century. During both his revolutionary and post-revolutionary careers, O'Brien was in contact with members of the political and military elites in Europe and South America, including San Martín and Simón Bolívar (the leaders of the independence movement in South America), British prime ministers and foreign secretaries, the king of France, and the presidents of the newly established South American republics. He not only crossed the Atlantic at least fifteen times, he also covered thousands of kilometres during military, commercial and scientific expeditions across South America, including the most inhospitable terrain in the Amazon and the Andes.

His entrepreneurial career highlights both the opportunities and obstacles faced by foreign capitalists in postwar South America. Initial successes could often be reversed by the vagaries of a chaotic and unpredictable postwar politics. Foreign veterans such as O'Brien enjoyed benefits and privileges from the new regimes that replaced Spanish colonial rule, but, in turn, were also most susceptible to the jealousies and suspicions of former comrades-in-arms.[2] In O'Brien's case, at least three of his commercial enterprises failed to get off the ground or were deliberately destroyed as a consequence of political enmities. His unrelenting energy and enthusiasm helped him to meet these failures with optimism.

O'Brien epitomises the kind of capitalist explorer who first appeared in South America in the post-independence era, convinced that the continent could be transformed through the introduction of British capital, expertise and technology. He belonged to what Karen Racine has called 'a community of purpose', comprising the political and military elites of the new republics and the representatives of British manufacturing and trade, who shared the aim of winning South American independence and 'embarking upon a bright new era of freedom, happiness and material progress for their citizens'.[3] O'Brien worked a mining concession in Peru; brought a steam engine from the north of England for use in his Peruvian mine; had a sailing ship dismantled and hauled across the Andes in order to transport supplies across Lake Titicaca; embarked upon prospecting expeditions in Brazil and eastern Peru in the 1830s, 1840s and 1850s; imported expensive sheep breeds for use on his Uruguayan ranch; and promoted the idea to British investors of opening up South America's rivers to steamships.

He became a relentless self-publicist, burnishing his image as a virtuous veteran of the wars of independence in the British and Irish press. He took advantage of modern communications and transport, including newspapers and steamships, which were ushering in a wave of globalisation. O'Brien was acutely aware of his public image, and succeeded, mostly, in shaping it, becoming inseparable from South America in the public imagination. This image was designed to appeal to the appetite of a mass-market newspaper readership;[4] hence, the biographical sketches written about him in the late nineteenth and early twentieth centuries emphasise the romanticism of his military career rather than his contributions to, for example, Amazon exploration, commerce or international diplomacy.

Because of this celebrity, O'Brien was able, in turn, to shape the British and Irish public's image of South America in the mid-nineteenth century, not least through his efforts, over the course of almost forty years, to promote Irish emigration to the continent. He contributed significantly to the utopian conception of South America forged in the 1820s by the leaders of the small Irish community in Buenos Aires, who, while ready to exploit the commercial opportunities offered by independence, were uncertain about the ethos of the new republics and desirous of moral guidance from the Irish Catholic Church.

This Catholic utopia, which was to be found on the Argentine pampas, was empty, fertile and religiously tolerant, in direct contrast with the overpopulated homeland of the Irish emigrant. Of course, there was no mention of the inhabitants who already lived there: the indigenous tribes. Like his revolutionary contemporaries, O'Brien was able to revere the civilisation of the Incas, in Peru, while advocating the removal or destruction of their descendants if they proved an obstacle to his enterprises.

The glimpses of O'Brien to be found in the handful of biographical sketches that have appeared since his death have tended to create a caricature in the public memory: that of the loyal, gregarious Irish soldier beloved of the Victorian and Edwardian eras. O'Brien was keen to foster this image in order to reap the rewards that came from being a hero of the wars of independence. It also served the nationalist regimes of the late nineteenth century, who preferred to emphasise his Gaelic ancestry and the romantic elements of his military career, and to downplay his more troubling connections to British capital. However useful it proved at the time, this caricature reduces O'Brien to a bit player, forever in San Martín's shadow, and tends to obscure the other parts of his fascinating life and career. The narrative that follows, therefore, is an attempt to separate fact from fiction, to rescue O'Brien from his self-created myth.

1
King Cotton

If it had not been for cotton, John O'Brien would never have visited South America. The cotton boom of the late eighteenth century was the source of his family's prosperity. This was an age in which the global demand for cheap calicoes and chintzes was upsetting the centuries-old rhythms of rural life. The invention of mechanised devices – such as James Hargreaves' spinning jenny, Richard Arkwright's water frame, and Samuel Crompton's spinning mule – had turned a cottage industry into the greatest manufacturing phenomenon the world had ever seen. Brooding factories employing thousands of workers, many of them women and children working back-breaking hours in horrendous conditions, were thrown up in the formerly tranquil valleys of the north of England, earning vast profits for their owners and giving them newfound political clout. Artisans who had traditionally spun and woven cotton and linen in the family home were given the choice of moving to the mill or going hungry. Cotton was not just the latest fashionable fabric on the streets of London, it transformed Britain into an industrial society and solidified its position as a great power.

If the Industrial Revolution took Britain by storm, in Ireland it was more like a gentle summer breeze. During the 1780s, native and foreign entrepreneurs developed an Irish cotton industry, which became successful enough to frighten its competitors on the neighbouring island, before sinking into irrelevance by the middle of the nineteenth century. The industry's success more or less mirrored the period of Irish legislative independence. In 1782 long-established restrictions on the ability of the Irish parliament to enact laws were removed. For a few years Grattan's Parliament introduced financial measures to stimulate Irish industrial development. The parliament reflected the interests of the Protestant landowning class, which could see the financial benefits of subsidising the textile industry in Ireland by leasing land at high prices to manufacturers. During the 1780s the parliament introduced subsidies and protections for the textile industry, including punitive duties on imports.[1] These measures changed the landscape in and around Baltinglass in west Wicklow, John O'Brien's birthplace.

The second Earl of Aldborough, Edward Augustus Stratford, was the principal landowner in Baltinglass. Aldborough was not popular with his peers; they regarded him as pompous, touchy and eccentric. As a young man Aldborough spent much of his time in England, despite representing Baltinglass in the Irish House of Commons. He was also something of a spendthrift, blowing money on rare coins, medals, books and antiquities, and throwing expensive parties. In 1774 he was elected MP for Taunton in the British House of Commons, but was removed after being convicted of bribery. On the death of his father, he returned to Ireland to discover that his younger brothers had been dividing up the estate for themselves, which led to a long family feud. He did not just fight with his family, he also relished rows with friends and political rivals.[2]

Yet for all his youthful impetuosity, Aldborough was an intelligent, forward-thinking man. He had seen how mass textile manufacturing was transforming the English economy, and he returned to Ireland with new ideas, including that of turning west Wicklow into the Irish equivalent of Lancashire, the great manufacturing region of the north of England. In 1780 he built a factory, a mill and a village for the workers on a parcel of land beside the River Slaney. He incorporated his own family name (Stratford) into the place name, calling it Stratford-on-Slaney in a nod to Shakespeare's birthplace on the River Avon in Warwickshire. By the end of the century, Stratford-on-Slaney had become one of the most important centres of the textile industry in Ireland.

West Wicklow had several advantages for manufacturers. It had a plentiful supply of water from the rivers and streams flowing down the Wicklow Mountains. It was close to Dublin, with its merchants and port, but far enough removed from the disgruntled hand-weavers in the city whose livelihoods were being destroyed by mechanisation and who had taken to destroying factories and issuing sinister threats. One such outbreak of violence took place on 17 January 1810 when rioting weavers set fire to a warehouse containing finished cotton goods on Ardee Street in Dublin. As part of the same campaign, anonymous writers sent threatening letters to the main cotton merchants and manufacturers in the city. One letter accused the Dublin firm of O'Brien and Meade of 'bloodsucking the poor', and warned: 'We intend to do your business shortly as well as every manufacturer who sends work to the country while we are starving, for we won't let one escape, for we may as well Dye [*sic*] for Shooting you as for Burning you, we will do either shortly you may depend.'[3]

Aldborough had built the village and factory at Stratford-on-Slaney, but it was the Orr family that was responsible for turning it into a thriving business. The Orrs were textile manufacturers from Paisley in Scotland who had operated a lucrative business importing finished items into Ireland. When the Irish parliament introduced tariffs on imported calicoes in the 1780s, the Orrs had established a factory for weaving and bleaching muslins in Hillsborough, County Down. In the 1790s they leased the printing works and mill at Stratford, where they began calico weaving and printing, having invested £20,000 sterling (€23,208) in the facility.[4] By the 1830s they were employing about a thousand workers at the Stratford factory and manufacturing around two thousand finished items a week,[5] making them one of the largest producers in Ireland. The goods produced at Stratford were primarily for the Irish market, but the Orrs also exported to the burgeoning South American markets, and members of the extended family worked as agents in Buenos Aires, Lima and Santiago.[6]

The Orrs' success at Stratford may have encouraged the Bryan family. In 1785 Sylvester Bryan[7] was among the manufacturers based in Stratford-on-Slaney who were advertising their wares in the pages of the Dublin-based *Saunders's News-letter*. Business was brisk, and potential investors in the textile industry were advised that the village was expanding:

> Stratford upon Slaney is in the county of Wicklow, on the great Road from the Metropolis to Wexford and Waterford, and twenty-four Miles from Dublin, which Town will next Year consist of several Squares and a Number of Streets connecting them, formed of various priced houses, all slated and fitted up for Manufacturers or Merchants; a Spire Church and a Chapel will be also complete next Year; Markets and a Town Hall ...[8]

The Baltinglass-based genealogist Paul Gorry writes that the Bryan family were 'substantial landholders before Penal times and managed to retain much of their wealth throughout the eighteenth century' as John O'Brien's father, Martin, and his uncles were able to acquire substantial leases between 1789 and 1796.[9] They were members of the Catholic middle class who were emboldened to search for new commercial opportunities following the easing of the punitive laws that, for much of the eighteenth century, had restricted

Catholics from buying land, running for political office, or entering the professions.[10]

Martin Bryan is described as a merchant and shopkeeper in deeds related to properties in Baltinglass. He and his brother Laughlin held a substantial amount of property in the town from the Earl of Aldborough, leased shortly after the lifting of a ban in 1778 on Catholics taking long leases.[11] The exact nature of the business is unclear, but there is no doubt that the Bryan family was involved in the textile industry. Samuel Lewis' *Topographical Dictionary of Ireland* noted in 1837 that extensive manufacturing of linen, cotton and diaper had previously taken place in the town.[12]

Much of what we know about O'Brien's family and early life comes from biographical sketches published respectively in the nineteenth and early twentieth centuries by Chilean historians Benjamín Vicuña Mackenna and Pedro Pablo Figueroa. In retirement in Santiago, O'Brien had long conversations with Vicuña Mackenna. Figueroa knew O'Brien's daughter, Isabel, and other members of his family in Santiago, including his great-grandson, Clemente Perez y Valdes O'Brien, who was keeper of the family archive.[13] While these sources must be treated with great caution, they do provide useful starting points from which to speculate about aspects of O'Brien's early life. Figueroa's work, in particular, is of value because he had access to documents in the family archive that have since been lost.[14]

Martin Bryan was a rich farmer who owned a cotton factory adjoining his property, according to Vicuña Mackenna.[15] Martin and his partner, Adam Mulholland, certainly owned a bleaching firm in Baltinglass.[16] Despite technological advances in spinning and weaving, bleaching was still a lengthy part of the process of turning cotton and linen yarn into finished items. Before the invention of modern chemical methods for cleaning textiles, cotton and linen were treated with sulphuric acid and left to dry in the sun on bleaching greens.[17] Martin Bryan and Adam Mulholland were the leaseholders of one of two bleaching greens in Baltinglass in the 1790s.[18] It is possible that Martin Bryan was supplying bleaching services to the Orrs at Stratford-on-Slaney. It is also probable, on the basis of Vicuña Mackenna's description of him as the owner of a cotton factory, that Martin Bryan was producing finished goods in Baltinglass and was aware of the demand for textiles in South America's newly opened markets. This resulted in John becoming the family agent in Buenos Aires. According to the economic historian Manuel Llorca-Jaña, thousands of small-to-medium-sized manufacturers across the United Kingdom were supplying textiles to British and Irish merchant houses in the half-century after 1810.[19]

Martin Bryan was sufficiently well-to-do to take the oath of allegiance to the British monarch on 2 May 1796,[20] a legal device that enabled prosperous Catholics to circumvent some of the onerous restrictions placed on them because of their religion. His pastimes were those of the typical country gentleman. He kept a couple of racehorses; there was a racecourse on the southern side of the town, near the bleaching green he leased at Lathaleere. One of his horses, Rosetta, won three times at Baltinglass racecourse in November 1791.[21]

Martin and his wife, Honoria O'Connor,[22] had at least six children: Laurence, John, James, Catherine, Mary and Anne. Laurence was the eldest son. Born in the mid-1780s, he was responsible for managing the family business after his father's death. He never married, and died young, before 1813.[23] The three sisters all married. Catherine wed John Peppard, a woollen draper from nearby Athy, County Kildare. She died on 18 January 1865, aged about eighty. Her obituary mentioned 'her sacrifices and labours for the relief of distress, during the terrible famine years', and how 'her faith and hope were beautifully exemplified by her cheerfulness under many a bitter trial'.[24] Mary married John Metcalf, and lived at Castleruddery Park, eight kilometres north of Baltinglass.[25] Anne married James Horan, and inherited from her father the lease to a house in Baltinglass called 'The Steps'[26] – the original lease from the Earl of Aldborough to Martin Bryan dated from 1794. James O'Brien followed his older brother John to South America to work as a merchant; he was moving between Buenos Aires and Chile in 1819, but returned to live in Ireland. When 'The Steps' was up for sale in 1851, the prospectus mentioned that James O'Brien was still alive and aged about sixty.[27]

John was born on 24 June 1786.[28] No documentary evidence concerning his childhood has yet been uncovered. Although he must have received some schooling – Vicuña Mackenna writes that he received the education that a career in commerce required[29] – his letters betray a less-than-perfect command of written English. Given his character, he was probably a restless student who preferred the outdoor life, but there may have been more to it than that. Vicuña Mackenna describes O'Brien as having a 'certain paralysis of the tongue', which, rather strangely, he attributes to the fact that he was 'genuinely Celtic',[30] and that 'he was as silent as a stone, or rather, an enigma, because, being Irish, he had forgotten English and had not learnt Spanish'.[31]

English was only beginning to displace the Irish language in the late eighteenth century, and it is possible that O'Brien, speaking Irish at home, struggled with spoken English. Or it may be that Vicuña Mackenna is referring to a speech impediment. Not only did O'Brien have difficulties with

English, despite spending the best part of his adult life in South America, he also struggled with spoken and written Spanish.[32] His inability to get his tongue around the most basic grammatical constructions left him open to teasing by his South American comrades and mockery by his enemies. That said, O'Brien was able to navigate his way around South America with no apparent difficulty, which suggests that, whatever the extent of his linguistic frailties, he was able to make himself understood. Criticism of his inarticulacy may have involved an element of racial or class snobbery, perhaps fostered by other foreign-born officers.

When he was not studying, John would have enjoyed the typical country pursuits of the son of an eighteenth-century gentleman, such as hunting, shooting and fishing. These were all pastimes he enjoyed during his spare time in South America. He also developed a passion for that great eighteenth-century vice, gambling.

South America and its extraordinary natural wealth may have first entered John's consciousness in 1795 when he was a boy of nine. In the last days of summer, news came from the south of the county that a local man had made a startling discovery while crossing the slopes of Croghan Kinsella, a peak at the southern extremity of the Wicklow Mountains. Walking along a narrow, shallow stream known as the Aughatinavought, the man noticed something glistening on the riverbed; it was a piece of gold weighing about half an ounce (14.2 grams). Rumours of the find spread across the district, the rolling countryside of south and west Wicklow and north Wexford.[33] Small farmers and labourers, who had been busy collecting the harvest, rushed to the scene of the discovery. They camped by the banks of the Aughatinavought, leaving the crops to rot in the ground. A letter in *Saunders's News-letter* reported that

> On Friday last a man not worth 5s. in the world, that was only an hour and a few minutes working, got in a slate stone a piece, which I saw, that weighs near three ounces; it was bought by a respectable gentleman of the neighbourhood out of curiosity, not for profit, as he gave the poor man rather more than the worth of it ...[34]

News of the Wicklow 'gold rush' lured speculators from across the water to Croghan Kinsella. County Wicklow was already the most important mining district in Ireland. As well as gold, there were rich deposits of copper, silver, sulphur and lead. Agents for English mining concerns bought lumps of the metal that were being pulled daily from the ground. The gold-diggers did not know how much their discoveries were worth, and were happy to give up the precious ore for a handful of coins. Charlatans and conmen swarmed around. One 'humane gentleman' promised a young boy who had escaped from the workhouse upon hearing about the gold rush that he would look after the nugget he had discovered. It was valued at £17 15*s* 3*d* (€20.64). He gave the boy's mother a cow and told her he would use the rest of the money raised from the gold to buy an apprenticeship for her son.[35]

By the middle of October, the first, popular flurries of the gold rush were over. The Kildare Militia ejected the gold-diggers from the estates belonging to the earls of Arran, Ormonde and Carysfort, taking possession of the mines in the name of King George III. The Irish government passed an act of parliament to reinforce the Crown's claim to the treasure trove, and awarded licences for their further exploitation. Professional mining companies were drafted in to survey and extract whatever remained beneath the Wicklow bog. Though the Croghan Kinsella mines continued in operation until 1830, they never produced the quantities of gold dreamed of in the wilder speculations of both company reports and newspaper articles that had dubbed this remote part of Wicklow the 'New Peru', 'Little Peru' and the 'Irish Potosí'.[36] These exotic names must have stirred up intense excitement among the young men and women across the district and beyond, and it may be supposed that, entering O'Brien's childhood imagination, they fuelled his later determination to find South American gold and silver.

There is no evidence that Martin Bryan or any member of his family were engaged in politics. However, the Bryan family would have struggled to remain aloof from the violence that engulfed west Wicklow in the late 1790s. The Society of United Irishmen began organising in the county in 1797.[37] Influenced by the American and French revolutions, a group comprised mainly of middle-class Ulster Presbyterian businessmen had founded the society in 1791 in Belfast. A Dublin branch swiftly followed, attracting both Catholics and Protestants. Though the final political aims of the society's members differed, the United Irishmen was broadly committed to radical reform of the Irish parliament, religious equality and the removal of British influence in Irish affairs. The society was adept at using propaganda, employing newspapers, ballads and pamphlets to spread its message. The outbreak of war with revolutionary France in 1793 persuaded the British government to suppress the organisation, which continued in existence underground after May 1794.

Baltinglass was strategically important in the 1790s. It was in the barony of Upper Talbotstown on the main road connecting Dublin with Wexford and Waterford. Cradled in the western foothills of the Wicklow Mountains, which run north–south from the Dublin suburbs to the border with County Wexford, the town is forty-five kilometres south of the capital in a shallow part of the valley formed by the River Slaney in west County Wicklow. The mountains divide west Wicklow from the eastern part of the county, which runs along the Irish Sea. Baltinglass looks west towards counties Kildare and Carlow, the borders of which meet that of County Wicklow about three kilometres south-west of the town. The soft bump of Cloghnagaune Hill overlooks Baltinglass to the east, the gateway into the Wicklow Mountains. To the north, on the east bank of the Slaney, are the remains of Baltinglass Abbey, a Cistercian monastery founded by Dermot MacMurrough in the twelfth century. John O'Brien's grandfather, Andrew, and his uncle Laughlin are buried in the graveyard beside the abbey.

There was strong support for the United Irishmen in Upper Talbotstown. The leadership used commercial networks linked to the textile industry to radicalise and recruit the local population. The Orr family, the owners of the factory and mill at Stratford-on-Slaney, were United Irishmen sympathisers. One of the first United Irishmen martyrs, the County Antrim-born William Orr, who was executed by the government in 1797, was a relative. After his death, 'Remember Orr' became a popular revolutionary slogan. Some members of the Orrs' workforce had fled the authorities' scrutiny in Ulster and been given shelter in Stratford.[38] William Putnam McCabe, the son of a Belfast cotton manufacturer, was one of the principal United Irishmen propagandists and recruiters in west Wicklow in the 1790s. McCabe's brother worked as a foreman for the Orrs in Stratford.[39]

In 1796 bad weather prevented a French fleet, accompanied by the United Irishmen leader Theobald Wolfe Tone, from landing an invasion force at Bantry Bay, County Cork. The British government responded with a repressive crackdown on the United Irishmen's leadership. For two years, armed yeomen led raids on family homes throughout the parishes of west Wicklow in search of arms. Many of Martin Bryan's neighbours were arrested and tortured. At the end of 1797, the authorities deemed the rebel threat to be serious enough to order the dispatch of the Antrim and the north Cork militias to the county.[40] These militia units were led by Protestant landowners and were comprised mainly of Catholic conscripts. They served in place of regular troops who had been sent to America to fight the rebellion in the 1770s and, later, to Europe in the campaigns against revolutionary France. The North Cork Militia, in particular, enjoyed a brutal reputation, resorting to pitch-capping, half-hanging and flogging to exact punishment and retrieve information in a campaign of terror designed to intimidate the local population.

On 7 May 1798, during the days leading up to the rebellion's outbreak, an anonymous informant in west Wicklow wrote to the undersecretary, Edward Cooke, about the state of Baltinglass. Cooke was based in Dublin Castle, the headquarters of the British government in Ireland and the site of its intelligence-gathering operation. He was not only the permanent head of the government's civil department but also its chief spymaster, charged with combating the threat of Irish republicanism. 'I have reason to think the parish of Baltinglass exceeded any other parish in that County in its number of United [Irish] men, arms etc.', the informant wrote. 'It may probably prove a Satisfaction by and to you, in case you should think proper to send an army into that Quarter to compel the Surrender of arms, to have a draft immediately taken of the extent [of sedition] and a few of the principal Inhabitants …'.[41]

The informant suggested arresting the local blacksmiths 'in order to get information of the number of <u>pikes</u> made', and the carpenters and sawyers, but submitted that it was 'from the keepers of whiskey, ales and porter houses alone that you could be able to collect a proper notion of their committees and horrid deliberations'. The informant presented a pessimistic picture to the authorities, convinced, as he was, that the rebels had secreted away large quantities of arms:

> The extent of this Conspiracy is such <u>through every description</u> of men, that if it be attempted to be suppressed <u>all at once</u> or <u>violently eradicated</u> the innocent and truly Loyal will suffer equally or even more than the guilty from the disaffected of the soldiery, and a most dreadful civil war may be blown up; which is all the Rebels now wish for, at the same time I lament to think that <u>no measures can be too strong</u> against the guilty; and that nothing but the strongest measures and immediate punishment can have any effect on the minds of the savage bloodthirsty Barbarians.[42]

The informant believed that five hundred pikes were ready for use in the parish of Baltinglass, and that the Roman Catholic parish priest, William Travers, was colluding with the rebels to prevent the weapons from being discovered.[43]

The Orrs were accused of being the chief ringleaders of sedition in the area around Stratford-on-Slaney. On 9 May another anonymous informant furnished Cooke with 'a list of persons who can give effectual information respecting the present Rebellion'. In the letter the informant listed a baker, Joseph Fox, from Stratford-on-Slaney as 'one of the first who swore united men in the County Wicklow'. The informant added: 'He has been committee man and secretary and can give Information of how the fugitive Rebels from Belfast, Lisburn, Hillsborough etc. etc., under the protection and influence of the Orrs, first introduced uniting in Stratford and spread it through all parts of the adjacent neighbourhoods.'[44] The same informant named Roger McGuire, a blacksmith living in Stratford-on-Slaney, as having 'sworn more men and probably made more pikes than any other smith in the County Wicklow'.[45]

On 19 May, five days before the rebellion began, an informant wrote to Cooke about the difficulty of uncovering concealed weapons: 'If it were possible to get an honest or loyal popish priest to put in place of William Travers, the arms would soon come in; but that I verily believe is impossible, as it is inconsistent with the very object and principles of their Religion.'[46] The informant accused the Orrs in Stratford and other United Irishmen sympathisers of screening 'the murderer, the assassin, the rank Rebel, by indiscriminately lumping him with the well-affected in each Townland, and gaining a general protection for all together'.[47]

Aided by a sympathetic population and favourable geographical conditions, the rebel leader Michael Dwyer was able to prosecute a guerrilla war in the hilly terrain of west Wicklow against the Crown forces for the next five years, long after the government had put down the rebellion in the rest of the country.

Aside from a small French expeditionary force under General Jean Humbert, which was defeated at the Battle of Ballinamuck in County Longford, the rebellion was confined to east and south Leinster and north-east Ulster after informers enabled the authorities to swoop on the leaders in Dublin. The rebellion in west Wicklow was brief but bloody. Rebel attacks on the garrisons at Stratford and Baltinglass failed. In Upper Talbotstown, forty-three prisoners suspected of United Irishmen sympathies were summarily executed at Dunlavin.[48] Public executions were also carried out in Baltinglass.

The failure of the 1798 rising led in 1801 to the introduction of the Act of Union, which abolished the Irish parliament and created the United Kingdom of Great Britain and Ireland. In 1803 Dwyer's surrender in the aftermath of Robert Emmet's failed rising marked the end of the guerrilla campaign in Wicklow.

It is unlikely that the Bryan family was involved in the rebellion, on either side, but they must have had close links to some of those who participated, not least the Orr family in Stratford. There can be no doubt that the violence with which Crown authorities sought to quell the United Irishmen insurgency in County Wicklow left an impression on the young John. He was twelve when the rising erupted, and, for the next five years, a low-level but occasionally bloody conflict was fought in the mountains behind the family home between the Crown forces and Dwyer's guerrilla fighters. It may also be imagined that, having been exposed to a discourse of liberty present in United Irishmen propaganda, O'Brien was particularly susceptible to the Buenos Aires government's call to arms in 1813. This political awakening would, by the 1820s, see him become an active supporter of Daniel O'Connell and participate in the campaigns for Catholic emancipation and Home Rule, both as a leading member of the Irish community in Buenos Aires and during his trips home to Ireland.

Martin Bryan died around 1805. His eldest son, Laurence, shouldered much of the responsibility of carrying on the family business after his father's death.[49] Like many second sons, John possessed something of a reckless streak. The Chilean historian Figueroa writes that Martin left some racehorses to John and that within two years he had squandered his inheritance at the racetrack.[50] He was in debt by his early twenties. According to a deed dated 4 March 1813, John was indebted to several individuals 'by losses in trade and otherwise', including a Dublin merchant called James Griffin. On 24 April 1811 Laurence was forced to mortgage various properties in Baltinglass that he had inherited from his father in order to pay John's debts.[51]

The exact circumstances of O'Brien's departure from Ireland are unclear. In his own version, repeated by his friend and admirer Vicuña Mackenna, he left Ireland directly for South America to pursue commercial opportunities on behalf of the family business. According to Vicuña Mackenna, O'Brien lived in the family home in Baltinglass until the age of twenty-five, when he convinced his family to give him a credit note worth 25,000 pesos (€5,800) to set up in business in South America.[52]

But there is another version of this period of O'Brien's life, related by two other historians, Figueroa and the Argentinian Juan Estevan Guastavino.[53] In their narratives, having lost all his money betting on horses, O'Brien travelled to London and enlisted as an officer in the Royal Artillery. He deserted soon afterwards, having read about the war of independence against the Spanish in South America. Elements of this account seem credible given the fact that O'Brien was undoubtedly struggling with debt.

Vicuña Mackenna writes that it first occurred to O'Brien that 'he was a soldier and nothing more' in Buenos Aires.[54] But either O'Brien had military experience or else he convincingly lied to San Martín when he sought a commission in the patriot army in Buenos Aires in 1813.[55] Thus it seems more probable that O'Brien served in the British army before arriving in South America. That he did not feel inclined to mention the fact in old age is understandable. When seeking pensions from the Chilean and Peruvian governments, he probably thought it best to forget that in a previous life he had been forced to leave Ireland because of gambling debts, and had joined the British army as a mercenary. Instead, O'Brien portrayed himself as having first been motivated to become a soldier in South America for selfless reasons and a love of liberty.

The most likely scenario is that O'Brien left Ireland to escape his debts, and convinced friends at home to lend him money to join the British army as a cadet – he had £500 (€580) with him when he left Baltinglass for England[56] – but that, having enlisted in the Royal Artillery, he realised that the strict hierarchy and discipline of the army were not for him, or as Guastavino put it, 'his arrogance alienated him from his commanding officers'.[57] No definitive evidence of O'Brien having served in the army has to date been uncovered, although there is a record of a John O'Brien having been commissioned an assistant staff surgeon in the Royal Horse Artillery in 1811.[58] The fact that this John O'Brien is listed as a surgeon undermines the case for him being the Baltinglass native. On the other hand, the fact that the Royal Horse Artillery O'Brien deserted within a year of being commissioned tallies with the date of the Baltinglass O'Brien's arrival in South America.

There remains O'Brien's motivation for choosing to emigrate to South America. This was a period when the newly independent republics of the continent were removing colonial restrictions on trade, opening up new markets for British and Irish manufactures. The years between 1808 and 1815 were crucial, because the Napoleonic Wars had closed European markets to British exports.[59] Buenos Aires and Santiago were of vital importance to British and Irish textile manufacturers, not least to the industry in west Wicklow. Wearing British and Irish clothing became something of a patriotic statement in the aftermath of the wars of independence, as the South American elites demonstrated their cosmopolitanism and rejected the imports of their former colonial masters.[60] As has been mentioned, the Bryan family was involved in textile manufacturing in the late eighteenth and early nineteenth centuries, but were probably reliant on middlemen or larger-scale manufacturers or merchants – such as the Orrs, who had representatives in the continent's ports – to access South America's newly opened markets.[61] It is a sign of the family's expansionary ambition that John O'Brien travelled to Buenos Aires to open a merchant house.

Through his family's connection to the Orrs, who exported textiles from their factory in Stratford-on-Slaney to South America, O'Brien was able to take advantage of a commercial network that extended across Britain, Ireland and South America. The Orrs had agents in Chile and Argentina. John Orr, a merchant based in Santiago,[62] and William and Richard Orr, merchants living in Buenos Aires,[63] were among the family representatives who lived in South America in the early decades of the nineteenth century. O'Brien was also acquainted with Robert Orr,[64] who had worked in Buenos Aires before returning to Ireland to take charge of the operation at Stratford-on-Slaney in place of his father, William, in the early 1820s.[65] In 1823, trying to convince the Lord Lieutenant of Ireland, Richard Wellesley, of the merits of a scheme to bring Irish emigrants to South America, O'Brien recounted his service in the armies of the new republics and claimed to have documentary evidence from the governments he represented in South America. He wrote that 'this can be attested by Robert Orr of Merchants Quay, Dublin, who has resided in those countries for many years and who is well acquainted with the signatures thereto, with such documents and the Rank of Colonel which I have held for some time in their Cavalry'.[66]

The Orrs facilitated O'Brien's entry into the world of South American commerce by giving him letters of introduction to General Frederick Caldwell and John McNeile.[67] Caldwell, who was in the service of the Portuguese royal family, was from an Anglo-Irish family whose seat was in County Fermanagh and which had a proud military tradition. He had served as an officer of dragoons in the British army during the Seven Years War before entering the Portuguese service. He was summoned to Rio after the royal family had fled to Brazil to escape Napoleon's armies in 1808.[68] John McNeile was a business partner of the northern branch of the Orr family. After amassing a fortune in South America, he became a partner, together with James Orr, in Montgomery's bank, the forerunner of the Northern Bank. These early financial institutions in Belfast were closely related to the needs of the textile industry.[69]

The fact that O'Brien was able to rely on these military and commercial contacts in South America in 1811 points to the strength of trading networks between Ireland and South America in the pre-independence era. Sporadic Irish migration to the Viceroyalty of the River Plate (modern-day Argentina) had been taking place since the end of the eighteenth century. By the time of the revolution in May 1810, there already existed a small but significant Irish community in Buenos Aires.[70]

The claims that 'generous and enthusiastic sentiments'[71] drove O'Brien to South America to join the patriot armies after he had read about their struggle in newspaper reports in London should not be discounted. In relation to the recruitment of foreign (predominantly Irish) volunteers in the northern part of South America in the early nineteenth century, Matthew Brown has demonstrated that 'the expeditions were much more about emigration and adventure than they were about experienced military professionals seeking remunerative employment. Socio-economic explanations for migration merged with cultural expectations about the rewards of adventure in South America'.[72] O'Brien's principal reason for emigrating to the southern part of the continent was financial, but it seems reasonable to suppose that this was reinforced by what Brown describes as 'a transatlantic ideological context in which "liberty" stood for a weakly defined opposition to tyranny, and a bundle of beliefs encompassing opportunity, prosperity, Romanticism and enterprise'.[73]

The precise date of O'Brien's arrival in South America is not known, but it was most likely in 1811.[74] O'Brien's initial destination in South America was not Buenos Aires but Rio de Janeiro, where Frederick Caldwell was attendant on the Portuguese royal family. O'Brien's first passage across the Atlantic was the most eventful of the many ocean-going voyages he was to make during his lifetime. The Portuguese ship in which he was travelling encountered a fierce storm a few weeks after leaving port, and was wrecked on the island of Fernando Po, some thirty-two kilometres off the coast of West Africa.[75] O'Brien was among the handful of survivors who made it ashore. They had no fresh water and little to eat, and spent two days wandering across the two-thousand-square-kilometre island. O'Brien was suffering from a strong fever and was close to death when the small party of survivors came across the port of Santa Isabel – present-day Malabo – and were able to get help. He spent a few weeks recovering his strength before embarking once more for Brazil, on a British ship. Aboard his new ship, O'Brien encountered another obstacle to his progress when he began a romance with a fellow passenger, a Quaker's daughter called Rebecca. Her father was enraged upon discovering that his daughter was carrying on an illicit love affair, and conspired with the captain, another Quaker, to have O'Brien transferred to a Brazilian ship in the middle of the ocean. O'Brien protested vigorously, but the captain told him that if he did not disembark, he would be arrested and thrown in the brig as a mutineer.

It was aboard this third ship that O'Brien arrived in Rio de Janeiro to discover that Caldwell had died three months previously.[76]

O'Brien turned to McNeile, one of the principal Irish residents in Buenos Aires in this period,[77] who gave him a credit note for 25,000 pesos (€5,802) to establish himself in Buenos Aires.[78] Having endured months of hardship on the ocean, the young Irishman reached Buenos Aires at some point in 1811. Here, he discovered a city at war.

2

The Mounted Grenadier

Buenos Aires stands on the south-western shore of the River Plate estuary, where the south Atlantic tears into the eastern coast of the South American continent. Like its northern cousin New York, it is an immigrants' city, its unique character shaped by an eclectic mix of European nationalities – mostly Spaniards and Italians, but also Germans, Croats, Poles, British and, of course, Irish – who have settled there over the course of its almost five-hundred-year history.

The term used to describe a resident of Buenos Aires is *porteño*, which translates as the inhabitant of a port. And it was the port that initially drew the British and Irish merchants to the city in the late eighteenth century. In 1776 Buenos Aires had become one of the most important ports in South America, displacing Callao, Lima's port, on the Pacific coast as the main point of entry for European goods. When John O'Brien arrived in 1811, the city was humming with commercial activity.

Manuel Llorca-Jaña has demonstrated the importance of British and Irish trade to the Southern Cone (Argentina, Chile and Uruguay) in the immediate postwar period, estimating that there were 260 British and Irish merchant houses operating in Chile and the River Plate between *c.* 1810 and 1859.[1] Agents were opening warehouses to contain the manufactures that were arriving from English factories to serve the markets of the independent states, which were beginning to emerge from the ashes of Spain's American colonies. The period in which O'Brien arrived in Buenos Aires was one of dynamic growth.

The bulk of the Irish who emigrated to Buenos Aires in the nineteenth century were farmers and labourers. They came during and after the Great Famine. But there was already a small Irish community in the city in the early 1800s.[2] Many of the Irish were involved in the meat-curing and rendering industries. There were Irish-owned hotels, shops and taverns in the city. Also present were Irish merchants, who belonged to the upper echelons of the city's expatriate community. They mixed with the British, becoming members of the British Commercial Rooms, a type of gentleman's club where they could read English-language newspapers and hear the latest commercial and political gossip.

O'Brien's journey did not end at the River Plate. The deep-drafted, ocean-going ships that plied the route between South America and Europe were obliged to cast anchor in the outer roads of the estuary, about six kilometres from shore. In bad weather, passengers might be forced to sit tight below deck for days before they were able to make the journey to shore by tender. Drivers lining the shore on their horse-drawn carts waited to bring the passengers the short distance into the city.[3]

Early nineteenth-century Buenos Aires was far removed from its modern incarnation or the teeming European metropolises of the day. Churches dominated the low-rise city. According to the first impressions of one traveller who arrived in 1817, its domes and steeples gave Buenos Aires 'a gloomy and monastic appearance', which was strengthened by 'the number of priests and friars who thronged the streets'.[4]

The fort dominated the centre of the city. It was located where today stands the Casa Rosada, the pastel-pink-coloured palace that serves as the offices of the president of the Argentine Republic. The Casa Rosada overlooks the Plaza de Mayo, the former *plaza mayor* – or main square – of the colonial era. In 1811 the square was divided in two by a *recova*, a covered arcade that was home to the city's central market. Whitewashed, one-storey, brick houses constructed around a central courtyard, or patio, often built of marble, lined the streets running parallel to the *plaza mayor*. O'Brien would probably have lodged at one of the neighbourhood's *posadas*, or boarding houses. A popular inn for foreign travellers was the English-owned Los Tres Reyes – The Three Kings – on the Calle Santo Cristo between the Plaza de la Fuerte and the fort.

The Plaza de la Victoria (Victory Square) was the city's nervous system. Its name testified to the pride and growing sense of nationhood felt by the people of Buenos Aires. The *cabildo*, or town hall, stood at the western side of the plaza, where, on 25 May 1810, shortly before O'Brien's arrival, the principal residents of the city had ousted the Spanish viceroy, paving the way for the emergence of the United Provinces of the River Plate, the forerunner of the modern-day Argentine Republic.

Citizens' militias patrolled the streets of Buenos Aires. This martial atmosphere had prevailed since 1806 and 1807 when the British had made two attempts to occupy the city, events that have become known in Argentinian historiography as the *Invasiones Inglesas* (English Invasions). But it was the arrival of South American-born officers who had served in the Spanish armed forces and who began returning from Europe to help defend the fragile government from Spanish-led counter-revolution that was to shape the course of the wars to come. Most significantly, on 9 March 1812 the *George Canning* landed in Buenos Aires carrying a small group of experienced, well-trained officers. They included Lieutenant Colonel José de San Martín.

The taciturn San Martín was in marked contrast to Simón Bolívar, his rival for the leadership of the independence movement on the continent. Whereas the latter was inclined to give free rein to his emotions, the former was cool and calculating. The English merchant Samuel Haigh described San Martín as

> tall and well formed, and his whole appearance is highly military; his countenance is very expressive; his complexion a deep olive; his hair is black, and he wore large whiskers without mustachios; his eyes are large and black, and possess a fire and animation which would be remarkable under any circumstances. He is very gentlemanly in his deportment, and, when I saw him, he was conversing with the greatest ease and affability to the company around; he received me with much cordiality, for he is very partial to the English nation.[5]

Born in Yapeyú, a former Jesuit mission station in the north-east of Argentina, San Martín had fought with the Spanish army against the French during the Peninsular War. In Cádiz, San Martín had become a member of the Lodge of Rational Knights, a quasi-Masonic secret society committed to the overthrow of Spanish rule in the Americas and to the installation of governments imbued with liberal principles.

San Martín understood that in order for the government of the United Provinces to defeat its enemies – the well-trained, well-equipped Spanish and Portuguese armies – it would have to create a disciplined army of its own. The government was suspicious of San Martín's intentions, but desperately required military know-how and experience. Within a few days of his arrival in the city, the government gave San Martín permission to create the *granaderos a caballo*, a regiment of mounted grenadiers. Because of its rigid discipline and modern military techniques, it swiftly became the army's elite unit. The regiment's austere code mirrored that of its founder.

O'Brien was captivated by the sight of the cavalrymen riding through the streets of Buenos Aires in their smart, dark-blue uniforms, and, in 1813, offered his services to the regiment. O'Brien impressed San Martín. On 24 September the latter wrote to the government with a list of three candidates to fill the vacancy of *alférez* – or second lieutenant, the lowest officer rank – in the 2nd Company, 2nd Squadron. San Martín stipulated that the successful candidate had to be of proven 'bravery and valour', and placed O'Brien at the top of the list: 'In first place, Don John O'Brien of the Irish nation who has offered his services to the state, whose aptitude and knowledge of the art of war could make him very useful'.[6] San Martín emphasised the point at the end of the letter: 'All the candidates are worthy of being selected but particularly John O'Brien, proposed in first place.'[7]

San Martín was hungry for experienced officers, especially those with European military training. His letter to the government suggests that O'Brien had military experience before coming to South America. It was the first of many encomia to be written by San Martín and other officers about O'Brien's military skills. O'Brien was to forge a close relationship with San Martín, which later developed into a friendship. He admired San Martín's soldierly virtues and was willing to forgive his faults. San Martín relied on O'Brien's loyalty and, in return, repaid him with rapid promotion. On 27 September 1813 O'Brien was accepted into the mounted grenadiers with the rank of *alférez* in the 2nd Company, 2nd Squadron.[8]

The following is O'Brien's description of his conversion from merchant to soldier:

> The military life was far from my mind, but agitated by a romantic spirit and being a staunch enemy of tyranny and oppression, hardly had the trumpet of [South] American independence sounded, when, abandoning my national immunity and the interests and affections of my homeland and family, I resolved to dedicate myself to the cause of liberty, and devote my life to the defence of the rights of the South American peoples [*a.t.*].[9]

This passage was contained in a petition to the Peruvian congress in 1851. The colourful prose and declarations of selflessness were designed to persuade deputies to award O'Brien a military pension, but there is no reason to doubt the sentiments.

The lure of adventure must have played a part in O'Brien's decision. The government was desperate for soldiers. Recruiters were scouring the streets of Buenos Aires looking for men. O'Brien possessed a restless, impetuous character, and would have found their appeals irresistible. It is also possible that O'Brien drew parallels between accounts in government propaganda of Spanish atrocities with those committed by loyalists during his childhood in west Wicklow. There were also more pragmatic considerations. The revolution had sounded the death knell for the Spanish trade monopoly. Commercial opportunity depended upon the military success of the newly independent governments. Irish merchants trading in the River Plate, such as O'Brien and William Brown,[10] had a material interest in enlisting in the armed forces of the new regimes.[11] Indeed, most of the Irish and British volunteers who crossed the Atlantic to fight in the South American wars of independence were motivated as much, if not more, by material gain – either as emigrants or investors in expeditions – as by romantic ideas of glory and liberty.[12]

The Irish merchants who enlisted were conscious of the value of a service record in the patriot armies in a climate where those who hoped to make a profit in the newly independent republics were required to demonstrate a suitable level of patriotic fervour. Foreign merchants applying for citizenship had to prove their adhesion to the patriotic cause. Evidence of this is found in the application for citizenship made by O'Brien's younger brother, James, who arrived in Buenos Aires in 1813, making John's decision to join the army easier.[13]

The mounted grenadiers were subject to San Martín's strict code of conduct, which articulated the obsession with honour among the early nineteenth-century officer class.[14] Officers in the mounted grenadiers merited dismissal for showing cowardice in battle; this could mean simply lowering one's head during a cavalry charge. Duelling was the first recourse when seeking to avenge one's honour, and was officially sanctioned in the code of the mounted grenadiers. An officer could lose his commission if he refused a challenge, be it just or unjust; failed to demand satisfaction when he was insulted; or failed to defend the honour of the unit when it was defamed in his presence or he knew it had been defamed elsewhere. Equally egregious sins were: cheating like an artisan; lacking integrity in the handling of funds; speaking ill of a comrade with members of other units; publicising the unit's internal discussions; showing familiarity with sergeants, corporals and privates in a shameful manner; putting one's hand on a woman, even if one had been insulted; failing to come to the aid of a comrade in battle when one was able; fraternising in public with known prostitutes; spending time in gambling dens with those not belonging to the officer class; and drinking immoderately in such a way as to dishonour the unit.[15]

On the first Sunday of every month, San Martín would sit in solemn judgement at the head of a disciplinary committee of his fellow officers to deal with infractions. After a brief discussion about the importance of the regiment in the prosecution of the war against the Spanish and the necessity of weeding out those grenadiers not worthy of belonging in its ranks, committee members were invited to point out breaches of the unit's code. This they did by writing their accusations upon pieces of paper, which were placed in a hat and handed to San Martín. A commission was then charged with investigating the alleged infractions, and, after the evidence had been presented at the following meeting of the committee, the officers voted by secret ballot on whether or not the perpetrator should be asked to resign from the regiment.[16]

At first the mounted grenadiers were headquartered in an area close to the Plaza de la Victoria. The headquarters were then moved to the Retiro area of Buenos Aires, the present-day Plaza General San Martín, where the soldiers used the adjacent bullring to stable their horses. The grenadiers were well drilled but often lacked weaponry. When sabres could not be found, they trained with machetes or short lances. They also carried pistols and carbines. O'Brien spent seven months drilling in the open ground in front of the barracks and learning how to handle a sabre and lance while at full gallop. He won rapid promotion both for reasons of competence and because of the demand for suitably trained officers.

While San Martín was campaigning in Upper Peru (modern-day Bolivia), O'Brien first saw action during the Siege of Montevideo. The city was the centre of the loyalist counter-revolution in the River Plate. The government in Buenos Aires had the advantage in manpower, but the loyalists in Montevideo had retained possession of the navy, the principal naval station in the River Plate, and all the naval officers. In 1813 royalist ships based at Montevideo and manned by experienced officers were blockading Buenos Aires, preventing the government from trading with the outside world or supplying reinforcements to the troops in the Banda Oriental.[17] It was only through the extraordinary efforts of the Irish merchant sailor William Brown, and the scratch navy he cobbled together, that the blockade was broken, allowing the transportation of troops from Buenos Aires across the River Plate.[18]

Colonia del Sacramento lies directly across the River Plate estuary from Buenos Aires. Founded by the Portuguese as a trading post, it had an important position on the River Plate, controlling access to the River Uruguay and River Paraná, vital trade routes that penetrated deep into the heart of South America and the markets of present-day Argentina, Brazil, Uruguay and Paraguay. The United Provinces' army was fighting on two fronts in the Banda Oriental, besieging the royalists in Montevideo and trying to destroy the *gaucho* leader José Artigas and his band of guerrillas, who controlled most of the rest of the Banda Oriental.

O'Brien played a brief but conspicuous role during the campaign in the Banda Oriental. He was the principal aide-de-camp to General Miguel Estanislao Soler when Montevideo fell to the Argentinians in June 1814, bringing to an end the royalist threat in the River Plate. The siege had lasted for almost two years; O'Brien recalled the suffering of the troops besieging the city, who had no shelter from the weather and were forced to wrap themselves in animal skins for protection during winter storms.[19] O'Brien impressed his superiors during the campaign. When Soler became nervous that one of his generals, in pursuit of Artigas' forces, would become encircled by the enemy, he sent O'Brien with a warning. O'Brien reached the general and returned to Montevideo with such speed that Soler initially did not believe he had carried out his orders. When he realised that O'Brien had indeed completed the mission, and with startling alacrity, he rewarded him with a bag of gold coins and a licence to return to Buenos Aires.[20]

After the campaign in the Banda Oriental, the army's commander-in-chief, Carlos María Alvear, appointed O'Brien as head of his personal escort with the rank of *sargento mayor* (between a captain and a lieutenant colonel).[21] But within months O'Brien sought a discharge from the army.[22] His decision was linked to the shifting political sands in Buenos Aires. According to Figueroa, O'Brien resigned because 'he had not liked' the conduct of Alvear during negotiations with Gaspar de Vigodet, the royalist governor of Montevideo who had surrendered the city.[23] Vigodet believed that Alvear had broken his word during the negotiations that preceded the entrance of the patriot army into Montevideo by taking prisoner the Spanish garrison instead of allowing it to sail back to Spain. O'Brien may also have been perturbed at Alvear's increasing authoritarianism, the consequences of which were an extensive network of spies operating in Buenos Aires, mass arrests, and summary executions of opponents.

O'Brien did not remain a civilian for long. His brief taste of action and disillusionment with his superior officer were only the preamble to the main act in his military career, the liberation of Chile from Spanish rule. Enlisting once more in the mounted grenadiers, O'Brien rejoined his old regiment in the city of Mendoza.

3
The Invasion of Chile

Mendoza province lies on the eastern slopes of the Andes. It is the centre of the Argentinian wine industry because of its warm microclimate. In the nineteenth century the principal houses in the city had their own gardens, orchards and vineyards, making it a comfortable respite for those making the bone-shuddering journey across the continent from Buenos Aires to Santiago. When O'Brien arrived in 1815, the town was humming with the sound of an army preparing for war. Armourers, uniform-makers, muleteers, provisioners and soldiers wove past one another in the streets. When not drilling the men, the officers spent their days riding and shooting. In the evenings they danced waltzes and minuets with the daughters of Mendoza's wealthiest citizens.

After campaigning in Upper Peru, San Martín had come to believe that the way to defeat the Spanish was not by a direct confrontation in their Andean heartlands but by launching a seaborne invasion of Peru from Chile. But first San Martín had to liberate Chile, which was in royalist hands. In order to achieve this, he had himself appointed governor in Mendoza and began creating the Army of the Andes.

An independent government had been established in Chile in 1810. However, the royalists had regrouped and defeated the government's army at the Battle of Rancagua in October 1814. The leaders of the Chilean independence movement, including Bernardo O'Higgins, the Chilean-born son of an Irishman, and the County Monaghan native John Mackenna, fled into exile across the Andes. In Mendoza, San Martín not only had to build an army from scratch but had also to contend with the poisonous rivalry between the Chilean factions in the camp. There were shortages of weaponry, artillery, uniforms, horses and mules. Differences of opinion with the government in Buenos Aires over strategy complicated matters, as did tackling the unrest that typically befalls soldiers forced to endure extended periods in camp. Even the strictly disciplined mounted grenadiers suffered from an 'excessive' and 'scandalous' desertion rate in the middle of 1815.[1]

San Martín overcame all these hurdles, and did so while battling serious illness. Throughout his life he had had to contend with various ailments, some of which left him in severe pain. He struggled with his breathing, leading some medical experts to suggest he had asthma. He also frequently vomited blood because of a duodenal ulcer (some historians suggest that he was coughing up blood because of pulmonary fibrosis). He fought these maladies with copious quantities of laudanum and liberal amounts of Mendozan wine.

The late-nineteenth-century Argentinian historian and politician Bartolomé Mitre described the organisation of the Army of the Andes as 'one of the most extraordinary events in military history'.[2] San Martín worked from morning to night. He rose early, drinking down his first draft of laudanum, and ate only one meal a day, at noon, standing up. When the government in Buenos Aires was unable to send him everything he required, San Martín improvised. He employed a miller to design the machines used to produce the army's uniforms. Deprived of ammunition and powder, San Martín turned to a Franciscan friar for help. Later described as the 'Archimedes of the Army of the Andes',[3] Fray Luis Beltrán was a mathematician, chemist and physicist who could turn his mind to most engineering problems. San Martín gave him the task of creating an arsenal for a five-thousand-strong army. During the day Beltrán's forges churned out bullets, grenades and cannons. At night he wrestled with technical and logistical problems, designing harnesses to carry the big guns over the Andes and a factory to produce gunpowder.[4]

O'Brien rejoined the 1st Company, 4th Squadron of the *granaderos* as a *teniente* (lieutenant), but was swiftly promoted to acting captain.[5] At the beginning of 1816, San Martín placed O'Brien in command of a party with orders to guard one of the Andean approaches to Mendoza. The Chilean resort of Portillo is about eighty-five kilometres north-east of Santiago. It is one of a handful of mountain passes connecting Chile with the west of Argentina. San Martín sent O'Brien and his men to the pass at Portillo known as Malpaso. O'Brien and the twenty-five men under his command set up camp almost three thousand metres above sea level in freezing conditions at the top of the pass. The small group of soldiers suffered terrible privations for six months. When a party of loyalist soldiers attempted to cross the Andes at Malpaso, O'Brien repelled them, taking prisoner a colonel. O'Brien led only fourteen men down the mountains back into Mendoza in July 1816; eleven had died either from hypothermia or altitude sickness.[6] In September 1816 José Matías

Zapiola appointed O'Brien *ayudante mayor* (principal adjutant)[7] of the newly created 5th Squadron of the mounted grenadiers.[8]

During the next six months, while preparations continued for the invasion, San Martín and his eighteen-year-old wife, María de los Remedios, organised banquets for the officers to relieve the tedium. O'Brien, now thirty, was a recognisable figure in the city. He enjoyed dancing, drinking and female company, but he was perhaps most famous in Mendoza for his exploits in the bullring. On the eve of the departure of the army for Chile, the officers organised a bullfight in a specially constructed ring in Mendoza's main thoroughfare. In South America, variations of the traditional Spanish *corrida* had developed. Not one to shirk a challenge, O'Brien decided that he was going to perform one of the most difficult feats. Having entered the arena to the acclaim of the spectators, he jumped onto a table that had been placed close to the gate through which the bull would enter the arena. He then produced a ribbon with which he bound his ankles. When the bull charged the table, O'Brien jumped in the air, landing behind the animal and earning thunderous applause from the Mendozans.[9] This single anecdote contributed greatly to O'Brien's romantic image, earning him a reputation as an accomplished bullfighter.[10]

Another oft-told anecdote that contributed to O'Brien's image concerned a duel with Juan Lavalle, a future Argentine leader.[11] Despite the best efforts of San Martín, the officers were often bored, and this led to rows and, all too frequently, duels. O'Brien was a shameless womaniser, and prone to sharing details of his conquests with his fellow officers. One day he began regaling them with indiscreet gossip about a woman in Buenos Aires, who, unknown to O'Brien, happened to be a relative of Lavalle, then a captain in the mounted grenadiers. Lavalle was enraged by the slander, and challenged O'Brien to a duel. The Irishman realised that he had mistaken the identity of the woman, but his sense of honour forced him to accept.[12] The men thrust and parried their sabres on the *alameda*, the elegant boulevard in Mendoza along which the officers and their female companions would take their evening perambulation and seek shade beneath the branches of the poplar trees. At the end Lavalle had exacted a small revenge, leaving a deep scar on the Irishman's right wrist which he was to show off for the rest of his life.[13]

As the date for the invasion of Chile approached, San Martín developed strategies to confuse the Spanish commander-in-chief in Chile about which route the liberating army would take across the Andes. The Spanish knew that the patriots were preparing to invade the country, but did not know the point of attack. In October 1816 San Martín decided to parley with the

Pehuenche tribes living on the eastern slopes of the Andes.[14] He sent O'Brien to organise the meeting. Carrying a flag of truce, O'Brien met Ñacuñán, the Pehuenche *cacique* (indigenous leader), to invite him to an assembly.[15] The meeting – known in Spanish as a *parlamento* – between San Martín and the Pehuenche warriors was held at the fort of San Carlos, about 100 kilometres south of Mendoza. San Martín travelled with about two hundred *granaderos* and mules laden with gifts for his interlocutors. These included hides, sweets, dresses, wine and *aguardiente*, the powerful South American spirit. An English artillery officer, William Miller, who had joined the patriot army in Mendoza, described the scene:

> The *caciques* approached the esplanade in front of the fort, with all the pomp of savage life, each at the head of his warriors; their wives and children bringing up the rear. Polygamy being practised, the wives were very numerous. The men wore their hair unconfined and long; their bodies, naked from the waist upwards, were painted with different colours. Their horses were also stained precisely in the same manner as when they go to war.[16]

The Pehuenche leaders sat around a cloth-covered table that had been placed in the fort's parade ground, with San Martín and his interpreter seated at the head of the table. The Pehuenche agreed to allow San Martín to cross their territory and promised to give all assistance to the patriot army. The business over, and having deposited their arms in one of the fort's barrack-rooms, the Pehuenche began to drink the alcohol. According to Miller:

> Two thousand persons (reckoning women and children, and servants or attendants) were seated in circles upon the esplanade. One of the first subjects of conversation was their own feats, or the deeds of the ancestors. Some were affected to weeping in relating family history. As soon as the liquor exercised its influence all talked together, and shouted and yelled with deafening din.[17]

When San Martín departed, O'Brien remained, in Miller's words, 'to do the honours of the palaver'.[18] O'Brien played an important role in the negotiations between San Martín and the Pehuenche – evidence of San Martín's growing confidence in him.

At the end of 1816 the Army of the Andes was ready: the men were uniformed, the warehouses containing the army's weaponry and provisions were full, and horses and mules had been commandeered. But the enormity of the task the army faced was undiminished. The soldiers and officers were reminded of this every time they glanced towards the snow-capped Andes during their strolls down the *alameda*. If the expedition were to be successful, San Martín would have to do something that had never been attempted since the Spanish had arrived on the continent: transport an army, and the supplies to feed it, with artillery, horses oxen, mules and forage, across some of the highest peaks in the world, on narrow, precipitous paths, along which the men had to walk in single file.

In January 1817 San Martín gave orders to march. The main force of the army crossed at two passes. The larger column, including the mounted grenadiers, left Mendoza on 19 January 1817. Its route took it across the *cordillera* at a pass named Los Patos. The other column crossed at the Uspallata pass, closer to Santiago and south of the Los Patos pass. San Martín sent four smaller parties through different passes to the north and south of Los Patos and Uspallata in order to create a diversion. The ruse was intended to force the Spanish commander-in-chief to disperse his forces.

Five thousand men climbed into the Andes, dwarfed like ants by the peaks as they marched over grey-brown stone, the wind whipping through the valley. Behind the men were the seven thousand oxen that were to feed the army and the nine thousand mules that carried the army's supplies and equipment. The artillery pieces were carried in Beltrán's harnesses and hung on rods that were attached to two mules walking in single file. When the mules died, the men slung the rods on their own shoulders.

At 2,500 metres above sea level, breathing becomes difficult, and the men slowed to a trudge. The unlucky ones suffered from headaches and heart palpitations, and coughed up sputum flecked with blood, the first signs of pulmonary oedema. Their lips and skin began turning blue, and they sat down on the boulders, stripped of their last ounce of energy and unable to speak. But still the path led upwards, for another fifteen hundred metres, before there was any respite.

The two main columns began descending into the Putaendo valley in Chile on 6 and 7 February. It was a triumph of military precision. After receiving word about the location of the patriot army and concerned about the threat to the capital, the captain general of Chile, Casimiro Marcó del Pont, sent a 2,500-strong force, under the command of Brigadier Rafael Maroto, to engage the enemy. The two armies met at Chacabuco, about fifty kilometres north of Santiago.

O'Brien distinguished himself at the Battle of Chacabuco, a seminal moment in the modern history of South America fought in the early hours of 12 February 1817. As San Martín's principal aide-de-camp, he was responsible for delivering orders to and from the commander-in-chief. However, during the battle O'Brien fought alongside the mounted grenadiers, in O'Higgins' division, and charged the enemy lines. He was one of the first to arrive at the ranch of Chacabuco in pursuit of the royalists. In a lane connecting the main road to the ranch, O'Brien came across a party of royalist soldiers and, after a brief skirmish, captured the royal standard.[19] San Martín later gave O'Brien the honour of presenting the standard to the people of Mendoza, where it was hung in the cathedral.

By the afternoon of 12 February, the patriots had won the field. O'Brien had no time to rest, however; San Martín ordered him to pursue Maroto. O'Brien galloped south with a small party of men. The following day, at the Cuesta Lo Prado, a hill to the west of Santiago, he learnt that Maroto had passed through on his way to Valparaíso the previous afternoon. O'Brien's horses were tiring, and he decided to return to Santiago. At a ranch called Pudahuel, close to the city, O'Brien and his men stopped to feed their horses. The royalists had stayed in some houses at the ranch the previous day. One of the sergeants noticed some leather bags and equestrian equipment. O'Brien had a closer look. There were a pair of epaulettes, a silver bit for a horse, and, in the bags, stamped gold pieces worth about 25,000 pesos (€5,802). O'Brien returned to Santiago with his haul, which he handed over to the new Chilean government, passing up the opportunity to take a percentage of the booty. In later years, when he had fallen on hard times, he cited this act of patriotism, not without regret, in a petition to the Chilean government for financial support.[20]

O'Brien's star shone brightly after Chacabuco, not least for his having captured the royalist standard. San Martín mentioned O'Brien's actions in dispatches and proposed that he be promoted.[21] The government in Buenos Aires and the new Chilean government in Santiago awarded him silver medals in recognition of his services.[22]

From San Martín's departure from Mendoza to his triumphant arrival in Santiago, the liberation of Chile by the patriot forces had taken less than a month. By any military standard, it was an impressive feat and sent a shockwave through Spain's creaking American empire. San Martín's strategy had paid off, and he was offered the position of head of the new Chilean government, which he refused. His next objective was to secure the independence of the continent by ousting the Spanish from their remaining strongholds. With San Martín refusing the position, Bernardo O'Higgins became the supreme director of Chile. O'Higgins now concentrated on prosecuting the war against the royalists, who were still in the south of the country, while San Martín began organising the next stage of his plan to rid the continent of the Spanish: an expedition to liberate Peru.

For the proposed expedition to succeed, it was necessary to solicit financial help from the government in Buenos Aires. Less than a month after the Battle of Chacabuco, San Martín and O'Brien set off on another gruelling journey across the Andes. In an essay about the journey, Vicuña Mackenna depicts San Martín as taciturn, uncompromising, obsessive in his determination to rid South America of the Spanish, and suffering from never-ending ailments, in sharp contrast to his Irish aide-de-camp, who is depicted as romantic, happy-go-lucky, and relentless in his pursuit of women. It is far from a convincing historical account. Since it is contrived to portray San Martín as the Spartan hero – the all-conquering general who forsakes comfort for speed and simplicity – the foppish O'Brien must act as his superior officer's foil. However, Vicuña Mackenna's imagining of their exchanges was based on his conversations with O'Brien, and gives a flavour of the dynamic between the two men.[23]

O'Brien travelled in advance of San Martín in order to make arrangements for food, accommodation and the mules that would take them across the Andes. San Martín joined O'Brien at Huechuraba, about eight kilometres north of Santiago, on the evening of 10 March; he had tried to leave Santiago surreptitiously but had been forced to make his way through a cheering throng. On their way north, San Martín and O'Brien stopped briefly in Chacabuco, where they saw the burial mounds of the dead, many of them black slaves recruited into the patriot and royalist armies as cannon fodder.[24] Neither man was well, San Martín suffering from his ulcer, O'Brien struck down by an illness that 'never ceased to reign' in Santiago.[25] This could have been one of any number of the diseases that ravaged the Chilean population in the early nineteenth century, among them tuberculosis, typhus, cholera and measles.

San Martín and O'Brien, led across the Andes by a Chilean guide, Justo Estay, completed the journey from the Chilean town of Los Andes in the foothills of the *cordillera* to the outskirts of Mendoza in seven days, San Martín suffering considerably during the crossing. They made the Uspallata pass by mid-March.[26] Two weeks later San Martín and O'Brien arrived in Buenos Aires, where the population welcomed them as the liberators of Chile. Having consulted with the government, and procured arms and ships for the invasion of Peru, San Martín and O'Brien returned across the pampas towards the Andes. They crossed the *cordillera* in early May,[27] the third time they had done so in four months.

Though the patriots were in control of Chile'ss capital, Santiago, the royalists – aided by reinforcements from Peru – were assembling for a counterattack in the south of the country. San Martín's failure to pursue the remainder of the royalist army after Chacabuco had allowed it to regroup around Talcahuano, the naval base outside the southern city of Concepción. At the end of 1817, O'Higgins marched south to flush out the royalists. O'Brien and two squadrons of mounted grenadiers were present on 5 December when the patriot forces attempted to breach the royalist defences.[28] The royalists fended them off in a bloody confrontation. O'Brien estimated the patriot losses at eighty killed and 150 wounded.[29]

The main body of the army was based at Las Tablas, a piece of high ground overlooking the port of Valparaíso. The officers enjoyed a relaxed atmosphere. In the mornings, before breakfast, they were awoken by a servant bringing them *mate*, a caffeine-rich infusion popular in many parts of South America. According to the English artillery officer William Miller, who arrived at Las Tablas in January 1818, food was plentiful. Dinner consisted of 'excellent soup, roasted strips of flesh, brought to table on a stick or ramrod, which answered the purpose of a spit, poultry, vegetables, and fruit in great abundance'.[30] Vegetables, fruit and bread were available in the camp market. During the day, the officers played practical jokes on one another or sat around chatting. Longer moments of leisure were spent horse racing and hunting. At night the officers fell asleep to the sound of the soldiers singing and playing the guitar.[31]

O'Brien kept a diary during this period, a fragment of which has survived and is held in the national archives in Santiago. He was bored, and attempted to divert himself by hunting birds – pigeons and partridges – often without success. 'Kept shooting all the Evening at the Pidgeons [*sic*] but killed none – then went to converse with the old Negro in the Garden', he wrote on 7 January 1818. On 10 January: 'Arrived at Las Tablas where we got the news of Commodore Bowles' arrival from Lima – Immediately set off for Valparaíso where the General [San Martín] was nearly lost going down the Precipice by his own bad management of his horse'. The next day: 'Went on bord [*sic*] [the *Amphion*, Bowles' flagship]. Dined and came to the governadores [*sic*] Ball. Supper and danced with the mad woman …'.[32]

O'Brien basked in his celebrity while living in Santiago. He was among the most famous members of the growing community of '*ingleses*' living in Chile.[33] O'Brien and his fellow officers were never short of female company. In Valparaíso and Santiago, the wealthy citizens held frequent dances for the officers. But it was not just the city beauties who caught O'Brien's eye. He was captivated by the women he met in the villages and towns he passed through during his trips to the south, keeping notes about them in his diary: on 23 February 1818 he wrote, 'met by the Governor of Melipilla where we spent the day accompanied by a number of fine girls'; on 4 February 1819: 'saw the finest girl in my mind in all Chilli [*sic*] but poor and honest'; on 16 February 1819: 'at four o'clock marched, but on my departure, was struck with the sight of a beautiful girl and wished I had not come away for that evening'.[34] This last encounter brought on one of the occasional bouts of melancholy that surface in the diary.

At six feet, two inches, O'Brien towered above most of his fellow officers, and became a familiar face in Santiago. He was a handsome, well-built man. His friends and biographers make frequent mention of his womanising. In 'El Jeneral San Martín después de Chacabuco', Vicuña Mackenna writes that O'Brien's two passions were 'battles and good-looking girls'.[35] The essay deals with General San Martín's trip to Buenos Aires in the aftermath of the pivotal Battle of Chacabuco to seek support for the invasion of Peru. O'Brien accompanied him as his aide-de-camp. Before setting off, O'Brien bade farewell to 'the most beautiful of his female acquaintances'.[36] In *El Jeneral O'Brien*, the biographical sketch of his friend written shortly after O'Brien's death, Vicuña Mackenna describes him as 'the worshipper of all women, without exception, but for the ugly ones'.[37] The Argentinian historian Juan Estevan Guastavino relates an anecdote, probably apocryphal, about O'Brien and the bishop of Lima. The bishop shows O'Brien around the cathedral in the Peruvian capital, and points out an exquisite religious image of which he is particularly proud. O'Brien concurs, but, glancing around the nave, spots a young woman kneeling before the altar. Dazzled by the vision before him, O'Brien turns and says to the bishop, 'but that *limeña* [a female native of Lima] is more beautiful and I like her more'.[38]

O'Brien was a sentimentalist. There is a verse written in O'Brien's diary: 'Nor joy, nor ease, that heart can know/ which like the needle true/ Turns at each touch of joy or woe/ But turning trembles too.'[39] It was from 'A Prayer for Indifference' by the Irish poet Frances Greville. Composed in the 1750s, it became one of the most famous poems of the eighteenth century, and obviously held some hidden meaning for O'Brien, the serial romantic. Typically, he had made an error when transcribing the verse into his diary, substituting 'joy' for 'peace' in the first line. O'Brien was 'deeply religious', according to Figueroa, noting that he would always say a prayer before setting off on a journey.[40] He was undoubtedly a convinced Roman Catholic, but there is no significant evidence of religiosity in his writings.

There was a vibrant community of British and Irish-born merchants living in Santiago and Valparaíso in 1819,[41] and there was much social intercourse between the native-born officers and the foreigners – both soldiers and civilians – arriving in Chile to take advantage of the opportunities created by the establishment of the new state. The British government had stepped up its involvement in the region, sending Commodore William Bowles to Chile to protect the country's commercial interests from the marauding Spanish fleet based in Callao, Peru. Royal Navy ships were scattered around the bay at Valparaíso. To keep themselves amused on shore, the British officers would arrange horse races and cricket matches between teams from different ships, as well as picnics and excursions to the nearby city of Quillota.[42]

The City of London and the northern English manufacturers had welcomed Chilean independence with enthusiasm, dreaming of the profits to be made in the new markets. A twenty-two-year-old clerk, Samuel Haigh, recalled being invited by a merchant relative to travel to Chile as his company's agent:

> He stated, that great news had just been received from South America, no less than the opening of Chile to foreign trade, in consequence of the victory of Chacabuco, gained by the patriots; that this was the time to make a push for a fortune, and as he and two partners contemplated sending out a cargo, to get the 'cream of the market,' if I would undertake its management, I should have an opportunity of filling my coffers with ingots of gold and silver, or, as he quaintly expressed it in his synonymous phraseology, of 'making a man of *myself*'.[43]

Haigh's was not an unusual experience. British companies rushed to send ships laden with manufactures to Chile in the expectation of exorbitant profits. For this they needed representatives or agents on the spot. John O'Brien's brother James – known in South America as Diego[44] – was among the Irish-born merchants working in Chile. James does not seem to have followed his brother into the military life, and it is reasonable to assume that he managed the family business while his elder brother went off to war. He was about twenty-two when he arrived. He first lived in Buenos Aires, working as a merchant, most probably importing textiles and exporting the many raw materials in plentiful supply in South America and which were in demand in Europe. In 1818 James was in Chile while at the same time applying for citizenship of the United Provinces of the River Plate. In his history of the Irish in Argentina, Fr Thomas Murray accords James O'Brien the distinction of being 'the first unmistakably Irish name' to apply for citizenship.[45]

John Orr was one of the witnesses who testified to James O'Brien's character and financial health during his citizenship examination. He claimed in 1818 that James had between 10,000 (€2,321) and 12,000 pesos (€2,785) at his disposal. Colonel Nicolas de Vedia of the army of the United Provinces was another witness to James' good standing. In a letter of recommendation, he claimed that James O'Brien had 'always demonstrated with good sense and reason his attachment to the justice of Americans fighting our enemies, the Spanish'.[46] This demonstration of patriotic enthusiasm was a prerequisite for achieving citizenship in the United Provinces.

The royalist threat in the south of Chile remained alive. On 19 March 1818 the army, led by O'Higgins and San Martín, suffered a disastrous defeat at the hands of the royalists at Cancha Rayada, close to the town of Talca. John O'Brien was present.[47] It was a demoralising loss, and the future of the government was in doubt. In Santiago, as fears grew about the expected Spanish occupation of the city and as rumours spread that O'Higgins was dead, there were calls for a mass evacuation. A profound gloom hung over the patriot forces after the disaster at Cancha Rayada, and the revolution seemed briefly in danger. But the royalists were incapable of pressing home their advantage.

Three weeks later, on 4 April, San Martín faced a royalist force, commanded by Mariano Osorio, at Maipú on the outskirts of Santiago. Osorio's manoeuvres enabled the patriots to charge the royalists' flank, giving them a decisive advantage. O'Brien rode into battle at the head of a cavalry division that included the mounted grenadiers. The action of the mounted grenadiers in charging the royalist Burgos regiment was one of the key moments in the battle. The patriot army suffered the loss of about a thousand men. Some two thousand royalist troops were killed during the battle, and most of the senior officers were taken prisoner.[48] The exception was Osorio, who managed to escape with two hundred cavalrymen. By the end of the day, the royalists were routed. It was the definitive victory in the war for Chile. Though the Spanish continued to resist the patriots in the south of the country, they would never again pose a serious threat.

On the evening of the Battle of Maipú, once victory had been won, and following San Martín's orders, O'Brien set off in pursuit of Osorio, accompanied by 150 mounted grenadiers. At Pudahuel he was led to believe that Osorio had taken the road to Valparaíso, and he tried to cut him off. On the summit of a hill known as the Prado, O'Brien decided to take a steep, winding path down towards the Valparaíso road. The path was treacherous and extremely difficult to negotiate on horseback, but it gave O'Brien the chance to intercept the royalist commander and his party. Once he and his forces made it down the hill, they laid an ambush and waited. But O'Brien's gamble failed. Instead of making for the Valparaíso road, Osorio and his party had travelled south-west in the direction of Melipilla and the coastal village of Bucalemu, from where the royalist commander escaped to the south of Chile. By the time O'Brien discovered his mistake, it was too late to give chase.[49] 'Indeed, O'Brien, by his excess of zeal in the completion of his orders, had committed an error which allowed Osorio and his companions time to escape' was the assessment of the nineteenth-century Chilean historian Diego Barros Arana.[50] Throughout his life O'Brien would recount the story of Osorio's escape to each and all, adding colour and indulging in some gentle self-mockery. In its telling he would credit San Martín for his benevolent spirit, believing that other superior officers might have shown more displeasure at the mission's failure.

Despite his failure to capture Osorio, O'Brien's mission did achieve an important result. Returning to Santiago, he and his men came across a large party of retreating royalists and their heavily laden mules. He captured four hundred troops and twenty-five officers. His men also found a suitcase containing Osorio's official dispatches and correspondence with the viceroy of Peru. Not only did this discovery give the patriots an indication of royalist strategy, it also unmasked several traitors in Santiago, men who, though outwardly sympathetic to the patriots, had turned coat after the Battle of Cancha Rayada, offering their services to the royalists.[51]

There has been some debate about San Martín's role during the Battle of Maipú. He did not physically take part in the fighting, and some of his detractors later claimed that he was drunk. The same critics levelled allegations after the wars of independence that San Martín was frequently drunk on campaign. José de la Riva-Agüero, writing under a pseudonym, made some of the most damning allegations about San Martín. Born in Lima, he was a liberal army officer who had fought against the French during the Peninsular War. He returned to Lima and conspired to bring about the end of Spanish rule in Peru, which brought him into contact with San Martín. Initially an ally, he later condemned San Martín for assuming power in Peru. In 1858 Riva-Agüero posthumously published a book in Peru containing a damning, if suspect, account of San Martín's behaviour during the Battle of Maipú. It is interesting not so much for what it tells us about San Martín – after all, Riva-Agüero is a prejudiced source – but the extent to which the Argentine general relied on O'Brien, or at least how the relationship was perceived by observers. Riva-Agüero claimed that during the Battle of Maipú, both officers and privates had seen San Martín 'at a great distance from the army, lying on the ground, and so drunk that he did not give the most minor order'.[52] According to Riva-Agüero, this was not untypical because San Martín would spend 'a great deal of the day sleeping off his drunkenness'.[53] Riva-Agüero contended that O'Brien had approached San Martín at Maipú and told him that Osorio's infantry were sweeping aside the patriots' forces, and that if he did not order a cavalry charge the battle would be lost. In Riva-Agüero's account, O'Brien saves the day by taking command:

> Then he noted that San Martín was totally drunk; as he had been before at Cancha Rayada, and he, that is O'Brien, returned immediately to the battlefield and, in San Martín's name, himself ordered the cavalry forward, with which the victory was won. The reply which San Martín gave captain O'Brien was to hand him a bottle of rum, saying: '*Take this and drink it in my name*' [*a.t.*].[54]

Riva-Agüero's book purported to be a collection of documents relating to the history of Peru. But the title – in English, *Memories and Documents about the Independence of Peru and the Causes of its Misfortunes* – pointed to its being a polemic, a virulent attack on those whom Riva-Agüero held responsible – chiefly San Martín and Bolívar – for Peru's woes in the post-independence era. Riva-Agüero himself had been appointed the first president of Peru, a position he held for less than four months, and felt that San Martín and Bolívar's autocratic tendencies had contributed much to the failure to embed democracy in the country. It seems unlikely that San Martín could have led the patriots to victory in Chile and Peru against overwhelming odds if he had been constantly intoxicated. It might have been that the effects of San Martín's heavy laudanum intake and his tendency to lie down on the ground – both the result of his efforts to alleviate the chronic pain he suffered due to rheumatism – were used by his enemies to support malicious rumours that he was a drunk.

The most interesting aspect of Riva-Agüero's account is that he credits O'Brien with the victory at Maipú, the battle that definitively turned the tide in favour of the patriots in the south of the continent. Even if, as is likely, his account of that day is invented, it still gained currency. Writing in the late 1850s, the German merchant Heinrich Witt noted that some accounts of Maipú that he had heard in Peru attributed the victory to O'Brien rather than to San Martín.[55]

After the wars of independence, O'Brien embarked upon various commercial projects. His ability to raise capital and gain access to the governments of the new republics was greatly aided not only by the fact that he was a veteran of the wars of independence with the rank of colonel – he was later promoted to general in the Peruvian army by President Andrés Santa-Cruz – but also because he had performed vital actions at Chacabuco and Maipú, which, as Witt recalls, entered folklore.

After Maipú, O'Brien was showered with honours. The Chilean government awarded him a silver medal,[56] and Bernardo O'Higgins presented him with the cross of Chile's Legion of Merit. He was promoted to the rank of *teniente coronel* (lieutenant colonel). The government of the United Provinces had awarded silver aiguillettes to San Martín in honour of the victory at Maipú. In 1820 San Martín sent them to O'Brien, writing that 'there are no better shoulders than yours, so that I have all confidence in sending them [the aiguillettes] to you to wear in my name'.[57] O'Brien treasured the letter. In the margin at the bottom of the letter, in red ink, he wrote that it was 'a very interesting document, San Martín declaring that no officer in the whole of his army was so well deserving of the cordones [aiguillettes] and honours as I for the battle of Maipo [Maipú]'.[58]

Shortly after Maipú, San Martín and O'Brien rode out to a waterfall called El Salto in the hills outside Santiago. O'Brien sat on a wooden bench watching San Martín burn the letters incriminating various citizens of Santiago as traitors that the Irish officer had discovered in Osorio's correspondence.[59] Mitre ascribes chivalrous motives to San Martín's behaviour,[60] and it is important to note that Mitre's principal source was a conversation he had had with O'Brien.[61] Other writers believe that it was a tactical gesture designed to keep the traitors within the fold, rather than open up bitter divisions within the patriot ranks. O'Brien believed that San Martín had acted from the purest of motives. For the rest of his life he regarded the burning of Osorio's correspondence as one of San Martín's noblest deeds.

In June 1818 O'Brien was granted leave for ten months to return to

Ireland. It was initially unpaid until San Martín intervened with the government, citing the fact that O'Brien was one of the officers 'who had proven themselves most during the Chilean campaign', whereupon he was awarded fully paid leave.[62] However, he was unable to travel. In April 1819 he once again solicited leave for a ten-month period. This second petition cited business related to the family estate in Baltinglass following the deaths of his parents.[63] Though leave was granted, he was again prevented from travelling, this time because San Martín was planning his next campaign, the liberation of the last important Spanish stronghold on the continent: Peru.

4
The Liberation of Peru

The joint Chilean-Argentine army departed Valparaíso to liberate Peru on 20 August 1820, with San Martín as commander-in-chief. Eighteen transports carried the four-and-a-half-thousand-strong force, with an escort of seven warships. The Scottish admiral Thomas Cochrane was commander of the fleet. Cochrane's fame had rivalled Nelson's during the Napoleonic Wars but, after falling into disgrace following a conviction for fraud, he had been dismissed by the Royal Navy. Lacking gainful employment, he had offered his services to the Chilean government.

Having been promoted to *teniente coronel*, O'Brien travelled with San Martín as his aide-de-camp.[1] The English army officer William Miller recalled the departure in his memoirs:

> It was in truth an imposing and an exciting spectacle to behold that bay crowded with shipping, under patriot banners, which formerly received only one merchant vessel annually. As the several corps, marching from cantonments, with music playing, through cheering multitudes, severally arrived upon the beach, they were taken off to their respective transports in the greatest order, and without the occurrence of a single accident.[2]

San Martín landed his army at Pisco, about 200 kilometres south of Callao. He remained there for six weeks, hoping to attract Peruvians to the cause of independence. Sending a small detachment inland with orders to march north, San Martín sailed with the rest of the army to Ancón, a fishing village about forty kilometres north of Lima, landing on 1 November 1820.[3] It was in Ancón that O'Brien played a vital role in preventing a disaster that might have had far-reaching consequences. He had been aboard the frigate *Águila* – which was carrying the artillery and significant quantities of ammunition and gunpowder – when a fire broke out below decks. The terrified crew, which had been preparing a meal below, ran onto the main deck. O'Brien, along with an army captain and an English sailor, raced below and managed to put out the fire before the ship exploded.[4]

From Ancón, San Martín ordered the fleet to the port of Huacho, 120 kilometres north of Lima. He established his headquarters at nearby Huaura. San Martín's strategy was to avoid a direct confrontation between the main armies. Instead, he spread propaganda and secured desertions to the patriot forces. At the same time he sent smaller parties of soldiers to attack royalist positions in the south of Peru – the north of the country had already declared its independence from Spain – and the outskirts of Lima.

The war in Peru was brutal, exacting a heavy toll on the civilian population. O'Brien took part in several expeditions into the back country. Marching through the Andean district of Huancavelica at the head of an advanced party, he witnessed the aftermath of a particularly violent encounter between marauding royalists and the residents of a small town. Upon entering the town, O'Brien asked for the parish priest in order to ascertain the enemy's movements. He was told that the priest had fled. When O'Brien asked for the church sexton, a local man pointed silently towards a tree. The dead bodies of the sexton and his wife were hanging from one of the branches, surrounded by their crying children. The sexton had earlier gone into hiding, while his wife had refused to divulge his whereabouts when questioned by a royalist officer, who wished to open the church to billet his men. When the royalists uncovered the sexton's hiding place, he and his wife were executed.[5]

The proximity of the liberating army and the *montoneras* – the local militias or guerrillas that sprang up among the indigenous population in opposition to the royalists – forced the viceroy of Peru, José de la Serna, to evacuate Lima. San Martín entered the city in triumph, and ordered a series of public ceremonies to mark the arrival of the liberating army. On 28 July 1821 O'Brien climbed onto a platform that had been erected in the Plaza de Armas in Lima.[6] He joined senior officers, members of the hierarchy, and other local dignitaries as San Martín proclaimed Peru's independence. Thousands of cheering soldiers filled the square to watch San Martín raise Peru's first national flag – a diagonally quartered design with white upper and lower fields and faced with an oval-shaped depiction of the sun rising over the Andes.

During the ceremony, San Martín presented O'Brien with the canopy under which the viceroys of Peru – the foremost representatives of the Spanish monarch – had entered Lima. The canopy was a sumptuous piece of red silk flecked with gold.[7] This was a significant honour. In the colonial era the viceroy of Peru was the most powerful man in South America, and enjoyed a quasi-monarchical status. The canopy, or baldachin, was a symbol of royal authority dating back to the medieval era. Pizarro himself was said to have been bestowed with viceregal powers under the same canopy. The fact that the viceroys were entitled to enter the city of Lima under a canopy symbolised their royal authority. This privilege was usually reserved for the Spanish monarch but had been extended to the viceroy of Peru in the sixteenth century. The privilege was rescinded in the seventeenth century, before being restored, indicating just how jealously the monarch guarded it.[8] O'Brien was also awarded a medal for his participation in the capture of Lima, and was admitted to the newly established Order of the Peruvian Sun, which San Martín had created to recognise the bravery of his officers during the campaign in Peru.

The declaration of independence in the Plaza de Armas had important political meaning. The ceremony there was the first of four that took place in the centre of Lima. It was a piece of theatre that marked not so much the ending as the beginning of the war, a nation-building exercise, which San Martín believed was as important as achieving victory on the field of battle. Chile had been receptive to the patriot cause, but in Peru there was a far larger, and stronger, element sympathetic to the Spanish Crown.

Captain Basil Hall, the British commander of the Royal Navy's HMS *Conway* – who was present at the 'rather imposing' ceremony – understood its purpose. He observed that, although 'San Martín's manner was graceful and easy throughout, unaccompanied by anything theatrical or affected', it was 'a business of show and effect, and quite repugnant to his taste'. 'I sometimes thought', Hall added, 'there might be detected in his face a momentary expression of impatience or contempt of himself for engaging in such mummery; but, if it really were so, he speedily resumed his wonted look of attention, and of good-will to all around him.'[9] San Martín may not have enjoyed the show, but he realised that, in Peru, nation-building – or what might have been described in a later era as winning hearts and minds – was as important as ambushes and cavalry charges.

San Martín's army held Lima, but the war in Peru continued. In Callao, the Pacific port that served Lima, twelve kilometres to the west, the royalist garrison was holding out. At the end of August, General José de Canterac approached Lima with a royalist division from Jauja, 170 kilometres east of the capital, but decided not to attack the city, sheltering instead under the guns at Callao. On 14 September William Miller was given command of seven hundred men to observe Canterac's movements. O'Brien was attached to this unit. On 17 September Canterac retreated south-west towards Cuzco. Miller's division did not pursue the retreating royalist force until three days later. Without provisions, Miller's division – which had been swollen by a group of five hundred *montoneras* – followed Canterac into the foothills of the Andes, O'Brien skirmishing with the rearguard.[10] On 22 September the patriot division began climbing, in single file, a narrow path up the side of a mountain called Puruchuco. Near the summit the men had lain down to rest when some royalist soldiers were spotted coming out of the undergrowth. According to Miller's memoirs:

> They called out that they wished to pass over to the patriots. O'Brien, accompanied by a trumpeter, rode forward to parley with them, but he had not proceeded far when the pretended deserters commanded him to halt. At this time, a royalist battalion issued from an ambuscade; but finding that the patriot party was not to be entrapped, they pursued their march to the summit of the mountain. The light infantry company of Numancia, commanded by the gallant Captain Saens, and some cavalry, were sent forward, under the orders of O'Brien, who skirmished for about an hour; but three royalist battalions having countermarched to support their rearguard, O'Brien was compelled to fall back, and the patriot division was drawn up so as to defend a strong pass; and they continued in this position all night, expecting to be attacked; but the royalists continued their retreat.[11]

The royalists attacked the next day, but O'Brien, 'with a small party of infantry, by a well-directed fire', kept them at bay and the patriots were able to retreat. Miller and O'Brien 'were more than once on the point of being made prisoners', but 'were saved by the goodness of their horses, and galloped down declivities that, at another time, they would hardly have descended on horseback at a walk'.[12] Realising that his division had retreated too far 'to continue an effectual pursuit', Miller ordered them back to Lima, except for thirty hand-picked dragoons and 'some montoneros [*sic*]'.[13]

Miller and O'Brien pursued the royalists by a different route, bivouacking by a stream that night. The next day they came across another party of *montoneras*, led by a man called Quiros, which 'consisted of men of lawless habits, wearing long beards, and dressed in the most grotesque manner'.[14] According to Miller, 'it was curious to hear the conversation of these fellows seated in groups around their fires. One avowed having committed seventeen murders, another having strangled a woman of seventy and violating her daughter. Almost every one boasted of some deed of darkness.'[15] Miller decided to retreat to Lima on 27 September, having failed to capture Canterac. According to his memoir, though the mission was 'not altogether successful in its object', it 'facilitated the desertion of above one thousand royalists in spite of the exertions and severities of their chiefs'.[16]

Eight years of warfare against the Spanish and their royalist allies came to an end for O'Brien in Peru in 1821, but not before he had again been granted permission to return to Ireland. Before he embarked for Europe, however, San Martín entrusted him with a last mission. As part of his efforts to bed down the revolution, San Martín ordered O'Brien – now holding the rank of colonel – to Chile and the United Provinces with the flags and standards that had been captured from the royalists in battle. O'Brien's first port of call was Santiago, where he returned to the government the patriot flags that had been captured by the royalist army at the Battle of Rancagua. In Mendoza he placed in the cathedral the red-and-gold royalist flag which he himself had captured at the Battle of Chacabuco. On 30 March 1822 he arrived in Buenos Aires. He carried with him the prized standards of the Spanish army's Light Battalion of Arica, the Battalion of the Reserve Grenadiers, the Chaupiguaranga Regiment, the Regiment of the Tarma Cavalry and the Caramo Dragoons. He had been given orders to hand the standards to the city's municipal council. But because it had been abolished in the intervening period, he instead placed the standards in the city's cathedral.[17]

This was the final scene in the first major act of O'Brien's life in South America: that of a revolutionary soldier. His mind now turned towards home.

5
The Emigrant's Dream

O'Brien's role as a facilitator of Irish emigration to Argentina, rather than his military career, has been of most interest to Irish and Irish-Argentinian writers and historians.[1] He has been credited with playing a direct role in persuading, and travelling with, the first families to emigrate from County Westmeath in the 1820s, setting in motion the large-scale, mid-nineteenth-century Irish migration to Buenos Aires province. Although these claims remain dubious, as has been recently highlighted by Patrick Speight,[2] there is no doubt that O'Brien was one of the foremost promoters of Irish emigration to Argentina in the mid-nineteenth century, that his name became publicly linked in both Argentina and Ireland with the promotion of the former as a destination for Irish emigrants, and that he helped to forge a vision of a South American utopia that was to become a powerful lure for Catholic Irish emigrants.[3]

O'Brien was already thinking about developing a scheme for Irish emigration to Argentina immediately after leaving Peru in 1821 when he sought a meeting with Ñacuñán, the *cacique* whom he had first encountered when organising the *parlamento* between San Martín and the Pehuenche in 1816. O'Brien had visited Ñacuñán on other occasions during his time in the south of Chile. Nevertheless, he took precautions, seeking permission first from the *cacique*'s son.[4] The importance O'Brien placed on this meeting may be gauged by the fact that, on his way to Buenos Aires from Santiago, he crossed the Andes at a pass called El Planchón before returning north towards Mendoza. This route not only added several hundred kilometres to his journey but also entailed considerable danger because it meant passing through the territory of the Pehuenche. Many of the *caciques* who lived on the slopes of the Andes to the south of Santiago and Mendoza, on both sides of the border, were hostile to the new patriot governments and were allies of the royalists.

O'Brien's interactions with indigenous communities during his travels through South America range from conciliatory to hostile. As has been seen above, San Martín trusted him to oversee the festivities with the Pehuenche on the eve of the invasion of Chile, which would suggest that he possessed a talent for diplomatic negotiations with the *caciques*. On the other hand, if the indigenous leaders were uncooperative, he viewed them as an obstacle to the continent's material progress, and advocated violence against them, as was later to be the case in Peru.

Evidence of the discussions between O'Brien and Ñacuñán is contained in a report in *The British Packet, and Argentine News*, the English-language newspaper in Buenos Aires. The story was based on O'Brien's own testimony:

> The reception he met with from the Indians was hospitable in the extreme: the country which they inhabit is both beautiful and fertile, abounding in game, and the animals, not fearing molestation, are in a manner tame. The Colonel's thoughts reverted to Ireland, its over peopled cities, and consequent suffering, and on his arrival [in Buenos Aires] he made a proposition to this Government, in order to bring out a number of Hibernians to people the interesting country he had just departed from.[5]

As may be seen from the above passage, O'Brien was an able propagandist: the reference to Indians who were 'hospitable in the extreme' did not reflect the reality of the indigenous tribes' reaction to the expansion of white European settlers on the pampas.

O'Brien's was not a novel idea; it had its roots in the late sixteenth and seventeenth centuries, when the Spanish monarchs, in desperate need of priests and religious, sent Irish missionaries, such as the Jesuit Thomas Fields,[6] to labour in their new colonies. In the early seventeenth century, Irish colonists – such as Philip Purcell, Bernard O'Brien and Jasper Sheehan – were already suggesting a policy of promoting Irish emigration to South America – in this case, the northern bank of the Amazon – in order to ensure the creation of a politically loyal, religiously orthodox settler community.[7] This policy was actively pursued in North America in the late eighteenth century, when Irish missionaries were sent by the Spanish Crown to Florida and Louisiana in the failed hope of converting Anglo-American and British settlers to Catholicism. During the same period the Irish-born viceroy of Peru, Ambrose O'Higgins, and his appointee as governor of the southern Chilean town of Osorno, John Mackenna, introduced Irish artisans to the south of Chile,[8] while Thomas

O'Gorman proposed a similar scheme for Paraguay.[9] In the post-independence era, veterans of the wars of independence – including John Devereux in Venezuela, Bernardo O'Higgins in Chile, Francis Burdett O'Connor in Bolivia, and, later on, the journalist William Scully in Brazil – promoted emigration schemes in Ireland.[10]

Throughout the colonial period, the Spanish government was attracted by the idea of sending Irish settlers to its American colonies because of their Catholicism and attendant political loyalty. In turn, promoters of Irish emigration to Spanish America constructed a Catholic utopia, which was defined by its contrast with the Protestant-dominated United States. These visions of South America – vast, rich, empty and tolerant of the Catholic religion – were a form of escape for Irish emigrants struggling with limited access to land, poverty, and the denial of religious and political liberties. As Laura Izarra has written in the context of late-nineteenth-century Brazil: 'The propaganda of agents in England and the United States who were recruiting labour for agricultural settlements in Brazil unconsciously fed the desire for the real existence of a place which until that moment had only taken shape in the imagination of Irish emigrants [*a.t.*].'[11] In order to attract emigrants, it was necessary, therefore, to construct a vision of a promised land, or, as Oliver Marshall has written, also in the Brazilian context: 'Before an immigrant-based community can assert its identity, be influential or assimilate, it has to be established. Before it can be established, it has to be imagined.'[12]

O'Brien, then, was not unique in selling a South American utopia to Irish emigrants, but his efforts, as a promoter, to cultivate the idea of the continent as a suitable new home for Irish emigrants were the most significant. That he played a crucial role in encouraging Irish emigration to the continent was due to several factors. First and foremost were his impressive credentials as a veteran of the wars of independence. He had played crucial roles in two of the most important battles in the southern half of the continent, Chacabuco and Maipú, he held the rank of colonel in the Argentine army and, later, general in the Peruvian army, and had served as an aide-de-camp to San Martín. This allowed him access to the highest ranks of the military and civil establishment in South America, which, in turn, gained him entrance to political and diplomatic circles in Europe. In the British and Irish press, from the end of his participation in the wars of independence in 1821 until his death in 1861, he was regarded as an authority on South America. In the late 1820s O'Brien was one of the prominent leaders of the Irish community in Buenos Aires. His support for Daniel O'Connell and the campaign for Catholic emancipation would have further boosted his credibility in Ireland. During his trip home, O'Brien appeared publicly with O'Connell. O'Connell was himself a supporter of South American independence, buying commissions for his son and nephew in John Devereux's Irish Legion, which travelled to Venezuela to fight for Bolívar.[13]

Another important factor was O'Brien's talents as a publicist, both for himself and for his various projects, not least that of promoting Irish emigration to South America, which was to be a constant throughout his career. Except for a brief period in the late 1840s and 1850s, when he was regarded as a threat to British interests in Argentina, O'Brien received mostly favourable publicity in the British and Irish press for the forty years after the end of his career as a revolutionary; he was portrayed as a distinguished veteran of the wars of independence and a shrewd purveyor of intelligence on all matters related to South America.

Finally, his indefatigable energy must not be underestimated, nor should the improved conditions in ocean-going travel, both of which enabled O'Brien to cross the Atlantic on at least fifteen occasions, and to communicate face to face with members of the British and South American governments.

During his travels in the southern part of the continent, O'Brien came to regard the rich agricultural land to the east and west of the southern Andes as perfect for an Irish colony. In later years he wrote:

> In all my occupations for the welfare of other Countries, I have never been forgetful of my own. One hope has been ever entertained by me, one thought has still clung to me, that I might live to benefit my unhappy Countrymen, and help to raise some, if it was not allowed to me to elevate all, from the slough of despondency and of misery, in which I knew them to be immersed.[14]

In 1821 the situation in the Irish countryside was dire, with the partial failure of the potato crop causing famine conditions. O'Brien was in Uruguay in 1822, having returned from military service in Peru, and on learning that subscriptions were being raised in England for the relief of Irish famine victims, he brought forward his plans.[15] On 3 June he signed a contract with the government in Buenos Aires to bring Irish emigrants to the province. The men were to be labourers between the ages of fifteen and twenty-five, and would be employed on public works. The contract stipulated that the government would pay them 100 pesos (€23) in cash upon their arrival and another 150 pesos (€35) within three months; they would be obliged to work for six years and five months; they would be provided with dormitory accommodation and cooking facilities; they would have access to the same healthcare in military hospitals as soldiers; they would be exempt from military service; and, having served their time as labourers, would be given a plot of land and a cash advance for supplies and equipment.[16] The government agreed to provide a piece of land close to Buenos Aires for the residential quarters of the immigrants.[17]

This contractual letter does not propose the number of emigrants that O'Brien planned to bring to South America. However, in 1848 he wrote that he was proposing to 'take out a few thousand families'.[18] He returned to Europe with £15,000 (€17,424) at his disposal to implement the scheme,[19] and spent several months travelling across the continent; however, his travel plans for Italy and Greece were disrupted by the French invasion of Spain.[20] In letters to the British foreign secretary, George Canning, and to the Lord Lieutenant of Ireland, Richard Wellesley, O'Brien extolled the climate and soil of Buenos Aires province. 'The means of emigration hitherto sanctioned by the Government have been all colonial and heavily expensive', he wrote to Wellesley on 30 September 1823. 'It is my object to propose to you a mode of Emigration different from Colonial emigration, with more than its advantages, and none of its expense, and I make the proposal with full authority and ample means to give it effect.' He added:

> Your Excellency knows the immense resources of Buenos Ayres for Colonization, with a climate like Italy or the south of France, having more than 3000 miles [4,828 kilometres] in circumference uninhabited: the greater part over run with wild horses, cows, oxen and sheep with the finest soil on the Globe, entirely uncultivated, tho' capable of producing every kind of grain, of vegetable, tree or plant. To a country so circumstanced, colonization is not less an object of national importance than emigration is to the superabundant population of Ireland and I beg leave to add that a kindred colony placed under circumstances so advantageous promises to be not less beneficial to the Individuals concerned than it must prove of National importance to the growing intercourse and rising commerce now existing and rapidly increasing between the British Dominions in Europe and the Territory of Buenos Ayres.[21]

O'Brien wrote that his scheme had no political motive. Its purpose was

> the pure mutual benefit of both countries grounded on their mutual wants and interests in order that by the Exchange of the superabundant soil and food of one nation for a part of the superabundant population of another, their great interests may be promoted without expense by a free exchange of their greatest wants, and both may thus be combined in the advancement of their mutual Commerce.[22]

Conmen and charlatans – such as John Devereux, the County Wexford-born founder of the Irish Legion that had fought for Bolívar in Colombia, and the roguish Scottish officer Gregor MacGregor – had promoted similar schemes to prospective emigrants in Britain and Ireland during the wars of independence in Colombia and Venezuela. They involved defrauding poor emigrants into handing over what little they owned by promising them non-existent land and livestock in South America.[23]

On 24 August 1822 London's *Morning Post* included a salutary article about returning emigrants who had landed in the United Provinces intent on settling but who, 'on witnessing the distressed state of many families who had been deluded thither from imaginary ideas of obtaining a more happy situation', had 'the prudence to return to their native country before their resources were exhausted'. The newspaper added:

> This striking fact will, we hope, produce its due effect upon our countrymen, and operate as a warning not to be led away by the deceitful representations of romantic or desperate speculatists [*sic*] to forsake their native land, and run after impracticable schemes of bettering their condition, which generally terminate in disappointment and ruin.[24]

In September 1823 O'Brien tried to reassure the British authorities of his credentials, claiming that

> no speculation of an individual or interested character makes any part of my object; that the gratitude of the states of Southern America has rewarded my services with an independent Fortune, and that with such means and placed in an intermediate relation between both countries, allied to the one by blood, and to the other by duty, I have no other object than the common good of the country of my birth and the country of my adoption, and I have no doubt of mainly promoting that object by establishing an important Irish settlement in the

> Territory of Buenos Ayres should that object be sanctioned by your concurrence.[25]

In Belfast and Dublin he recruited skilled tradesmen. He toured the Irish countryside, attempting to persuade small farmers of the opportunities that existed on the other side of the world. O'Brien believed that the climate and soil in the province of Buenos Aires were perfect for the production of hemp, so he travelled to Ulster to find skilled textile workers who knew how 'to cultivate and manufacture [the plant] from the moment when the seeds were sown until it was turned into a ship's cable'.[26] Though he realised he was not going to be able to fully honour the contract without the support of the British government, O'Brien wrote to the government in Buenos Aires in January 1824 claiming that he was ready to sail from Dublin with two hundred artisans and farmers who would take on native-born apprentices in Argentina to teach them their trades. According to O'Brien, they were 'honest', 'virtuous', the 'chosen' few who were the 'flower of Ireland'.[27] He also intended to travel with an Irish chaplain,[28] indicating that the principal members of the Catholic Irish community in Buenos Aires already believed in the importance of having their compatriots minister to them.

Because the number of emigrants was substantially lower than had been hoped, the cost to the government would be reduced. 'My compatriots always expect the Government of Buenos Aires to be generous', O'Brien wrote, 'so that when they arrive, they will have to receive their citizenship papers and the same monthly salary earned by the country's workers'.[29] In order to win public opinion to his side, he began a publicity campaign in the British and Irish newspapers in which he outlined the benefits of his scheme. He was to remain a prolific letter writer to the press for the rest of his life.

At the same time that O'Brien was attempting to persuade the British government to back the scheme to transport Irish emigrants to the United Provinces, he was working on a similar project for the Chilean government. As the son of an Irish emigrant who, from humble beginnings, had risen through the ranks of the Spanish administration to become the most powerful man in South America, Bernardo O'Higgins felt a deep connection to his ancestral homeland, and was an enthusiastic supporter of Irish emigration to Chile. Indeed, Ambrose O'Higgins had been an enthusiastic proponent of Irish emigration to Chile. Bernardo was a great admirer of his father's achievements, and hoped to build on Ambrose's limited successes.[30]

In 1821 O'Brien offered to send British and Irish emigrants to Chile.

O'Higgins replied positively. Chile was in need of expertise to develop industry, and he asked O'Brien to enlist a range of professionals and skilled workers, including chemists and mineralogists, cotton and linen manufacturers, porcelain-makers, glass-blowers and paper-makers. In exchange for their services, the emigrants would be given Chilean citizenship, the protection of the government, and tools and equipment.[31] O'Higgins considered using part of a $5 million loan obtained in London on behalf of the Chilean government to finance the colonisation scheme.[32]

In January 1822 O'Higgins wrote to Antonio José de Irisarri, a Guatemalan-born journalist who had been appointed Chile's minister for foreign affairs and sent to Europe with a roving brief to negotiate support and a loan for the new government. O'Higgins urged Irisarri to help O'Brien. Irisarri was sceptical of the scheme and its promoter:

> I very much doubt this plan will take effect, at least to a large extent, given that to transport useful people, which are not in excess in their own country, the outlay of large sums is necessary, which I don't believe has entered into Colonel O'Brien's calculations; but, as it is your wish, I will try to make sure that the good intentions of this distinguished servant of the state are not all fantasies.[33]

But while promising to help, Irisarri refused to spend any money on the scheme, and requested details about how the Irish emigrants would be employed.[34] O'Brien was equally contemptuous of Irisarri. He met him in Europe, but told O'Higgins that 'he would not even listen to me. He is gone to Paris and thinks never more to return to Chili [*sic*]. He has got money enough and he does not care for you or the country.'[35]

O'Brien called upon some of O'Higgins' relatives in Ireland. He told O'Higgins that he had 'met a good many – and asked some of them to go out to see you but they say Chili [*sic*] is to [*sic*] far away'.[36] O'Brien visited the Chilean leader's former haunts in Richmond, outside London, the scene of O'Higgins' happiest days in England. O'Higgins had attended a college in Richmond and fallen in love with the master's daughter, Charlotte Eels. O'Brien gave O'Higgins news of the family in the same letter:

> I have been to Richmond where you first received your education. I enquired particularly after the proprietor of the college, Mr Eels. He is long since died at the Island of Madera [*sic*]. His wife is now living

> in London, No. 100 Crawford Street. She is very old but remembers you very well. Her daughter, Miss Charlotte Eels is also dead very soon after you left this country. She never married and the mother says it was her last request to be remembered to you. And she was interred at Richmond hill. I have sent by the ship Sesotros her likeness which very probably you may remember when you see it.[37]

Political events in Chile were to put a brake on the plan to recruit Irish settlers. In Santiago, O'Higgins' enemies were circling. In January 1823 he resigned as head of the Chilean government under pressure from his former comrade-in-arms Ramón Freire. O'Brien sympathised in a letter written from Liverpool in May: 'I am very sorry for any dissension between two of the men who has [*sic*] for ten years fought together and were such good friends but we are told Freire does not declare war against you but that it's your ministers.' He ended the letter: 'Dear O'Higgins, every success and that the enemies which rise up against you may meet the death they deserve.'[38]

O'Brien's scheme to bring Irish emigrants to Buenos Aires also failed. The British government's policy towards South American independence was conditioned by its diplomatic efforts in post-Napoleonic Europe and the continuation of the Anglo-Spanish alliance. The government had maintained a policy of non-interference in the conflict between Spain and her former colonies, and had passed the Foreign Enlistment Act in 1819 to prevent British and Irish soldiers from enrolling in the patriot armies. Despite the efforts of representatives of the government in Buenos Aires, most notably those of the United Provinces' minister for foreign affairs, Bernardino Rivadavia, Britain had still not recognised the regime in Buenos Aires in 1823 – it would take another two years.[39] It was in this context that the British foreign secretary, George Canning, objected to O'Brien's Buenos Aires scheme. According to O'Brien, he had been 'on the point of making a selection of emigrants, when Mr Canning, apprehensive that it might be said that he was permitting a political object to be gained, rather than sanctioning the accomplishment of a benevolent purpose, interfered, & the Emigration I then suggested was rendered abortive'.[40] The chief secretary of Ireland, Henry Goulburn, brushed aside O'Brien, replying that '[the Lord Lieutenant] does not deem it to be one to which he could properly give any sanction or with respect to which it is necessary to express any opinion'.[41]

Disillusioned that he had not been able to persuade the British government to support his scheme, O'Brien embarked for South America in September

1824.[42] He arrived in Buenos Aires on 18 January 1825,[43] and sought permission to re-enlist in the army. In a petition to the government, he lamented the losses he had accrued in trying to bring Irish emigrants to the province. He claimed that he had spent 16,000 pesos (€3,714) chartering ships and buying provisions and supplies for the journey to South America. The British government's decision to prohibit the sailing of these ships had forced him 'to return to this country for which he had made so many sacrifices, with the object of continuing his military career, to which he had given his best years [*a.t.*]'.[44] He also requested payment of the portion of the salary he would have earned had he remained in the army. This request was refused, the Buenos Aires government arguing that it had not been a condition of the licence granting his discharge. The government was also unable to find O'Brien a place in the army, despite recognising his 'commendable and distinguished services [*a.t.*]'.[45]

There remain the confused claims in some of the literature that O'Brien was involved in persuading Irish emigrants to travel to Argentina at a later date in the 1820s. Patrick McKenna has written that, in 1826, 'it was decided to send Thomand [*sic*] O'Brien back to Ireland to recruit Irish immigrants'.[46] In another work, McKenna writes that the 'Irish elites in Argentina' sent O'Brien to Ireland in 1828 'to select only a type of emigrant that would suit their purposes'.[47] Another Irish writer, Pat Nally, has written that O'Brien met John Mooney of Streamstown, County Westmeath and travelled with him, his sister Mary, and her husband, Patrick Bookey, to Argentina in 1828.[48] Although O'Brien did travel to Europe in September 1827, returning to South America a year later, there is no documentary evidence supporting the claims that he was involved in promoting another scheme to bring Irish emigrants to Argentina in 1828.[49] There is also no mention in O'Brien's correspondence of his having been involved in a later scheme, which, if it were the case, would seem to be a strange omission.

Further muddying the waters is O'Brien's contention, in a letter to the Earl of Clarendon in 1848, that, after he returned to South America in 1825, he did not visit Ireland until the mid-1840s.[50] This is demonstrably untrue, because he is reported as having been in Ireland in the late 1830s. However, the fact that no mention is made of a visit to Ireland in 1828 is interesting, given that O'Brien, in trying to persuade Clarendon of the merits of a new Irish emigration scheme to Uruguay, relates the history of his involvement in efforts to bring about Irish emigration to the River Plate.

Though he was denied permission by the British government to implement his plans, O'Brien had succeeded in awakening interest in Ireland to the opportunities available to emigrants in Argentina. James M. Ussher provides probably the fairest summation of O'Brien's efforts:

> His [1822–25] mission, as such, was a failure; but it advertised the advantages offered to settlers in the River Plate; it effected a permanent contact between the two nations; it encouraged aspiring young men to seek their fortunes over here, and it inaugurated a current of Hibernian immigration that lasted for a full half century.[51]

For the rest of his life, especially in the 1840s, when O'Brien represented the government of Montevideo in Europe, he promoted and advertised the benefits of emigration to South America.

However, in 1825 O'Brien's fortunes were at a low ebb and, frustrated by the refusal of the Buenos Aires government to offer him a position in the army, he returned to Peru. It was a decision that would bring him into contact with Simón Bolívar and open up a range of new commercial opportunities.

6
Laykakota

O'Brien returned to Lima in 1825. Much had changed in his absence, not least the fact that his mentor and commanding officer San Martín had left the political and military stage. While San Martín had been leading the armies that liberated Chile and much of Peru from Spanish rule, Simón Bolívar had been fighting the Spanish forces in the north of the continent, in Venezuela and Colombia. San Martín and Bolívar's armies had eventually converged in Peru. During a famous conference with Bolívar in the Ecuadorean city of Guayaquil, San Martín ceded overall command of the patriot army in Peru to Bolívar and, after a brief spell living in Mendoza and Buenos Aires, retreated into exile in Europe. On 9 December 1824 Bolívar led the patriot armies to a decisive victory at the Battle of Ayacucho, bringing an end to Spanish rule in Peru.

O'Brien and Bolívar met in the first half of 1825, most probably in Lima.[1] O'Brien needed help: his project to settle an Irish colony in Buenos Aires had been frustrated by the British government and, once back in South America, the government of the United Provinces had refused him a position in the army. From Buenos Aires, O'Brien had travelled to Peru to offer his assistance to Bolívar.

Both San Martín and Bolívar relied upon Irish officers – a reflection, perhaps, of the military reputation of the nation in the early nineteenth century, especially in the Hispanic world. Two of Bolívar's most loyal aides-de-camp were Irishmen, Daniel Florence O'Leary from County Cork and William Owens Ferguson from County Antrim. Bolívar must have been aware of San Martín's regard for O'Brien's talents. Not long after the two men had become acquainted, he gave the Irish officer a pair of silver spurs as a gift, and appointed him as an aide-de-camp. O'Brien was therefore in the rare position of having served alongside the two most famous generals of the South American wars of independence. According to Vicuña Mackenna,

> O'Brien always kept a place in his heart for the two great warriors of our hemisphere, whom he always compared to each other, giving his preference to San Martín. He used to say that Bolívar was America's Napoleon and, in order to make greater his praise, that San Martín was the Wellington of her wars [*a.t.*].[2]

In May 1825 Bolívar and O'Brien left Lima for La Paz, Bolivia on a triumphant procession through the recently conquered Andean territories. The route took them down the Pacific coast towards Arequipa before they headed inland towards the Andes and the Inca capital of Cuzco. From Cuzco they travelled west towards the city of Puno, and then on to the Isla del Sol (Island of the Sun) on Lake Titicaca.[3]

The Isla del Sol is one of the most important sites in Inca mythology. The Incas believed that, after a devastating flood, the world was shrouded in darkness, until the creator god, Viracocha, arose from the lake and commanded the sun to rise from the Isla del Sol. At the same time Viracocha created the first two Incas from the island's rocky earth: the legendary king, Manco Capac, and his wife, Mama Ocllo, both deities in their own right. The legend of the sun rising from Lake Titicaca symbolised the triumph of Inca civilisation over barbarism. This vast expanse of water, some 3,810 metres above sea level, became the wellspring of an empire, which at its peak, in the early sixteenth century, covered much of present-day Ecuador, Peru, Bolivia and northern Chile. There were about twelve million inhabitants, mostly self-sufficient farmers linked by a common dialect, Quechua, and an advanced road network.

When O'Brien and Bolívar approached the Isla del Sol, fourteen hundred Indians in canoes paddled out to salute them. They were wearing traditional dress and singing victory songs in honour of Bolívar, the Liberator of South America. In the ruins of the palace, O'Brien knelt in the earth and buried his sword, medals, epaulettes and the other military insignia he had been awarded over his twelve-year career in the service of the armies of Argentina, Chile and Peru.[4] The ceremony O'Brien performed on the Isla del Sol coincided with the end of the military campaign against the Spanish; by 1825 the Spanish royalists had been comprehensively defeated in nearly all of South America. It was also evidence of a Bolívarian narrative that sought to portray the liberating armies as restoring the Andean republics to their pre-Columbian purity.[5]

O'Brien and Bolívar headed south towards La Paz. This was mining country. For hundreds of years, indigenous and *mestizo*[6] miners had been forced to work as little more than slaves for the mine owners. But the once-booming industry, which had long represented the essence of Spanish America in the European mind, was a shadow of what it had been during the colonial era. During the wars of independence, many of the miners had been conscripted into the armies, while the mines had been looted, vandalised or left abandoned. Once the wars were over, the cash-strapped governments of the Andean republics looked at new ways of tapping the natural resources beneath their countries' mountains and deserts. They had neither the capital nor the expertise to exploit the ore, so they turned to foreign companies, granting them valuable licences and concessions.

There was a scramble to invest in Latin American mines in the years following independence. British companies poured millions of pounds into mining enterprises in Bolivia, Brazil, Chile, Colombia, Mexico and Peru. An anonymous letter writer, whose correspondence appeared in *The Morning Chronicle*, depicted the rush to invest in Peruvian mining:

> Agents from London are seen or heard of in every province of this Continent, bargaining for mines; they have turned the brains of the Spaniards, who had long given up mining, in despair. Potosí, they write, is all in an uproar, with the competition of Englishmen for pits full of water.[7]

Agents for British companies were flooding into Chile, Peru and Bolivia, desperate for mining concessions. Captain Joseph Andrews, who had travelled to South America on behalf of the Chilian and Peruvian Mining Association, described the frenzy that had descended upon the City of London in response to a newspaper article about the first returns for a British mining company: 'The public, without inquiring into facts, conceived that South America was the scene to realize all their golden dreams. The scrip of the company to which these riches belonged, mounted five or six hundred per cent., while that of others, catching the excitement, became proportionably [*sic*] elevated.'[8]

Potosí was the centre of this heady mix of revolution and commerce. In 1825 victorious patriot and defeated royalist officers, exhausted from the harsh Andean campaigns, consorted with competing mining agents from Europe and Buenos Aires in the shadow of the *cerro rico* – Potosí's fabled 'rich mountain'. Since the arrival of the Spanish in South America, Potosí silver had created unbridled wealth for some and misery for others. The ore dug from the ground by indigenous labourers had paid for the baroque luxuries of the mine's Spanish owners during the colonial era. In the early seventeenth century, hundreds of thousands of miners and their families had lived in abject poverty in the hovels that grew up around the mine, making it one of the most populated cities in the world. Under the notorious colonial system of the *mita*, Indians from across the Andean region of southern Bolivia were required to provide labour in the mines to the Spanish. When they died from exhaustion, mercury poisoning, pneumonia or disease, African slaves were transported to Potosí to replace them. Night after night, thousands of smelting furnaces would light up the mountain in an eerie glow. Hundreds of thousands died in accidents or from silicosis. In 1825, after a period of colonial decline and the chaos of the wars of independence, the population of Potosí was about eight thousand. 'The turrets and edifices rise heavily and ominously, while not a bush or streak of green enlivens the neighbourhood of the ugly and crime-stained capital', Andrews wrote after first seeing Potosí in October 1825. 'It looks like the city of a prince of sin, strange, desert, solitary, mysterious; a place of evil enchantment.'[9]

There were thousands of mine openings on the *cerro rico*. The individual mines were named after the saints, Catholic virtues, or apparitions of the Virgin Mary, among them Rosario, San José, Purisima, San Miguel, San Juan de Dios, Esperanza and Mercedes. In 1825 the authorities constructed adits – canals – to drain the inundated mines, using prisoners of war for labour. The most important building in Potosí was the mint; it dated from the middle of the eighteenth century.

British and Irish veterans were conspicuous in Potosí in 1825 – evidence of the opportunities opening up to those foreign soldiers who had served the patriot armies during the wars of independence. General James Paroissien, an Englishman and one of O'Brien's comrades-in-arms during the wars in Chile and Peru, was appointed the chief commissioner of the Potosí, La Paz and Peruvian Mining Association at the invitation of one of O'Brien's old enemies, Antonio José de Irisarri.[10] William Miller, the English veteran of the campaigns in Chile and Peru, beside whom O'Brien had served, was the governor of Potosí and presided over the events laid on to welcome Bolívar to the city. For the celebratory dinner, Miller refurbished the governor's house, covering the floor with scarlet cloth in place of carpets, sending to nearby Tacna for plates, glasses and cutlery, and buying large quantities of 'wine, liqueurs, English porter and cider'.[11]

O'Brien realised that there were plentiful opportunities in the new climate prevailing in post-independence Peru and Bolivia, not least the valuable mining concessions. Around him, at the soirées held in the governor's house, desperate agents of European companies charged with sinking capital into the mining industry circled the revolutionary generals like the condors in the Andean valleys in search of a fresh carcass. And O'Brien had access to the best of all sources of governmental largesse, the Liberator himself.

In 1826 O'Brien persuaded Bolívar to give him a twenty-five-year licence to reopen an old mine at Laykakota, near Puno. For the privilege, O'Brien agreed to pay 10,000 pesos (€2,321) – in annual instalments of 500 pesos (€116) – in the form of a subvention to the College of Arts and Sciences in Puno. O'Brien's Irish agent, Michael Crawley,[12] handed over the first payment to the authorities in Puno on 18 March 1826.[13] Crawley had served as a staff surgeon in San Martín's army, and made 'a good fortune' in Lima before entering the mining business. He was prefect of Lampa, sixty-four kilometres north-west of Puno, and lived in a fine brick house full of expensive furniture and exotic items he had collected on his travels. He was politically influential, as is made clear from the fact that when, in 1843, the Peruvian treasury ministry issued a decree establishing a mint in the town, it was located in Crawley's house.[14] Even by the standards of the sprawling, mountainous Peruvian landscape, Lampa was remote. According to Francis Burdett O'Connor, an Irish officer who had served under Generals Bolívar and Sucre, and who visited Crawley in Lampa, such was Crawley's joy at seeing one of his compatriots that he broke down and cried.[15]

O'Brien settled in Puno in 1826 and spent much of the next ten years in Peru.[16] The city is built on hills overlooking Lake Titicaca. In the 1820s most of the dwellings in the town were single-storey adobe huts. Puno is 3,810 metres above sea level, and new arrivals tended to suffer from altitude sickness. The cathedral, with its simple Andean baroque façade, dominated the main square. Many of the Indian workers lived on the higher slopes overlooking the town, where they tended to small patches of potatoes, barley and quinoa.

The mine at Laykakota had a fabled history. In the 1650s two brothers from Andalusia, José and Gaspar de Salcedo, arrived in Puno. José fell in love with a local *cacique*'s daughter by the name of Malika. In 1657 she told José about the existence of a vein of silver in Laykakota. Malika's father had created a small artificial lake to hide it from the Spanish fortune-hunters who, from time to time, would pass through the district. Directed to the mine by Malika, the Salcedos drained the lake and began digging. They became extraordinarily wealthy, which inevitably attracted the jealousy of other European colonists. Their fellow Andalusians poured into San Luis de Alba, a town that had sprung up to serve the miners.

The Salcedos welcomed the first influx of miners from Andalusia – there was more than enough silver to go around. But they were less pleased by the arrival in San Luis of Basques who had travelled north from Potosí in Upper Peru, where the veins of silver were beginning to wane, and the Andalusians and Basques engaged in a violent dispute. Given the importance of the mines at Laykakota, not just to the regional economy, but to the viceroyalty of Peru, the authorities in Lima watched the events in San Luis de Alba with some distress. They were worried not only about the violent inter-Spanish disputes but also about the possibility that the destabilisation of the region could lead to a *mestizo* uprising. In 1668 the new viceroy of Peru, Pedro Castro, intervened, travelling from Lima by way of Cuzco to Puno. The Salcedos had prepared an extravagant welcome for the viceroy, but their Basque enemies were determined to use the occasion to be rid of them. Castro took the side of the Basques, and set about destroying the Andalusians, ordering the arrests of Gaspar and José de Salcedo. Gaspar was sent into exile, while José was garrotted at a place called Orkapata, close to Puno. José's wife Malika, having watched her husband being taken away and put to death, swore that the viceroy and his henchmen would not get their hands on a single piece of silver from the mine at Laykakota. In revenge for the execution of her husband and the destruction of her home, a furious Malika ordered that the mines be flooded.[17]

O'Brien would have been well aware of the Salcedos and Malika's curse when, 150 years later, he entered the mine at Laykakota (also known as the Salcedo mine, after the Spanish brothers) and saw nothing but dark green water. But though he could not see it, he knew that beneath the water's surface lay great quantities of silver. The problem was how to extract it. In order to turn the mine into a profitable business, O'Brien required capital and technical expertise. He turned to John Begg, a Scottish merchant based in Lima, whose company was the most profitable foreign merchant house in Santiago. Like most of the foreign merchants trading in Chile and Peru, Begg was involved in many different enterprises, including contracts with the newly independent governments for arms, ships, uniforms, provisions and the raising of foreign loans. As well as being in the import–export business, Begg also had interests in mining and ranching. Having first established himself in Santiago, Begg had followed in the wake of the patriot army, establishing trading posts in Guayaquil and Lima immediately after they had been liberated from the royalists. In 1821 he had moved from Santiago to Lima within weeks of San Martín entering the city.[18]

The first task was to drain the mine, which required the construction of an adit. In order to penetrate the hard, porphyritic rock, O'Brien and Begg decided they needed a steam engine, together with the means to transport it to the remote *altiplano*. O'Brien wrote to a manufacturer in England and ordered the construction of a specially designed engine, which was transported across the Atlantic and around Cape Horn to the Pacific coast, from where it was brought by mules across the Andes to the mine. The Peruvian government met the expenses.[19]

Once the steam engine was in place, construction of the canal commenced. It was an ambitious undertaking: when completed, it measured two kilometres and had nine locks. In order to transport the ore from the entrance of the mine to the refinery further down the mountain, O'Brien and Begg constructed a railway.

Another problem was how to import the provisions needed to feed the army of miners. The hinterland on the western side of Lake Titicaca yielded little in the way of foodstuffs. Potatoes, fruit and corn had to be imported from the other side of the lake, which involved hauling them hundreds of kilometres across difficult terrain around the southern edge of Titicaca. O'Brien realised it would be quicker and cheaper to bring supplies across the water, but the only vessels on the lake were *balsas*, the light canoes made of rushes that had been used by the indigenous people for centuries. These were not practical for transporting the requisite quantities of wood and food. At O'Brien's suggestion, he and Begg came up with a solution in partnership with Robert Page, who had come to South America as the agent of Rundell & Bridge, the famous London jewellery firm patronised by the British royal family. In 1826 Rundell & Bridge had invested in Bolivian mines, buying a gold mine at Tipuani and an emerald mine in Illimani, both close to the eastern shore of Lake Titicaca. The company appointed Page as its South American representative, and he travelled to Arica on the Pacific coast, where he bought a broken-down brig named the *Santa Maria*, which had been condemned as unseaworthy. He had the eighty-one-tonne ship dismantled, and the hull, sails, rigging, cables and ironwork transported by mule across the Andes to the eastern shore of the lake, where there was a plentiful supply of good timber. He hired a group of skilled shipwrights to return with him to Lake Titicaca, and a shipyard was built near the point where the River Suches entered the lake. Over the course of two years, the workmen from Arica toiled to rebuild the sailing ship; when the work was complete, the ship was perfectly seaworthy. The only hindrance to her captain was the lack of adequate anchors; Page had been unable to bring the original anchors across the Andes because of their weight. The vessel was renamed the *Julia* and plied the lake for many years, bringing foodstuffs and wood from the eastern shores to the mining villages on the other side.[20] At an altitude of 3,810 metres, the *Julia* operated at a higher elevation than any other ship in the world.[21]

Transporting the *Julia* was a feat of logistical daring that bears comparison to the events portrayed in Werner Herzog's 1982 film *Fitzcarraldo*, though with wildly different results.[22] O'Brien's evident pride in the *Julia* is captured in the following passage:

> Visiting in her *myself* every town and village connected with it [Lake Titicaca], and considering the imperfect manner [in which] the vessel was put together, the expense attendant upon it, and the means at our disposal, it was only surprising she floated at all. As it was, no vessel on the face of the earth paid so well, or made such freights, and had she been perfect, there would have been ten thousand times over profitable employment for her.[23]

The work at Laykakota took many years, and progress was painfully slow. 'All in all, I do not flatter myself that I am going to become richer than the Peruvian government', O'Brien told the *Gaceta de Lima* newspaper in 1830, 'but I declare myself satisfied to see that the great sacrifices I have made to benefit the Salcedo mines have not been unfruitful.'[24] During one lucrative two-month period, the mine produced ore worth 96,000 pesos (€22,283).[25]

The mines were drained by November 1830, according to a letter published in a Buenos Aires newspaper.[26] At the beginning of 1831, five years after work had begun at Laykakota, O'Brien expressed himself confident that he would be able to make a success of his mining venture in Peru, but political instability in the region threatened the enterprise. 'There has been a considerable property [capital] advanced to finish the works, but I feel now assured of commensurate advantage', he wrote. 'If the Republic of Peru was at peace within itself, fortunes might yet be made in it.'[27] In fact, O'Brien spent less than a year in Peru overseeing the initial works at the mine before he was in the saddle once again. The years of campaigning had taken their toll on his health, and the harsh Andean climate in Puno was not conducive to his recovery. Though he would return to Puno sporadically, he left the management of the mine to Begg, while retaining a financial interest. In 1826 O'Brien was planning to return to Europe to seek investors for his mining business. But first he returned to Chile, dipping his toe into its febrile politics.

O'Brien retained a special affection for Chile. He had spent almost four years in the country in his early thirties, at the peak of his military career. As an elderly man he would recall his triumphs on the battlefield and his love affairs in Santiago. No matter where his wanderings took him, he would always return to Chile. When he arrived in 1826, however, he was appalled by the political crisis in the country, which was on the brink of civil war between supporters of the country's leader, Ramón Freire, and the exiled Bernardo O'Higgins. O'Brien found himself in a difficult situation. Both men were former comrades-in-arms whom he admired, but he came to believe that, because of the political crisis in Chile, it was necessary for O'Higgins to return from his exile in Peru to restore order.

In a letter to O'Higgins' secretary, John Thomas, O'Brien wrote of the 'many strange things' happening in Chile. He added that 'I am almost afraid to begin because if I do, the people you might speak to, why they will say it is because O'Brien is a friend of O'Higgins.' O'Brien said that he was 'sorry' to be shortly leaving Chile 'because I think I could do a great deal … I think I could have no difficulty in sending O'Higgins the *Aquiles* brig'.[28] In the event, O'Higgins' supporters' bid to restore him to power failed, and the former supreme director never returned to Chile.

Despite his support for O'Higgins during this period, O'Brien remained an admirer of Ramón Freire; he was later responsible for erecting a monument in Santiago in his honour. It was during this visit to Chile that O'Brien secured possession of the piece of land in the hills outside Santiago known as El Salto. In November 1826 the Chilean lawyer and politician Manuel Salas donated it to O'Brien for his use during his lifetime.[29] In his creaking Spanish, O'Brien renamed it 'La Salta'. It was here that San Martín burnt the correspondence O'Brien had recovered from Osorio after the Battle of Maipú. For O'Brien, the destruction of Osorio's correspondence was the act that, more than any other, demonstrated San Martín's greatness, and he erected a plaque near the spot recalling the famous deed. He also built a cabin at El Salto, to which, in later years, he would retreat from the world. It was then a rural area, dotted with fig trees and vines, where the *santiaguinos* (Santiago residents) would go to hunt partridges. O'Brien honoured Salas' generosity by erecting a stone pyramid to his memory in the vicinity. These were all signs of O'Brien's lifelong determination to sustain public memory of the leaders of the revolutionary generation. During the same period, when the Scottish businessman and author William Parish Robertson paid a visit to Chile, O'Brien went out of his way to escort him around the battlefield at Chacabuco.[30]

After his brief sojourn in Chile, O'Brien spent a few months travelling in Argentina's wild frontier country, where the ongoing confrontation between the indigenous peoples and the livestock-rearing settlers flooding into the area was similar to that taking place in North America. The pioneering *estancieros* (ranchers) who worked the cattle ranches and sheep farms on the pampas outside Buenos Aires lived in fear of raids from tribes that had been migrating east from Chile for decades.

In Buenos Aires on 11 September 1827, O'Brien embarked for Europe, 'proceeding to London on official business for this government, and carrying despatches to the house of Baring and Co. in London'.[31] He sailed aboard the barque *Lord Melville*. His business with Baring Brothers most likely related to the £1 million (€1,161,493) loan the bank had issued to the Buenos Aires government in 1824 and on which it had defaulted in 1828. His involvement in the negotiations over the Barings loan illuminates the elite circle of British and Irish-born merchants living in Buenos Aires. This group, which included John Parish Robertson and Thomas Armstrong, were instrumental in contracting the loan.[32]

O'Brien visited San Martín in Brussels. The Argentinian was mourning the death of his wife and was in constant pain from his rheumatism. Often, he would be unable to move from his bed, and would try to alleviate the pain with leeches and frequent visits to the baths at the spa town of Aix-la-Chapelle. His glittering military career had ended in ignominy, and his domestic happiness had been destroyed by disease. He was tortured by illness and forced to decamp to wherever a friendly government regarded his presence as an honour, not a threat. O'Brien's visit must have reminded San Martín of happier days and eased the homesickness from which he constantly suffered. They reminisced about past campaigns and discussed the political upheavals that continued to afflict the young South American republics. But San Martín was not up to receiving visitors for long, and O'Brien left for London after two days.

The nine to ten months that O'Brien spent in England and Ireland in the late 1820s coincided with the growing clamour for Catholic emancipation. O'Brien gave his support to O'Connell's campaign at home and, on his return to Buenos Aires, made sure that the small Irish community there would play its part.

7
The Irish Community in Buenos Aires

O'Brien embarked for Buenos Aires on 14 September 1828, sailing via Rio de Janeiro aboard the packet *Swallow*.[1] Upon his return, he enlisted in the Buenos Aires cavalry and travelled south to Bahía Blanca. It is tempting to see this decision as emerging from his continued determination to settle Irish emigrants in the province of Buenos Aires.

In the 1820s Bahía Blanca was a military outpost. The settlement had been founded to protect the port that had been developed in the southernmost extremity of the province to export the rich produce of the pampas. It was also the furthermost point at which the government in Buenos Aires exercised authority. Further south were the expanses of Patagonia. In the European imagination, Patagonia had been a land populated with giants and strange beasts. It was only in the late eighteenth century that scientific accounts of the region had begun to be published in Europe. By the early nineteenth century, indigenous tribes began moving across the Andes from Chile into Patagonia and the adjoining provinces. They were hunters who lived off the wild animals that roamed the pampas, and were understandably hostile to the spread of the *estancias* (ranches). They picked off isolated *estancieros*, robbing them of their livestock and possessions. In response, the Buenos Aires government sent soldiers to the frontier lands. 'A man at his estancia will tell you that fear of the Indians deprives him of his natural rest; that his property is not secure, and that he is kept in continual alarm', *The British Packet* editorialised in February 1829.[2]

O'Brien loved these wild borderlands. He enthused about the herds of deer – 'so numerous as to exceed belief' – the grey foxes, the hares and the exotic birds, including the thousands of scarlet flamingos 'whose plumage (as they rise from the banks of the Lakes) glittering in the sun produces an effect beautiful in the extreme'. He believed that this was a land in which the Irish immigrant could happily settle:

> It is true that immediately upon passing Tandil and near the coast, the land is very barren, and strong winds prevail all the year round, but this is compensated by afterwards meeting with a rich and luxuriant soil, which continues for many thousand square miles, intersected by large lakes and small rivers of excellent water, until the approach to the Andes, and indeed there is only 12 leagues of desert country.
>
> The traveller need not burthen himself with provisions; with his gun he can amply provide himself with choice fare. The game is so abundant in the lakes that in emerging from the water they in a manner darken the horizon.[3]

The British Packet reported that O'Brien wished 'to show the facility [by] which that country might be occupied, and cleared of a powerless enemy which at present prevents its prosperity'.[4]

O'Brien did not stay long, perhaps becoming disillusioned at the prospect of bringing his dream of an Irish colony to fruition. Conflict between different tribes, deserting soldiers, militiamen and out-of-work gauchos brought an unrelenting cycle of violence to the countryside, which was further complicated by the struggle for power in Buenos Aires between rival political factions. O'Brien returned to the city in early 1829.

O'Brien was a celebrated figure in Buenos Aires and, along with Admiral William Brown, the naval hero, and John Oughan, the doctor and academic, was one of the leaders of the city's small but thriving Irish community.[5] In addition to those involved in the import–export business, there were Irish grocers, butter merchants, tailors, spirit dealers, brewers, liverymen and bootmakers with premises in Buenos Aires.[6] Every St Patrick's Day, this small Irish community would congregate at parties in private houses or at James Willis' Naval Hotel – known as Irish Jemmy's – to eat, dance and toast their patron saint.[7]

Unlike those who had emigrated to the United States, the Catholic Irish who arrived in South America did not face racial or religious discrimination, as Oughan wrote enthusiastically in a letter to the archbishop of Dublin, Daniel Murray, in 1828. Oughan contrasted the experience of emigrants to South America with those who had gone to the United States: 'Numbers of our countrymen have settled in the North and there find shelter from the storms of discord. But, North America is not a country proper for Irish settlers.' Oughan argued that 'their identity, their ancient faith, and the peculiar cast of their national character, in the mixture of many nations, is totally confounded and lost for ever'.[8] On the other hand, adopting a millenarian style, Oughan extolled the virtues of this new colony to the south:

> Thanks to providence a very different destiny awaits them here. It would seem that Heaven had at length interposed to protect some remnant of her faithful followers, and created this new world, as the land of promise, where harassed Irishmen may 'pause from the toil', and Christianity divested of all its sectarian impurities may flourish again and become infallible. This country, fertile and vast beyond limits, abounding in all that nature can furnish for the support of man with a race of people, hospitable and congenial in faith and social feeling, seems, of all the earth, the most likely to satisfy the wants of the Irish wanderers.[9]

Oughan's language bears a notable similarity with that of William Scully, the Irish promoter of an emigration scheme to Brazil in the 1860s. Scully also directed himself to the Catholic Church in Ireland, portraying Brazil as a Catholic utopia in contrast with a religiously hostile United States.[10] While the majority of the Irish emigrants professed the common religion of Argentina, there were concerns about the absence of Irish-born priests to minister to the growing Irish-Catholic community in Buenos Aires. Oughan believed that 'the awful grandeur of the churches here and the long-established splendour of the Spanish rites' were designed to 'inspire the Catholic mind', but that 'without a knowledge of the Spanish language', they were 'but bad substitutes for the well-directed exhortation delivered in our native tongue'.[11]

This feeling provoked a campaign to raise funds in Buenos Aires to pay the travelling expenses for an Irish priest to come to the city; over £270 (€313) was subscribed. Oughan asked Murray 'to select such a person as may be qualified, not only to guide us spiritually but politically versed in the institution of a Catholic rent which we intend to establish for the relief of our Catholic freeholders'.[12]

Oughan was not convinced of the merits of the new governments that had come to power in South America. He was concerned about anti-clericalism in Argentina, and believed that it was up to the Irish Church to fill the spiritual void created by the destruction of the Spanish Empire:

> For my own part I beg leave to inform your Lordship, that the Catholic Bishops together with the authority of the King of Spain,

> have disappeared from this land, in the year 1806. Since which period, not one priest has been ordained in this country and as the decline in the Ecclesiastical body here cannot, for very powerful political motives, be supplied by priests from Spain, Ireland … is now destined to supply the new world with her ecclesiastical saints.[13]

Fr Patrick Moran was the first official chaplain to arrive in Argentina from Ireland. He wrote to Murray in February 1829, shortly after arriving in the city, describing the warm reception he had received from the citizens of Buenos Aires. Moran arrived at a moment of political crisis. At the end of 1828, General Juan Lavalle, O'Brien's former comrade-in-arms in the mounted grenadiers and with whom he had fought the duel in Mendoza in 1816, had ousted Manuel Dorrego as the governor of Buenos Aires province. This was the beginning of the civil war between Lavalle's *unitarios* (unitarians), who argued for Buenos Aires to control a centralised, unitary Argentinian state and who were opposed to peace negotiations with Brazil, and the *federales* (federalists), led by the authoritarian figure of Juan Manuel de Rosas, who were in favour of greater autonomy for the provinces. During his absence from the city, as he led the *unitario* army against Rosas, Lavalle had appointed Admiral Brown as the *pro tempore* governor of Buenos Aires province.

O'Brien introduced Moran to the leading citizens of the city, including the chief of police and members of the government. The new priest lived with Oughan, and frequently dined with Brown. 'This, My Lord, is the country for Irish farmers to emigrate to', Moran wrote to Murray; 'the most productive soil in the world … and a people who will show themselves more friendly to Irishmen than to any other nation'. But he shared with Oughan similar concerns about the impact the revolution had had on faith and morals: 'The people are a kind-hearted polite people with a strong sense of religion, excepting some of the young men. Who thro' French reading and intercourse with foreigners have lost their own religion and not substituted any other in its place.'[14] He also referred to the exertions O'Brien was making 'to interest this people for his ill-fated country. He is collecting the [Catholic] rent'.[15]

In February 1829 O'Brien began raising money for Daniel O'Connell's campaign for Catholic emancipation.[16] He advertised in the newspapers and personally collected subscriptions between 10 a.m. and 2 p.m. at the bar in Faunch's[17] on the Calle de la Catedral, which had replaced the Tres Reyes as the most popular hotel for travellers to Buenos Aires. He appealed not only to the Irish but to the wider British community in Buenos Aires, believing that, as Protestant emigrants in a Catholic country, they were ideally placed to understand the Catholic position in the United Kingdom. 'An Irishman, ardent in the cause of civil and religious liberty, acting from the impulse of the glowing feelings which devotion to such a cause naturally inspires, takes the liberty of soliciting you in [*sic*] behalf of *seven millions* of his oppressed countrymen', he wrote in a letter addressed to prominent members of the British community, which was published in *The British Packet* on 28 February 1829. He continued:

> An impartial view of the Catholic Question will convince every reflecting mind, that it is not the cause of Irishmen alone, but that of *civil and religious liberty* throughout the world. … Independent of general principles, it is peculiarly the cause of the Englishman who, led by commercial or other pursuits to visit foreign countries, finds the reproach of intolerance awaiting him wherever he goes. How often in conversation, perhaps in the heat of argument, when expatiating upon the superiority of the laws and civil institutions of his country, he is rudely silenced by adverting to the bigoted oppression of the Irish Catholics![18]

O'Brien reassured potential subscribers that he was personally acquainted with O'Connell, and that he was 'fully acquainted with the uses to which the product of the Catholic subscription is applied'.[19]

The British Packet carried weekly reports about the progress of the campaign for Catholic emancipation, and supported the bill going through the British parliament, telling its readers that 'every liberal minded person will rejoice if that measure is effected, more from the positive *justice* of the case than from any menace'.[20]

In a letter to O'Connell, dated 18 March 1829, published in the *Dublin Morning Register*, O'Brien wrote that 'subscriptions are augmenting every day' and that he was confident that 'England must, from her present political situation, grant emancipation this session'. However, if this were not to be the case, it was his 'fixed determination to use all my influence in these countries – even to Chili and Peru, where I expect it will meet with equal success'. He concluded:

> I cannot close this letter without mentioning an instance of patriotism worthy of consideration. I was met a few days since by an Irishman of

> the name of Patrick Moyler, a native of the county of Wexford, who told me he arrived in this country a few years ago, a poor man, and now that he had saved something by his industry, wished to dedicate a part of it towards the liberation of his country. Without further preface, he handed me a hundred dollars, and desired to be enrolled as a monthly subscriber. For the honour of our countrymen here, I must say, they are most enthusiastic in supporting our little Association; what they give, they give it with the greatest cheerfulness imaginable.[21]

The Roman Catholic Relief Act was passed by parliament and signed into law by George IV on 13 April 1829. In the pages of *The British Packet* O'Brien was jubilant that the Irish community in Buenos Aires had contributed in its own small way to the success of the campaign. He described the enacting of the legislation as a 'signal overthrow to the powers of darkness, bigotry, and its gloomy train of malignant attendants', and extended his 'most heart-felt thanks to his friends, and the generous public of this city, who have manifested their friendship to his person, and their ardent attachment to the principles of civil and religious liberty, by liberally subscribing in aid of the fund for the advancement of that great cause'.[22] The fund was closed with a balance of $6,230.

In August 1829 O'Brien participated in ceremonies to mark the end of the civil war, including a solemn High Mass in the cathedral in Buenos Aires.[23] But the city's residents were to enjoy only a short-lived peace. The arrival of one of O'Brien's old acquaintances, Juan Manuel de Rosas, to the office of governor heralded the beginning of a tempestuous period in Argentinian history. Whether he had a premonition of the troubles ahead, or the old itch to be on the move had returned, O'Brien decided to leave Buenos Aires for pastures new.

8
El Dorado

In 1829, his body showing the stresses and strains of the gruelling campaigns in Chile and Peru, O'Brien, now in his mid-forties, began a new career as an explorer and gold prospector. From Buenos Aires and the borderlands of the windswept Patagonian steppes, where he had spent much of the late 1820s, he travelled north to the muggy Amazon basin. During the next five years he led stamina-sapping expeditions in search of gold and other precious natural resources through some of the most hostile environments on the continent. The glamorous Irish cavalry officer who had helped liberate four republics might have been expected to enjoy a sedate retirement, enjoying the perks of a fabled reputation in the company of businessmen and politicians. Instead, he spent his middle-aged years tramping through dangerous, disease-infested tropical jungles.

The time was ripe for exploration. Scientists, botanists, gold prospectors, rubber merchants and miners from across the world were flocking to the Amazon, a region of the world Europeans regarded as possessing the same mystique as the polar extremities. Brazil had long been known for its rich gold reserves, but by the 1830s European industrialists had also become interested in the rainforest's other treasures. These included commodities such as rubber, timber and quinine, the latter the most effective treatment for malaria.

In late 1829 O'Brien travelled to the Gongo Soco mine in Minas Gerais in Brazil. He was determined to enter the gold-mining business, and wished to see for himself the modern enterprise that his travelling companion, an English industrialist, Edward Oxenford, had described to him on their trip across the Atlantic. Oxenford was a roguish character who had been involved in several financial frauds in the course of his career. During this period he was engaged in a bitter row with the directors of the Imperial Brazilian Mining Association over the ownership of the mine. Once Oxenford had realised the extent of the profits that might accrue to the shareholders from Gongo Soco, he was determined to secure a greater share of the spoils.

O'Brien had first encountered Oxenford in London in 1828 while meeting representatives of British mining companies, and the two had travelled together to South America.[1] Oxenford was one of the first foreigners to negotiate mining licences with the Brazilian government. In 1825 the London-based Imperial Brazilian Mining Association had employed him as their representative in South America; his job was to find and assess mines in Brazil suitable for investment. He came across the Gongo Soco mine, an old claim close to the Brazilian city of Belo Horizonte, about 350 hundred kilometres north of Rio de Janeiro. His company bought the mine for £70,000 (€81,291), and sent a team of mining experts from Britain to supervise work on the claim. Most of the men were from Cornwall. They brought their families with them, and established a thriving Cornish colony in the Brazilian countryside. The village was about a kilometre from the mine; in fact there were two villages, one for the Cornish and one for the Brazilians. The Cornish men built a library and a school for their children, and on Sundays the Cornish men and their families attended service in the Anglican church; there was also a Catholic chapel for the Brazilians in their village. The centre of the colony was the Casa Grande (the Big House) where the company's chief representative lived and worked. There was a company store and a market on Saturdays selling fresh produce.[2]

Though the Cornish experts made conditions as pleasant as possible for themselves, life for the miners was very different. Mining in Brazil was still reliant on slavery. About five hundred black slaves and two hundred free men worked the mines under Cornish supervisors.[3] The Cornish miners introduced the latest techniques in deep-shaft mining and milling, and by the 1840s Gongo Soco was one of the most modern and most profitable mines in Brazil. However, forty years after its sale to the Imperial British Mining Association, it lay worn out and abandoned, while the small villages where the Cornish emigrants and the Brazilian workforce had lived were overgrown and falling into ruin.

When O'Brien arrived in Gongo Soco, the British owners had been operating it for a little more than four years, and it was far from the peak of its production. O'Brien was well versed in mining technology from his time developing the mine in Laykakota. He spoke to the Cornish miners about the machinery they were importing from England but, more importantly, he chatted to some of the older, native miners, hoping to find a nugget of information. One elderly miner, a man by the name of Marcos Lisboa, told him about some hills in the far west of the Amazon, thousands of kilometres from

Gongo Soco, in the area around the Paucartambo valley in eastern Peru. Close to these hills were said to be flood plains covered in gold. Lisboa told O'Brien that, in 1754, a band of Portuguese explorers had arrived in the area with a hundred slaves. Before they could begin removing the gold, the local tribes had slaughtered them. The story left a deep impression on O'Brien.[4] Shortly afterwards he and Oxenford began an expedition into the Amazonian interior.

Oxenford and O'Brien journeyed through 'the Brazilian borderlands, towards the source of the Amazon'.[5] They had inherited the dream that had haunted the Spanish conquistadors as they hacked their way through the jungle: El Dorado. O'Brien and Oxenford's El Dorado was not a mythical Indian chief or city but the source of the precious metals that flowed through the Amazon and the mother river's thousands of tributaries. The two men scoured the remote tropical region at the confluence of the borders of modern-day Brazil, Peru and Bolivia. They navigated the Madre de Dios, the Beni, the Mamore and the Madeira rivers. They may even have travelled as far north as the Orinoco River in Venezuela.[6]

O'Brien emerged from the Amazon rainforest convinced that any speculator who wished to get his hands on the gold that flowed down the rivers of Brazil had to explore its source in the Paucartambo valley to the north-east of Cuzco in Peru. And he was one of them:

> Whoever has once seen the profusion of gold that decorates the palaces and temples of Rio de Janeiro, its beautiful plate and ornaments made from this precious metal, will not easily forget it, nor will the natural desire leave them of knowing how such a magnificent collection of gold, which shines so fabulously, came to be gathered in that privileged place [*a.t.*].[7]

O'Brien was convinced that the future development and trade of South America depended on making the Amazon river system navigable. Instead of bringing minerals, rubber and other raw materials down the Andes to the Pacific coast and, from there, around Cape Horn into the Atlantic, it made more sense to bring it directly east, down the great rivers of the continent and into the Amazon delta. Up to then this region of western Brazil, eastern Peru and northern Bolivia had been a backwater. During the colonial era the Andean regions had looked west towards the Pacific. O'Brien believed that the modernisation of the transport network, based on steamships plying the river network from one side of the continent to the other, would open up trade and communication between South America and Europe. During these frenzied years of activity, he saw parts of the South American continent that few Europeans had ever set foot in. 'Probably it might be said of Colonel O'Brien that no one has travelled so much in South America: he has, in fact, for the last twenty years, been almost solely occupied in one pursuit or other in the regions in question', *The British Packet* reported in 1833.[8]

A new spirit of inquiry was propelling European adventurers into the jungles and mountains of South America. They measured, classified, observed, sketched and, above all, collected. The fruits of these expeditions were displayed in mahogany cabinets under the roofs of sturdy, temple-like classical edifices, the new churches of the rational mind. Nineteenth-century explorers were collectors, mineralogists, naturalists and taxonomists.

O'Brien was among a group of Victorian-era collectors who responded to the insatiable demand in the United Kingdom for exotic specimens of flora and fauna.[9] He financed his expeditions into some of the most hostile environments on the continent by selling artefacts. Like many of his fellow explorers, he brought to Europe the exotic birds, animals, minerals and plants he discovered on his journeys, donating or selling specimens to private collectors or the new museums beginning to appear in British and Irish cities. These institutions became the symbols of the British Empire's dominance of the world's resources. But they also appeared in South America as part of the new republics' drive to awaken national consciousness. Throughout the 1820s and 1830s, natural-history museums opened in Latin America's principal cities, and European experts were invited to direct their activities.[10] In contrast to British museums, whose varied artefacts from every corner of the globe glorified the imperial project, the South American states, by establishing these museums, were reappropriating the continent's resources from their former colonial masters to make nations from the ashes of empire.

O'Brien's collecting activities were a response to a demand from both the South American governments and British and Irish scientific institutions. As Helen Cowie has written, the new governments of the South American republics viewed the patronage of natural history as serving 'both to effect and to showcase Spanish America's march towards modernity'.[11] At the same time, an insatiable demand for specimens from British and Irish scientific institutions was fuelled by an increasing awareness of, and interest in, the continent's resources. O'Brien's exhibits appeared in museums throughout Britain and Ireland. He presented the Glasgow museum with one of the pieces of silver that had been thrown into the crowd at the ceremony to mark Peruvian independence in 1821.[12] Condor skins previously belonging to a collection assembled by O'Brien in Peru were donated to Belfast's museum in 1835.[13] O'Brien was in contact with important private collectors, such as the Earl of Derby, the father of the future British prime minister, who kept his own natural-history museum and a one-hundred-acre menagerie at Knowsley Hall, the family seat near Liverpool. Derby was the president of the Zoological Society of London and bred many rare species in captivity for the first time.[14]

The collection of relics and specimens had important financial consequences, and the meaning attached to them was often the subject of fierce debate, as may be seen from the evidence given during a London court case involving O'Brien, which was widely reported in the British and Irish newspapers. O'Brien had bought a nugget of pure gold in Peru for £100 (€117), believing that it bore an uncanny resemblance to the Duke of Wellington. In London he showed the nugget to John Laurie, a well-known saddler in the city. Laurie asked to borrow it so as to show it to his uncle, and O'Brien agreed. But when Laurie returned the nugget, O'Brien noticed that it was two ounces lighter and that the 'nose of the Noble Duke' was missing, and he took Laurie to court. It was heard in evidence that a friend of Laurie's, a refiner, had believed that the nugget had been tampered with in some way and that its appearance was not the work of nature. Laurie had allowed Roberts to take the piece home to test it in his workshop, where it had accidentally fallen into the fire. O'Brien told the court that Laurie had 'appeared to have sliced away a Prime Minister's nose and chin with as little compunction as he would feel in lopping off the corner of a brass candlestick'.[15] At one point during the case, O'Brien produced a plain-looking stone from his pocket and showed it to the magistrate, claiming that he had taken it from the ruins of the Temple of the Sun in Cuzco. The point of this piece of theatre was to demonstrate that it was not always a simple matter to measure an object's value. But the magistrate was unimpressed and, to O'Brien's disappointment, refused to award more than the £8 (€9.30) he adjudged the missing golden nose to be worth in purely material terms. His honour offended, O'Brien refused the award.

In the 1840s O'Brien used his expertise on South American fauna to become closely associated with the burgeoning alpaca wool industry in Britain and Ireland. Having seen the practical benefits of the alpaca as a beast of burden at first hand while serving with the patriot armies in the Andes, and having later put the animals into service at his mine in Puno, he now became a champion of its wool. Along with sugar, guano and cotton, alpaca wool was to become one of Peru's most important export commodities in the mid-nineteenth century, with British merchants opening trading houses in Arequipa in the post-independence era to buy fleeces from Andean producers.[16] By the 1840s, with the expansion of alpaca wool manufacturing in the industrial heartlands of Britain, O'Brien was one of the foremost promoters of introducing and acclimatising the animal to Britain and Ireland.

O'Brien supplied much of the information used by William Walton to extol the benefits of the alpaca in a book published in 1845. O'Brien suggested that the mountainous terrain of County Wicklow, especially the 'hilly lands' belonging to the estates of Lord Wicklow and Earl Fitzwilliam, would be ideally suited to the raising of the alpaca:

> I can venture to affirm that, if the animals are only properly chosen, and then prepared some little time previous to their embarkation for this country, they would arrive in good health, and eventually became a source of great national wealth, besides promoting the interests of a certain class of our manufacturers.[17]

In the event, Robert Bell of Listowel, County Kerry was the first to introduce the alpaca to Ireland.[18] As Helen Cowie has noted, 'the naturalization of the alpaca was presented as an important boost to the British textiles industry, a boon to agriculture and an antidote to various social problems'.[19] O'Brien urged his friends to help British importers make a success of the species. He entered into correspondence with William Danson, an entrepreneur from Liverpool who was planning to import a few hundred Peruvian alpacas to Britain and who had also written a book about the animal. O'Brien asked the British consul in Arica, Peter Murphy, and the prefect of Lampa, Michael Crawley, to help Danson source the best-quality animals.[20]

Bradford was the centre of the British alpaca-wool-manufacturing industry. In 1845 the city's manufacturers organised a public dinner to celebrate Queen Victoria's patronage of the alpaca trade. The event took place in the city's Exchange Rooms and epitomised the stolid triumphalism of British imperialism. The chairman of the dinner sat beneath a richly draped canopy, perhaps the only concession to frivolity. Above him was a banner on which 'The Throne and the Cottage' was written in gold letters. Portraits of Queen Victoria and Prince Albert hung on one wall, accompanied by the inscriptions 'God bless her' and 'Long life to him'. A large painting of Britannia, with figures representing commerce, peace and plenty, hung beside the royal personages, over which 'Manufacturing and commerce' was written. The opposite wall was decorated with the Bradford coat of arms and a painting of an alpaca. According to *The Leeds Intelligencer*, one of the most characteristic features of the decorations was 'a bridle belonging to General O'Brien, and the workmanship of native Indians, mounted with silver, the reins of which were formed by the skin of the Alpaca'.[21] O'Brien was engaged in a performance before the British and Irish public. His many roles – military hero, scientific savant, vendor of commercial intelligence – were designed to win financial and political favours. The artefacts and specimens, while often of significant monetary value, also served as props in these performances, conferring authenticity on their owner.

After exploring the interior of Brazil in 1832, O'Brien embarked upon a bird-collecting expedition along the Pacific coast of Peru. Ornithology had become a profitable business. Both institutional and private collectors in Europe and South America were willing to pay handsomely for exotic specimens. According to *The British Packet*, an avid reporter of O'Brien's expeditions, this was to be the first leg of a four-thousand-mile (6,437-kilometre) journey. The itinerary would see the intrepid Irishman travel along the coast to Arequipa before heading inland towards La Paz in Bolivia. From La Paz he intended to return westwards, in the direction of Lake Titicaca. From there he was going to head into the tropical Madre de Dios region, where he would pass the rainy season, before finishing in Cuzco.[22]

O'Brien set off from Lima in December, accompanied by an Indian manservant who could speak Aymara and Quechua, and who was described in *The British Packet* as a descendant of the great Inca warrior Túpac Amaru, a prime example of O'Brien's talents as a self-publicist. Their provisions included brandy, tea, salt, red pepper and *charqui*, a type of salted meat. The party travelled south towards Arequipa, a distance, as the crow flies, of 765 kilometres. The coast was home to many species of seabirds, including cormorants, petrels, boobies, oystercatchers, terns, Humboldt penguins and pelicans. In the Andes O'Brien collected specimens of llama, vicuña, guanaco, red fox, alpaca and 'other choice productions of the country'.[23]

Preserving the specimens was an elaborate, time-consuming process, and required a set of special instruments to clean, skin and stuff the bird or animal once it had been killed. The next stage involved the application of a preservative, such as arsenic; the preservative had to be applied over the course of several days to prevent decay.[24] It was a difficult enough job preserving one specimen in the comfort of a laboratory or study, much more so when trying to preserve the specimens while on the hoof in the Andes or the Amazon.

Once he had returned to the house he kept in Puno, O'Brien would carefully pack the specimens he wished to send to Lima, Buenos Aires or Europe.

O'Brien's specimen-collecting expeditions, which covered thousands of kilometres, and his frequent contacts with British scientific institutions, to which he supplied countless exhibits, exemplify the strength of these networks in furthering the study of South American natural history in Britain in the early Victorian era. These expeditions had not only monetary value but also played an important role in developing O'Brien's public image as an expert on South American scientific matters. As Helen Cowie has written, European natural historians in post-independence South America 'aspired, primarily, to secure their reputations back in Europe by procuring novel specimens and conducting exciting new research in countries that had previously been out of bounds'.[25]

O'Brien spent weeks exploring Lake Titicaca during his expedition through Peru and Bolivia. Two other Indians had joined the party, and they helped build traditional *balsas*. These six-metre canoes were made by fastening reeds of *totora*, the species of bulrush that grows on the banks of the lake, with cords fashioned from local grasses. O'Brien and two of the men travelled in one canoe; his Indian manservant travelled in the second canoe with the provisions. O'Brien began his trip on the shores of Lake Titicaca exploring Capachica and Chucuito, the isthmuses that form the bay at Puno. 'The country in its neighbourhood is well cultivated, and interspersed with small towns', reported *The British Packet*. 'After visiting the whole of them, our traveller bid adieu to the Indian beauties; and having received a good supply of provisions, sailed for the island of *Navio Blanco*, so called from its appearing, at a distance, like a large frigate under full sail.'[26]

Once the boats were on the water, a storm began to blow, forcing O'Brien and the other men to do their best to keep themselves dry and to preserve their provisions. When the wind abated, one of the men steered the boat with a wooden pole. When the wind got up, they used the pole as a mast, hoisting a sail made from reeds. At night O'Brien and his companions used the sail as bedding. *The British Packet* described O'Brien's visit to the Isla del Sol:

> ... which he had previously visited in the year 1825, with General Bolívar; at which period they were received by 1,400 Indians, seated in their canoes and singing songs of triumph in honor of the *Libertador*: rendering it altogether a most imposing affair, taking into account the beauty of their feathered dresses, the enthusiasm they evinced, and the

> charming view which the lake presented. But now all was silent; and the music, the song, the dance, the great feasts, the swimming in old Burgundy and Champaigne [*sic*] brought many hundred miles for the occasion, – placed to the account of by-gone days.[27]

On the Isla del Sol, O'Brien fished and took potshots at the seabirds resting in the rushes along the shores or flying overhead. He sketched the ruins where he had performed his solemn ceremony with Bolívar in honour of the Inca gods. And, occasionally, he sat reading the two books that he had brought with him: a Thomas Moore collection and Byron's *Don Juan*. No doubt Moore provided nostalgia, a reminder of faraway home. The choice of *Don Juan* is more interesting: he must have seen something of his own life in Byron's poem, that of a peripatetic voyager cast about on life's rough seas, a slave to feminine charms. It was perhaps during these moments of O'Brien's life that he was happiest, such as when he sailed contentedly around Titicaca, far away from the internecine squabbles of post-independence politics and the worries of commerce, or when he sat on the shore of the Isla del Sol as the sun set, a fishing line in the water, a glass of brandy in hand, pondering the fate of the Incas.

The weeks on Lake Titicaca were spent in pleasant reveries. However, at Copacabana, on its southern shore, O'Brien was met with hostility. The inhabitants of Copacabana 'conceived him to be attached to Bolívar, – and Bolívar, they said, was not a "*biracocha*" (caballero) nor their *libertador*'.[28] After explaining that he was a friend of San Martín's, O'Brien was allowed to leave, returning to Puno by land. The contrast between this and the welcome O'Brien and Bolívar received in 1825 is striking, and perhaps points to the alienation of the indigenous communities from the Peruvian state in the early years of the postwar era as a consequence of Bolívarian land-reform legislation.[29]

In Puno O'Brien visited the Laykakota mine and sorted through the specimens he had collected, before returning west towards Cuzco. He was now determined to begin preparations for an expedition to discover the source of Brazil's mineral wealth, which he believed was located on the other side of the Peruvian border.[30] This was Madre de Dios (Mother of God), the low-lying, tropical Amazon region that lay on the eastern side of the Andes, north of Lake Titicaca. Madre de Dios had been one of the most important coca-growing areas at the time of the Inca Empire. The Spanish had recognised the region's significant economic value, and made efforts to control the local trade. When O'Brien travelled to Madre de Dios, many of the coca plantations had been abandoned, in part because of conflict between their *criollo* owners and the indigenous Harakmbut people.

The indigenous labourers on the few coca plantations still in operation endured a miserable existence. The plantation owners exploited them, doing nothing to improve their material circumstances. 'A labourer earns two shillings a day; a woman, a boy, or a girl, who picks coca leaf, earns two rials (1*s*.)', William Miller observed in his travels through the Paucartambo valley. He continued:

> Yet these people are always considerably in debt to their employers, and live so wretchedly, that they suffer dreadfully from ague and fever, and there being no medical attendance they die off numerously. The stewards are so incurious, that not one of them has ever penetrated a mile beyond his own estate. There is neither a priest, nor a chapel, nor a clock, nor a watch, in the whole valley, although the number of the inhabitants on the six estates amounts to at least 600.[31]

The Harakmbut was comprised of several tribes sharing linguistic ties and religious beliefs. O'Brien made careful preparations before venturing into their territory:

> First, in order to prepare for such a gruelling expedition, I equipped myself in Cuzco with objects of witchcraft which were most valued among the savages, and I launched myself towards their frontier. I had an interview with the tribe called the Chunchos [the Harakmbut], who predominated in that area, and started talking with their warriors, familiarising them with my character and teaching myself the steps that safety required on that risky path. This was a walk rather than a journey. My formal journey, which I undertook immediately upon my return [to Cuzco] has been of four months of constant and laborious travels in those remote places, recording the rivers and streams of all those valleys and mountains, and with the most satisfactory results.[32]

In July 1834, before leaving for the valleys of the Amazon, O'Brien attended a feast held in the fabled Temple of the Sun at Cuzco to honour the visit of General Mariano Necochea, an Argentinian veteran of the wars of independence. Many of the guests were Argentinian officers who were in Peru to lend their support to the government. During the feast they shouted lusty toasts to the Argentinian heroes of the revolution, including the Irish admiral William Brown.

O'Brien's remarks at the feast were carried in the pages of the newspapers. Having 'recalled to mind the encampment of Mendoza, the passage of the Andes, the battles of Chacabuco and Maypú [*sic*] which at once gave liberty to Chili and Peru', O'Brien's first toast was to 'the Hero of the Andes, General San Martín; and that even Manco Capac, could he now rise out of the Temple of the Sun, would be proud to embrace the hero'. O'Brien's second toast was to the health of Thomas Moore, 'a poet whose fame will be eternal; and whom he now saluted in the Temple of the Sun, in gratitude for the pleasure the perusal of his works had afforded him in the valleys of Cusco'. But O'Brien was not finished:

> The enthusiastic applause which accompanied the following toast, it is stated, absolutely shook the very Temple of the Sun to its centre: – 'To the lovely *porteñas*, whose beauty, and amiable qualities, are at once honourable to Buenos Ayres, and to human nature; and whose eyes rival in brightness the sun that now shines before us.'[33]

In 1834 O'Brien travelled into the valleys north of Cuzco, and down the eastern slopes of the Andes into the Amazon basin. He spent months living with the Harakmbut and exploring the almost impenetrable rainforest for gold and other riches. He came across three rivers rich in gold-bearing sand: the Ninto, the Milagro and Erin's Golden River, the latter he named after his homeland. He returned to Cuzco convinced of the region's economic potential. From the Peruvian government, he sought mining licences and military support:

> I know well those fine lands and abundant gold rivers which form the best ornaments of the vegetable and mineral kingdoms; I have seen precious agricultural fruits, cascarilla [a medicinal herb], cinnamon, cacao and cocoa, and the inexhaustible valuable resins which sweat from their leafy stalks; I am much persuaded that the powerful mountain of gold, Camanti, and the numerous rivers and streams which flow to the Brazilian sea, which contain nuggets of this precious metal in their sands, if worked with constancy and regularity, in place of being held in scorn by their owners, the Ch'unchu, would soon satisfy the enormous national debt contracted with England, and

> would present us with Peru's wealth, which unfortunately exists solely in the rugged sierra and the streams and rivers of the desert.[34]

In order to bolster his case, and timed to coincide with the visit to Cuzco of the president of Peru, Luis Orbegoso, in January 1835 O'Brien published a pamphlet outlining the economic benefits to the Peruvian exchequer of a government-backed expedition to Madre de Dios. He wrote of the opportunities for developing gold mining and an export trade in commodities such as cacao, coca, cinnamon and various resins. The pamphlet contained letters of support from residents of the valley who wished to see the region developed and who bemoaned the local lack of technical expertise.[35]

That same month William Miller arrived in Cuzco. Miller had served with distinction in Chile and Peru, rising to the rank of general of division and commander-in-chief of the cavalry. In 1825 he had been appointed governor of Potosí. In 1826 he had returned home to England, suffering from the injuries he had sustained in battle. Three years later he had returned to Peru and been given command of the garrison at Lima and Callao. After a spell in Chile he was appointed military governor of the southern provinces of Peru in October 1834.

Miller was the very picture of the wounded war hero. He was facially disfigured, having suffered horrendous burns in an accident during the blockade of Callao in 1819; he had been cleaning and loading a cannon with powder when it had exploded in his hands and face. He had been temporarily blinded and was delirious for several days, and had to be fed through a quill. He later lost the use of a hand when a musket ball passed through his palm.

Miller's presence in Cuzco riled O'Brien. Not only had the Englishman served as a general on the battlefield, he also enjoyed considerable celebrity in Britain and South America. After Cochrane, he was probably the most famous British officer to have served in South America. Peru's leading newspapers celebrated his return to Lima in 1830. His residence in Cuzco diluted the attention bestowed on O'Brien, arousing the Irishman's jealousy. O'Brien was also annoyed with Miller for planning a parallel expedition to explore the Paucartambo valley. Miller's idea was to plant a military colony of about one hundred soldiers and their families on the banks of one of the navigable rivers on the eastern side of the Andes

> with a view, first to facilitate the discovery or examination of the vast pampas or plains lying between what may be called the civilized

> confines of Peru and Brazil, leaving an immense intervening breadth; and, secondly, to endeavour to open a direct communication with Europe by means of the river Marañon or the Amazons.[36]

In other words, Miller was proposing an identical scheme to O'Brien's.

O'Brien was incapable of holding fire. He focused his attack on Miller's memoirs, which Miller's brother, John, had published in London in 1828 and which described Miller's exploits during the wars of independence in Chile and Peru. The book had been translated into Spanish and distributed in Peru. In January 1835 O'Brien launched a tirade against William Miller in a pamphlet published in Cuzco, which he addressed to his old comrades-in-arms in Argentina, Chile and Peru. He accused Miller of 'portraying himself as the principal agent of the glories' won on the battlefields of Chile and Peru, and of ignoring the achievements of his fellow soldiers in order to burnish his own reputation – this despite the book containing the following description of O'Brien, albeit in a footnote: 'This officer, by birth an Irishman, has displayed a noble and disinterested enthusiasm, during ten years of active service, in the cause of South American independence, equalled only by his courage and humanity, which have acquired for him universal esteem.'[37]

O'Brien described himself in the pamphlet as 'one of the aggrieved', along with 'his comrades-in-arms, and the widows and orphans of the illustrious dead', and declared that history would do justice to the important achievements of 'my countrymen (the Irish) and of the brave Argentinians, Chileans and Peruvians who have worked on the grand edifice of liberty and independence and whose glories this gentleman had wished to attribute to himself alone'.[38] Such was O'Brien's annoyance that he publicised the fact that he was going to burn every copy of Miller's book that he could find in Cuzco. On 20 January 1835 he set fire to a pile of copies of the book in the main square, an event that was the talk of Cuzco for years.[39] Bizarrely, while attacking him in the press in Cuzco and publicly destroying his memoirs, O'Brien maintained that he entertained 'the most sincere friendship for General Miller' and highly appreciated 'his virtues and amiable character'.[40]

O'Brien's bonfire of the vanities provoked a mixed response. The writer of a letter to a local newspaper mocked O'Brien, calling him 'Don Juanito', ridiculing his poor Spanish, and making fun of the stories the Irishman would tell about his time with the Harakmbut. The letter was signed the 'Victors of Ayacucho' – the famous battle that had sealed Peruvian independence, at which Miller had been present and O'Brien had not.[41] Another letter writer called O'Brien 'an unfortunate *sansculote* [*sic*]', 'a plague on society', 'a lying rogue' and 'a demented adventurer [*a.t.*]'.[42] But O'Brien does not seem to have suffered any repercussions from the authorities. President Orbegoso was in Cuzco at the time of the bonfire and, while he did not attend the burning of Miller's memoirs, the authorities did nothing to prevent O'Brien from carrying out his threat. This has been accepted by one historian, Luis Miguel Glave, as a tacit acceptance that the Englishman's book 'was not very eloquent about the achievements of others and extremely laudatory, to the point of exaggeration, about his own, which rightly deserved the Irishman's anger and the understanding of Orbegoso, who did not prohibit the ceremony [*a.t.*]'.[43]

The principal reason for O'Brien's enmity would seem, at first glance, to have arisen from the fact that he and Miller were vying for commercial backing for competing expeditions to eastern Peru. Miller undertook two scouting expeditions in 1835 to find a location for his military colony. During the first, in April, he travelled north-west from Cuzco along the River Urubamba, skirting the site of the ancient Inca ruins at Machu Picchu, which was then still unknown to Europeans. The second expedition, in July, brought Miller eastwards towards the Madre de Dios region. But underlying the conflict was a deeper struggle to protect and shape both men's military reputations. Reputation was a vital asset to foreign-born veterans of the wars of independence, which could be translated into material reward and honour, not only in South America but also in Europe.

O'Brien appealed to the Peruvian authorities for support on the basis that he had already explored the region and had developed contacts with the indigenous tribes who lived there. In a letter of January 1835, contained in a pamphlet addressed to the authorities, he pointed to his friendship with the *cacique* Huya Mesenonga, whom he had met during his stay in Madre de Dios. This would explain the letter mocking O'Brien's contacts with the Harakmbut.

The outbreak of civil war in Peru and Bolivia upset O'Brien's plans. When General Agustín Gamarra seized power in Cuzco, O'Brien tried to gain his support for his expedition to Madre de Dios. He requested permission to form a company in England, with a capital outlay of £50,000 (€58,000), or 250,000 pesos, to exploit the rivers he had discovered. He asked the government to provide his company with a small army: two hundred soldiers, artillery, a surgeon and medicine. O'Brien claimed that his friendship with the Harakmbut people would allow him to easily reduce them to working on plantations. But if he could not achieve his objectives by conciliation, he was prepared to conquer them by force. The company would pay double wages and provide double rations to the soldiers. The government would grant the sole concession to O'Brien's company in exchange for a tenth of the profits. O'Brien claimed that the profits accruing to the government would enable it to pay off the Peruvian national debt within three years. He recalled:

> Such was the abundance of precious metal in that privileged region, and such was my conviction about the facility of extracting it, with the necessary protection of arms, that I did not hesitate then in proposing to President Gamarra that the Government send without delay a military and mining expedition to occupy those valleys, being so close to the populous region of Cuzco, and the Indians who lived there being so few and weak, their conquest required little more than some effort [*a.t.*].[44]

Though Gamarra responded positively to O'Brien's request, he wrote that he was unable to provide any assistance to the expedition until the war was over.[45]

In the meantime, O'Brien offered his services to Gamarra's Bolivian enemies. General André Santa Cruz was from a village close to La Paz in present-day Bolivia, the son of a Spanish father and a *mestizo* mother. Though he was born into a wealthy family, and was classified as *español* (Spanish) on his birth certificate, his enemies gave him the nicknames *el indío* (the Indian) and *el cholo* (the half-breed). He was educated at the Franciscan college in La Paz before continuing his studies at a seminary in Cuzco. He entered the Spanish army in his early twenties, and fought against the patriot armies that were trying to spread the revolution to Upper Peru. But he switched his allegiance to San Martín in 1821.

Santa Cruz crossed into Peru with five thousand Bolivian soldiers. O'Brien knew Santa Cruz from fighting in Peru in the early 1820s, and asked to serve alongside the Bolivian president in a private capacity and without military rank. On 13 August 1835 Santa Cruz defeated Gamarra's forces outside Cuzco at the Battle of Yanacocha.[46] O'Brien served as an aide-de-camp to Santa Cruz, and was lucky to emerge unscathed; his horse was shot twice and a bullet passed through his poncho. During the battle, Gamarra's troops hoisted a black flag with a red skull at its centre and the declaration 'Ni pide ni doy cuartel' (I neither ask for nor give quarter). Despite the brave words, Gamarra fled north after the battle and into exile. Santa Cruz commended O'Brien's bravery during the battle, and gave him the flag as a prize.[47]

After the battle O'Brien accompanied Santa Cruz to Arequipa on the Peruvian coast.[48] While Santa Cruz could muster a good-sized army on land, and had the advantage in terms of troops, the opposition forces under General Felipe Santiago Salaverry controlled the Peruvian navy. Santa Cruz asked O'Brien to use his contacts in the Chilean government to buy ships and recruit naval officers. O'Brien spent the early part of 1836 in Santiago, negotiating on behalf of Santa Cruz. In a newspaper report he was quoted as saying that 'if he had his friend and countryman Admiral William Brown with him, he had little doubt that the naval part of the warfare against Salaverry would be promptly brought to a successful close'.[49] He was desperate to return to Puno and his Peruvian mining interests, not least because he was financially hard up, and was forced to borrow money from friends.[50]

In February Santa Cruz defeated Salaverry's forces at the Battle of Uchumayo. He now began to put in place his plan to create a confederation of Peru and Bolivia. Santa Cruz awarded O'Brien the Peruvian Legion of Honour and the rank of brigadier-general in the Peruvian army. In October 1836 the Peru–Bolivian Confederation came into existence. Santa Cruz became its supreme protector.

O'Brien was now living in Lima. He is listed in parochial records as a merchant. At the age of fifty, having spent most of his life in the army or travelling across the continent, it seems that he had finally decided to settle down. On 3 September he married sixteen-year-old Manuela de la Herrán y Leon. Not long afterwards, Manuela gave birth to their daughter, Isabel. There is some confusion in the sources about whether O'Brien had any other children. His biographers relate that he had just one daughter. However, in 1863, two years after O'Brien's death, the British diplomat William Garrow Lettsom, in a communication about O'Brien, referred to 'the two children of the deceased in Chile',[51] while Thomas Murray, in his history of the Irish in Argentina, mentioned 'two daughters surviving him'.[52] The letter O'Brien wrote to Isabel on his deathbed suggests that if there had been any other children, Manuela was not the mother. It is unclear what happened to Manuela. She most likely died young. It is possible that she may have died in childbirth – either giving birth to Isabel or to a subsequent child who died – because she seems to disappear from O'Brien's life immediately after their marriage. She was certainly dead by 1861 because O'Brien's burial certificate records him as being a widower.[53] Isabel was educated in Santiago. She married José Antonio de Valdés Aldunate in 1857 and settled in Chile. Valdés was from a distinguished family in Santiago. His great-uncle was Mateo de Toro Zambrano, the president of the first independent junta in Chile. One of Valdés' uncles was the revolutionary leader José Miguel Carrera. The couple had four daughters.

O'Brien's domestic happiness was short-lived. The governments of Chile and Argentina greeted the emergence of the Peru–Bolivian Confederation with alarm, believing that this new superstate threatened the regional balance of power on the continent. In 1837, in order to dampen down the simmering tensions between the new Peru–Bolivian Confederation and Buenos Aires, Santa Cruz asked O'Brien, who was about to return to Europe, to deliver a diplomatic message to the Argentine government. O'Brien agreed. It was a decision that marked the beginning of the bitterest period in his life.

9
The Restorer of the Laws

On 24 April 1837 O'Brien set off from the town of Tacna in southern Peru for Buenos Aires. His orders from Santa Cruz were to sign a treaty with the Argentine Confederation, the object of which was to obtain free access to the market in livestock, mules and foodstuffs in exchange for silver from the mines at Potosí.[1] O'Brien later wrote:

> This proposal was most willingly acceded to by the governors of the different provinces, and they evinced their feelings in marked demonstrations of their affection, respect, and regard for him who had been entrusted to make it. In every great town through which I passed, from Lima to Buenos Ayres, public entertainments were given to me by their governors, my old associates in the war of independence.[2]

However, on 19 May the Argentinian leader Juan Manuel de Rosas declared war on the Peru–Bolivian Confederation, citing the fact that Santa Cruz was allowing *unitario* armed forces cross the border between southern Bolivia and north-east Argentina. Rosas claimed that Santa Cruz had 'promoted anarchy in the Argentinian Confederation [the successor to the United Provinces], consenting to and allowing military expeditions, which, armed on Bolivian territory, had invaded the Republic'.[3]

Rosas remains a controversial figure in Argentinian history. Depending on one's perspective, he was either a brutal tyrant who used a secret police force to spy upon, murder and terrorise the citizens of Argentina, or a nationalist hero who stood up to and defeated British and French economic imperialism. He was born in Buenos Aires on 30 March 1793 into a wealthy family. His father was a soldier. It was through his mother, Agustina, that the family inherited their wealth; she had been left a profitable *estancia* in Buenos Aires province. Agustina left her mark on Rosas. She was an autocratic, cruel woman who dominated her children. She gave birth to twenty children, ten of whom survived, and was unrestrained in her use of corporal punishment.[4]

Although Rosas was born in the city, having spent much of his early life on the pampas, it was the countryside that moulded his character. He started his career managing the family *estancia*, before deciding that he wished to branch out on his own. His purchase of two *estancias* in frontier territory was the beginning of a property empire that was to see him amass millions of acres of territory in Argentina. Throughout his life he had an unquenchable thirst for land.[5]

Rosas was a haughty and arrogant young man. A landowning conservative, he was disdainful of economic liberalism and the merchant middle classes. Rather than being thankful for being born into a wealthy family, he believed that his exalted position in the social and economic hierarchy was preordained. This belief in the primacy of the land and the conservative values underpinning the place of the landowner in the economic system was at the heart of his political thinking.

Rosas helped repel the British invasions of Buenos Aires, which took place in 1806 and 1807, but took no part in the revolution of May 1810 that led to Argentinian independence, of which he was suspicious. Instead, he spent the next decade amassing a fortune, not least by marrying Encarnación Ezcurra y Arguibel, a wealthy *porteña* heiress. He helped develop the infant export trade in beef and hides that revolutionised the Argentinian economy in the late nineteenth century.[6]

Rosas first tasted political power in 1820 when he raised a militia comprised of gauchos. The United Provinces was in chaos, divided between *unitarios*, who wished to see a strong central government in Buenos Aires, and *federales*, who were in favour of a loose federation of provinces. Rosas led five hundred men into battle on behalf of the Buenos Aires government against the invading provincial armies. They were recruited from the labourers on his *estancia*, and became known as the *colorados del Monte* because of the red (*colorado*) shirts they wore. The Buenos Aires government accorded Rosas military honours and grants of land in gratitude for his help.[7]

In 1827 Rosas switched sides, joining the *federales*. The government appointed him commander of the rural militia in Buenos Aires province, during which time he may have come into contact with O'Brien. On the back of his new-found military might, Rosas was elected governor of Buenos Aires in 1829. He relinquished office in 1832, during which period he prosecuted the war against the *unitarios*, but returned to the governorship in 1835. This time he maintained an iron grip on power.

Rosas derived his power from the countryside and the urban poor. His wife, Encarnación, was an important political ally, especially during the years when Rosas was out of office. Prefiguring the mass appeal of Eva Perón in Argentina in the late 1940s and early 1950s, Encarnación welcomed the destitute into her house in Buenos Aires, dispensing small favours in return for their support.[8]

Rosas built his regime upon law and order – which earned him the title of Restorer of the Laws – and the need to stamp out anarchy. His method of achieving this political objective was state terror. He wielded extensive powers and employed summary justice in dealing with his political opponents. In Buenos Aires Rosas' agents murdered dissidents in their beds. Soldiers cut the throats of their prisoners, and sometimes decapitated them. Rosas would order the execution of the countless inmates in his prisons without a second thought or due process. Torture was common.

The instrument with which Rosas applied the terror was his political organisation, the Sociedad Popular Restauradora (the Popular Society of the Restorer). The society had an armed wing, a much-feared paramilitary force called the Mazorca. In Spanish, *mazorca* means 'head of maize', a symbol of union and strength; but *mazorca* also sounds like *más horca* (more hangings), *horca* being the Spanish word for gallows.[9]

The regime articulated its political agenda through a bluntly effective propaganda campaign. The mantra '¡Viva la confederación argentina! ¡Mueran los salvajes unitarios!' (Long live the Argentine Confederation! Death to the savage unitarians!) was used to rally, or terrify, the population. Men wore badges with the slogan, and it appeared at the beginning of all official correspondence. Citizens were expected to wear red ribbons, the *federales*' colour.

The outbreak of war might have dissuaded O'Brien from completing his mission. Instead, he decided to defy Rosas' declaration of non-communication between the Argentine Confederation and the Peru–Bolivian Confederation. O'Brien was delayed at the border for twenty days before the governor of Jujuy granted him permission to enter Argentinian territory. At Salta the authorities laid on a reception for O'Brien. According to the British minister in Buenos Aires, John Henry Mandeville: '[O'Brien] was fêted and feasted by the authorities of this town, for they looked upon him as the Harbinger of Peace and the war with them is very unpopular.'[10] The authorities in Salta and Jujuy, the north-western states of Argentina adjoining the border, had good reason to welcome O'Brien's peaceful overtures. They stood to suffer the most from a war; both provinces benefited from a strong export trade to the mining territories in Peru and Bolivia.

O'Brien arrived in Buenos Aires in early July, seemingly unaware of the danger to his life. He had known Rosas for the better part of two decades:

> I had been an acquaintance of Rosas at a former period of my life; I might even say his friend. No thought had ever entered my mind of injuring him in any way. I could not believe it possible that he could thus act towards one whose life was so well known to him, and to whose opinions and habits he could not be a stranger.[11]

The nature of O'Brien's mission to Buenos Aires has been the subject of speculation. According to Mandeville, O'Brien had come 'to refute the charges which General Rosas has brought publicly against General Santa Cruz and to ask at the same time for an explanation of the measure of non-communication by which he has interdicted the Argentine Confederation from holding intercourse with Bolivia and Peru'.[12] Mandeville attended a dinner in O'Brien's honour, 'given to him by one of his fellow countrymen', shortly after his arrival in Buenos Aires. Among those present was General Carlos Alvear, under whom O'Brien had served in the mounted grenadiers in Uruguay. Alvear was an ambitious man who dreamt of leading a federal state in South America – comprising modern-day Argentina, Uruguay, Chile and Bolivia – to rival that of the United States. Some have implicated Alvear in a plot to overthrow Rosas with the help of the Bolivian army and Argentinian exiles living in Montevideo. But in June 1837, just a month before O'Brien's arrival in Buenos Aires, Rosas appointed Alvear as minister plenipotentiary to the United States. This appointment has led some to believe that Alvear was a traitor who double-crossed those comrades who wished to overthrow Rosas. Others believe that Alvear continued planning Rosas' downfall while representing his government in the United States.[13] Either way, Rosas did not trust Alvear and O'Brien's presence at a dinner attended by the dictator's arch-rival, and rumours of conspiracy have contributed to that which followed.

Mandeville reported that, during another dinner on 11 July, O'Brien

> spoke freely upon the State of the Interior and of the Extreme Unpopularity of the War, and declared upon his Conscience that he believed that Genl. Santa Cruz never encouraged any plot or Party against Rosas, and if he could only see the Governor and have half an hour's conversation with him, he would open his Eyes to the good faith of Santa Cruz with regard to him, – and the folly of the War.[14]

O'Brien's reception at Rosas' mansion gave no indication of the looming threat. 'He did not see the Governor but Doña Encarnación, his wife, her sisters and the daughter kissed and embraced him and could not make enough of him', wrote Mandeville.[15] The following day the foreign minister, Felipe Arana, called on O'Brien, who was getting ready to travel to Europe. Arana offered the Buenos Aires government's financial assistance, and told him that Rosas would visit him the next day. But instead of Rosas, the chief of police, Bernardo Victorica, accompanied by a Colonel Pereira, both of whom were armed, arrived at O'Brien's hotel. They told him that they were escorting him to see Rosas.[16] 'I followed them', O'Brien recalled,

> but instead of conducting me to his residence, they brought me to the Cuna – a prison of the worst description – and there, without a charge made against me – I was placed in a cell measuring six yards by five [5.5 by 4.6 metres], and from that cell I was never permitted to stir for six months and twenty-five days.[17]

Mandeville went to the theatre that evening to gather information about the reasons for O'Brien's arrest. The British minister was a fixture on the Buenos Aires social circuit. He was 'a cultured man with an intriguing personality, physically small, bald, and with tiny penetrating eyes', and was 'dashing in both his attire and his social life'. He regularly attended the theatre, and was close to the Rosas family, 'despite the fact that the dictator treated him with a certain mockery'.[18] Mandeville wrote in a report to his superiors in London:

> Seeing Doña Encarnación, Rosas's wife, in her Box with her Daughter I joined them, and after going through the long category of Spanish Compliments, she asked me if I knew that Genl O'Brien had been conveyed to Prison. – I said yes, the whole town knew it I supposed, for half a Dozen people had stopped me on my way to her Box to tell me so. – I did not enquire what for, altho' the Question was burning on my Tongue, but I said, did not he bring Despatches to the Governor from Genl. Santa Cruz? – She said no, – then recollecting herself, – and the untruth she was telling, – I know not, I know nothing – presently after, as if tired of waiting for my Question – What for? – She said it appears that he had a mission here, – and here the Conversation ended.[19]

O'Brien's health was already fragile, and it quickly deteriorated. After a month in prison he believed himself 'so dangerously ill, that he thought his end was approaching'.[20] He had no access to medical treatment, and was worried that, not being allowed pen and paper, he would be unable to make a will in order that his younger sister might inherit his estates in Chile, Peru and Ireland. But he remained confident that the British government would come to his rescue:

> Patiently, and even calmly, had I waited out each slow and lingering hour, and watched the tardy pace of every tough and dreary day, hoping, calculating, self-convinced, that the next must bring with it the appearance of the British minister to my cell – to hear him say that the meanest subject of the British crown should not be thus treated, unaccused, untried, unconvicted. I waited, and – alas! I grieve to say it – I waited in vain. I was personally known to the British minister. I came at last to the conclusion that he must be utterly ignorant of my arrest – of my incarceration – and of the frightful torture that was inflicted upon me.[21]

O'Brien contemplated escaping – 'the sole amusement of my prison hours' – but claimed later that he had dismissed each plan he dreamt up as cowardly.[22] Instead, he managed to smuggle out a few lines to Mandeville. Though denied writing materials by the prison authorities, he carried a small memorandum book and pencil in the pocket of the coat he had been wearing when arrested, and he concocted a plan to communicate with the outside world. Each day his meals were brought to his cell from the British Hotel – 'the only favour conceded to me' – in a *portaviandas*, a contraption for carrying five or six dishes one on top of the other, fastened with a strap, and which contained a type of brazier underneath to keep the food hot. Before it was handed through the door of the cell, the guards would check each dish to make sure no messages were being smuggled in to O'Brien. The same 'rigid examination' took place when he handed it back. However, O'Brien realised that the guards did not check the brazier, and he managed to slip a note into it for Mandeville.[23] O'Brien wrote that his health was 'fast declining' and that his continued imprisonment would result in his death. The hotel employee charged with cleaning the *portaviandas* found the note addressed to Mandeville and passed it on the manager, who delivered it to the British minister.

Mandeville contacted members of the Rosas government, including Arana, demanding that O'Brien be given access to a doctor and writing materials. O'Brien had requested that Mandeville visit him in prison; instead, the chief of police, Victorica, arrived at his cell and threatened him for having communicated with the British minister. 'I denied the fact – I pretended that the communication was the invention of that gentleman's brain, and I denounced him in the strongest terms I could use, calling him "a humbug of a British minister"', he wrote.[24] Rosas finally consented to allow a doctor to visit O'Brien in the company of Victorica and a lawyer.[25] The doctor 'found him much indisposed but by no means dangerously ill, nor attacked by disease that would endanger his life'.[26]

O'Brien might have conjured up mock anger in front of the chief of police to extricate himself from a difficult situation, but, in truth, he was furious with Mandeville:

> He committed, I think a great error, and one that might have cost me my life, by thus betraying my act to the ministers of a man that he knew had acted outrageously towards me – who could not allege any excuse for my detention, but that it was a '*precaucion*' [*sic*], because he had heard and believed that I came to Buenos Ayres to make a revolution![27]

O'Brien condemned Mandeville as a stooge of Rosas, and suggested that the British minister had gone to the authorities in order to save himself: 'He could not but be aware that frightful atrocities were committed under the special direction of Rosas, and it might be that apprehension for his own safety induced him to apprise the minister of a fact that might subsequently be learned through spies …'.[28]

In the aftermath of the events arising from O'Brien's smuggled communication to Mandeville, security was tightened in the prison, and, according to O'Brien, Rosas contemplated moving him to the Retiro barracks, 'as I there could be with greater facility deprived of my life, and my death attributed to illness'.[29] Though other members of his government argued that it was a mistake to execute a British subject, Rosas was at one point determined to shoot O'Brien for plotting revolution against the government of Buenos Aires, and it was only the intervention of the governor's wife, Encarnación – who on her knees begged her husband to spare his life – that saved O'Brien from the firing squad.[30]

At one point, O'Brien was certain that his hour had come:

> I did not at the time know any of these circumstances. I had never been spoken to; but from the moment I had written to Mr. Mandeville, and that he had mentioned it to Rosas's Minister, I regarded my death as inevitable. I was treated as a man doomed to death, and I prepared for death. I expected to be taken out and shot, and I cut down a light green surtout, that I had brought with me to the prison, into a jacket – so that if I were given a soldier's death, I might appear as a soldier, with that care bestowed upon my habiliments which becomes a soldier, and that in my last moments it might be seen, I was not unworthy of those companions in arms, with whom I had often faced that danger, which was now inevitable.[31]

O'Brien was right to be terrified. A French inmate by the name of Baclé had died shortly after arriving at the prison, while a German prisoner, who 'had not been long confined before he was driven to despair', had cut his own throat. O'Brien watched the latter's body being removed from the prison.[32]

Arana admitted to Mandeville that no charge existed against O'Brien except that he had entered the country after the decree had been published prohibiting all communication between the Argentine Confederation and the Peru–Bolivian Confederation, and that O'Brien's imprisonment had been 'merely a measure of precaution' and intended 'to show General Santa Cruz that no one will be allowed to come to these Provinces and infringe the Decree with impunity'.[33] Mandeville replied that O'Brien was the bearer of a letter from Santa Cruz and in possession of a passport granted to him by a general of the army of the Argentine Confederation. He argued that the Argentine government had a right to expel O'Brien but not to detain him.[34] Arana later told Mandeville that 'there were many circumstances' attending O'Brien's arrest 'which he did not feel at liberty to communicate', but also mentioned the fact that O'Brien had previously purchased ships in Valparaíso on behalf of Santa Cruz's government, and 'therefore it was natural that his movements here [Buenos Aires] would be looked after, and stopped, if it was thought that they would take him to any Port in South America where he could execute a Similar Commission'.[35]

Mandeville condemned O'Brien's imprisonment, as did San Martín from exile in Europe.[36] But it was the intervention of the British foreign secretary, Lord Palmerston, that secured O'Brien's release on parole on 24 December 1837.[37] The government agreed to free O'Brien on a number of conditions. He was to leave Buenos Aires province, and was not allowed to travel to any of the other provinces of the Argentine Confederation or any other country in

South America during the period of the war. He was also bound not to work in any capacity for the 'tyrant' Santa Cruz in whichever country he chose as his residence.[38] O'Brien recalled his release:

> The doors of my prison were thrown wide – wide open for me – and the cold, sweet, fresh air was at last permitted to penetrate the foetid atmosphere in which I had been expiring. I thought I should never have enough of air – I tore open my jacket, that I might feel it on my skin; that it might be as a balm to my body, which had been withered and wasted without it. This is all I can recollect; for I am told I was delirious with pain, with misery, and suffering. I could not walk – the nerves had become torpid – my flesh so incapable of pain, that I could prod my thigh with a nail and not feel it.[39]

Suffering from pneumonia, O'Brien was helped to the carriage that was waiting outside the prison to take him to his hotel, 'as if I were a child'.[40] A friend, Dr Hogan, ministered to him during his initial weeks of recovery. When he had regained some strength, O'Brien boarded a ship to England. Despite Palmerston's intervention, O'Brien was far from grateful to the British government. He believed that, as a British subject who had not violated any laws, he was 'entitled to the protection of the British flag, and to the interposition of the British minister on my behalf. My former friend was my gaoler, and the representatives of the British crown did not enforce for me the rights of a British subject.'[41]

After his traumatic experience at the hands of Rosas' gaolers, he was anxious to return to Ireland, where his presence was necessary on account of business affairs.[42] He sailed for England at the beginning of March 1838, arriving in Liverpool at the end of May.

The Chilean government forced Santa Cruz to resign as the supreme protector of the Peru–Bolivian Confederation at the beginning of 1839 after defeating his army at the Battle of Yungay. Peru and Bolivia went their separate ways, becoming once more two sovereign nations. In an ingratiating letter written to Bernardo O'Higgins from Baltinglass after Santa Cruz's downfall, O'Brien argued that he had 'never liked' the Bolivian. 'There was too much India cholo[43] about him and after the battle of Yanacocha, I there saw he was no General in the field, and on the whole he was only an intrusive [*sic*] on Peru. He would have been a proud Tyrant, although he might have governed and done good for the country.'[44]

The Chilean government had succeeded in breaking up the Peru–Bolivian Confederation, the creation of which it had regarded as disrupting the regional balance of power. O'Brien predicted: 'Chili will now become a great country of commerce, while I fear Peru will fall off. Certainly, there must be a great deal due to the Chili troops for their success in beating Santa Cruz as he had a fine army.'[45]

The events surrounding his imprisonment in Buenos Aires have been shrouded in mystery. Vicuña Mackenna believed that Santa Cruz had entrusted O'Brien with a 'secret diplomatic mission' to Buenos Aires and to 'some of the courts of Europe'. Figueroa dismissed Vicuña Mackenna's claim of a 'secret diplomatic mission', arguing that O'Brien was nothing more than Santa Cruz's messenger. 'Because of incorrect diplomatic reports, some historians have attributed to this mission a significance which did not exist in reality', Figueroa concluded,[46] referring to a note written by José Joaquín Pérez, the Chilean minister to Buenos Aires and future president of Chile. In the note Pérez opined that O'Brien's ostensible return to Europe may have been a cover for a conspiracy dreamt up by Santa Cruz.[47] Given that Figueroa was a Chilean and his purpose was to depict O'Brien as a national hero, it is not surprising that he was quick to dismiss any suggestion that the Irishman was working against the interests of Chile. 'O'Brien loved our country, for which he conserved the most profound and indelible affection', Figueroa wrote. 'O'Brien proved his loyalty at every occasion and never gave a motive to doubt him.'[48]

O'Brien wrote that his arrest arose from the fact that he had been welcomed by the other provincial governors of the Argentine Confederation. He traced 'the motives for the conduct of Rosas' to the 'testimonies of affection' he had received from them. His warm reception, according to O'Brien, had excited Rosas' 'jealousy – they had perhaps aroused his fears – and they had induced him to believe that a plain man bent on extending the benefits of a free intercommunication between the provinces of South America was a formidable political agent'.[49] Certainly, Rosas would have viewed with suspicion the fact that Santa Cruz's representative – a decorated general, no less – was negotiating with the provincial governors behind his back. Under these circumstances, it is not surprising that he viewed O'Brien as a hostile agent.

Beyond his belief about O'Brien's involvement in a plot to bring down his government, Rosas would have viewed O'Brien's political views with suspicion. O'Brien was an agent for foreign capital, agitating for the removal of tariff barriers, the opening up of South America's waterways, and the expansion of trade. Rosas was a landowning conservative, a protectionist whose political success rested on denying the European powers access to the River Plate and its waterways, without which trade with the heart of the continent was impossible.

O'Brien was not to forget his humiliation at the hands of Rosas; this was an era when the loss of one's honour was a grave matter. Following his imprisonment in Buenos Aires, O'Brien spent the next few years in Europe, recuperating and pondering his next move, but it was not long before he crossed paths with Rosas once more.

10
The Great War

O'Brien spent his first months back in Europe in convalescence. After suffering for five months in a damp, dirty prison cell, he arrived in Liverpool in the spring of 1838 a sick man. He was shattered physically and mentally, not least from the effects of his pneumonia. He spent the early weeks of his recovery in Leamington Spa, Warwickshire. According to O'Brien, his doctor told him that his was a 'hopeless' case, and that 'he could not guarantee his life'. Despite the gloomy prognosis, which may well have been exaggerated as part of an efficient anti-Rosas propaganda campaign, and owing, perhaps, to his generally optimistic disposition, after three months he was 'restored to my usual health'.[1]

In December 1838 O'Brien returned to Ireland, where the press welcomed him as a national hero. 'With no inconsiderable delight should we hail the arrival amongst us of one of our most gallant countrymen, General O'Brien', a letter to the editor of *The Dublin Evening Post* suggested.[2] O'Brien revelled in the attention. He was in the habit of carrying around with him some of the exotic artefacts he had accumulated in South America. In Dublin he exhibited the viceregal canopy, the present from San Martín upon the declaration of Peruvian independence.[3]

Having raised money for the campaign for Catholic emancipation in Buenos Aires in the late 1820s, O'Brien now lent his support to the campaign to repeal the Act of Union. In Dublin's Pro-Cathedral, he presented a 'generous contribution' to Daniel O'Connell. According to the aforementioned letter-writer to *The Dublin Evening Post*,

> Be assured, in person as well as in purse, General O'Brien is resolved, during his sojourn in Ireland, which it is hoped will be for the balance of his life, to evince his very marked devotion to his country's advancement that fired his early youth, and that neither years, 'or feats, or

> broils, or battles,' have lessened that energy of spirit which, to his last breath, shall be up and stirring in endeavouring, by every legal means, to throw off those galling fetters that still oppress a loyal yet a generous nation.[4]

In view of his enthusiasm for the South American patriots, O'Connell must have welcomed the association with O'Brien, one of the most visible and successful of the Irish-born revolutionaries who had fought in Latin America.

In May O'Brien once again visited San Martín, who was now living in Paris. They spent two days together. 'I had long conversations with him', O'Brien wrote to Bernardo O'Higgins;

> He often times talked of you, and your family. He is very comfortably living there but I think he is disappointed and very unhappy in his mind. He would like to go back to America and I think he will do so the first opportunity, but it would be to Buenos Ayres.[5]

O'Brien may have considered remaining in Ireland, or, at least, this was what he told the press, which reported that he was planning on devoting the remaining years of his life to the repeal campaign. His experience of having been imprisoned in Buenos Aires may have given him pause for thought. In July 1839 he was living in Baltinglass at a property his father had left him. 'I suppose I must now for ever give up the Idea of seeing Peru again', he told O'Higgins. 'I am quite happy in my native land, with every comfort I can wish for.'[6] O'Brien spent three years in Europe, mostly in Ireland. But it was not long before he became restless and yearned to return to South America.

In 1841 O'Brien spent four months in County Cork.[7] It was perhaps during this sojourn that he decided to return to South America. His delicate health would have dissuaded him from settling in the Andes, where he continued to have an interest in the Laykakota mine. Instead, he decided to buy a sheep farm. Unable to return to Argentina because of the presence of Rosas, he chose to establish the farm in Uruguay, the country where he had first seen action with the patriot armies.

Sheep farming was enjoying a boom on the Argentinian and Uruguayan pampas in the 1840s. In Argentina the export trade in wool rose from 1.6 million kilograms in 1840 to 45 million kilograms twenty years later.[8] Sheep farmers were making great fortunes. O'Brien was interested in the possibility of importing merino sheep to the River Plate in order to supply the textile industry in the north of England with fine wool. Before leaving Europe he entered into a partnership with a group of Yorkshire textile manufacturers.

In September 1841 he purchased an *estancia* in Mataojo de Solís Grande near the town of Las Minas in the department of Maldonado, about 110 kilometres east of Montevideo. During the first three years of his stay in Uruguay, O'Brien poured money into the enterprise. He spent £4,000 (€4,642) building sheepfolds and sheds, importing merinos and other fine breeds from England,[9] and employing British and Irish shepherds and servants.

While the economic climate was propitious for O'Brien's new venture, the political situation in the River Plate was not. In 1838 the former president of Uruguay, General Fructuoso Rivera, had ousted his successor, General Manuel Oribe. Rivera and his Argentinian allies in the *unitario* party invaded Buenos Aires province. This was the beginning of what became known in the River Plate region as the Guerra Grande, or Great War, a series of internecine political and military confrontations in Argentina and Uruguay that lasted until 1853.

Irish immigrants became embroiled in the violence that swept the countryside. The Irish owner of an *estancia* called Las Averías in Buenos Aires province was a notable victim. On the morning of 7 November 1839, an officer under the command of General Prudencio Rosas, the brother of the dictator, stabbed James O'Neill to death with a lance. He died in front of his wife, Bridget, and their two children, seven-year-old Patricio and four-year-old Mary. In a claim for compensation submitted to the British government, his widow wrote that 'the murder of my husband was perpetuated by the Commander of the Troops', who, before killing him, had described James O'Neill as 'an English Barbarian'.[10] According to Bridget O'Neill, there had been no political motivation behind the killing, and the troops had plundered money, clothes and cattle worth $26,340 from their home 'immediately after executing the execrable crime of the barbarous murder of my husband without the shadow of cause, and whilst his blood still continued to warm the stones of the pavement'.[11] The indomitable Bridget O'Neill confronted Prudencio Rosas after the killing, but was given no redress.

The war spread to Uruguay. Rosas gave Oribe command of an army to bring Uruguay under the control of Buenos Aires; this was despite the British having warned Rosas that the government would intervene if he threatened Uruguay. Oribe's forces quickly overran most of the country; only Montevideo held out, but was under siege.

Known then as the Banda Oriental, Uruguay derived its strategic importance from its position at the entrance to the River Plate. Control of the River Plate allowed access to the River Paraguay and River Paraná, the primary transport routes for foreign merchants seeking access to the inland markets of the continent. The collapse of Spanish power in the region and the subsequent development of international trade had transformed Montevideo from a provincial backwater into one of the most important entrepôts on the continent. In 1843, at the time of the siege, over half of the fifty-thousand-strong population was foreign-born. They were mostly French and Spanish Basques, and Italians, but there were also hundreds of Irish-born, English-born and Scottish-born residents, most of whom were engaged in the import–export business.

What was essentially a civil war in the River Plate was complicated by the involvement of Britain and France. The French government was keen to protect the substantial French Basque population in Montevideo, and was more aggressive in its dealings with Rosas. The problem for the British government was that, though many of its citizens lived and traded in Montevideo, it also had to protect the large British community and its commercial interests in Buenos Aires. Between 1838 and the end of the Guerra Grande, British policy with regard to Rosas wavered between conciliation and confrontation, much to the annoyance of British citizens living in both Buenos Aires and Montevideo.

The groups that coalesced around Oribe and Rivera became known, respectively, as the *blancos* (whites) and *colorados* (reds)[12] – a political divide that continues in Uruguay to this day – from the coloured armbands they wore into battle. The *blancos* represented the conservative, rural class, while the *colorados* were the liberal party of the country's business class, which included the large foreign merchant community resident in Montevideo. O'Brien came to be associated with the *colorados*.

Despite the volatility surrounding him, O'Brien wrote with typical enthusiasm to San Martín in Paris about his new enterprise. San Martín was less sanguine, expressing foreboding about O'Brien's decision to settle in Uruguay. In a letter to William Miller, he wrote that 'if, as it is to be believed, Rosas defeats Rivera's forces, poor O'Brien will lose his new establishment'.[13] San Martín clearly believed that Rosas, if he had the chance, would come after O'Brien again.

Disaster struck at the beginning of 1844. On 12 February the *alcalde*, or mayor, of Mataojo de Solís Grande, Anacleto Fernández, arrived at the *estancia* and asked to see O'Brien. The overseer, John Larkin, told him that his employer was on business in Montevideo. Fernández informed Larkin that he was communicating an order on behalf of Colonel Manuel Melgar, an officer in Oribe's army, to the effect that everyone on the *estancia* had three days to leave. In a deposition, one of O'Brien's employees, a fifty-year-old Irishman named Patrick O'Donoghue, who was in the main house on the *estancia* at the time, later testified that Fernández had warned Larkin that 'if he or any other person in his employment or under his control should be found in the house or upon the estancia after the expiry of said term … they should be murdered'.[14] Larkin called on Melgar at his camp in order to request more time to remove livestock and other property from the *estancia*. Melgar refused and reiterated his warning that he would punish anyone on the *estancia* who did not leave within three days. Larkin, O'Donoghue and the rest of O'Brien's employees initially resisted Melgar's threats, but when they realised the seriousness of the situation, they fled to Las Minas in fear of their lives.

When he received the news in Montevideo, O'Brien wrote to Ángel Pacheco, a former comrade in the mounted grenadiers and now a senior officer in the Buenos Aires army, pleading with him to intervene with Oribe in order to make sure that 'my interests – which are worth more than 20,000 pesos [€4,642], and which is all I have in the world for the last days of my life – will be respected by him and that he frees my caretaker and two other *ingleses* who are in my house in Mataojo de Solís Grande'.[15]

O'Brien also sought the protection of the British government, writing repeatedly to John Pownall Dale, the acting consul general in Montevideo, and Commodore John Brett Purvis, the commander of the Royal Navy's squadron off Montevideo. Purvis sent the sloop HMS *Racer* to the port of Buceo, which served Montevideo, in order to allow O'Brien to circumvent Oribe's besieging troops and travel to the port of Maldonado and from there to Mataojo de Solís Grande. But O'Brien was prevented from visiting his *estancia* by the authorities, who told him that he needed a pass from Oribe.

O'Brien returned to Montevideo, and managed to arrange a passport for one of his employees, Edward Connell, 'with orders to investigate the nature and extent of the injury done to the estates and to use whatever measures might be practicable to save the remaining property'.[16] Connell left Montevideo for Mataojo de Solís Grande on 10 April, arriving two days later. He visited the *estancia* on 14 April, accompanied by O'Brien's neighbour, Benjamin Edwards.[17] On his return, Connell had grim news for O'Brien: despite protests from the British government's representatives in Montevideo, including one from Commodore Purvis,[18] Oribe's troops had run riot. O'Brien's house and farm had been vandalised, and what heads of livestock were still alive were close to death.[19] O'Brien assessed the damage to his property in Uruguay at between £20,000 (€23,212) and £25,000 (€29,007).

O'Brien saw the hand of Rosas behind the destruction. The Argentinian dictator had failed to kill the Irishman in Buenos Aires – or at his *estancia* in Uruguay, which O'Brien suspected was the purpose of the raid – but he had managed to destroy all that the Irishman had worked for in the intervening period. 'There can be little or no doubt whatever that these acts have been committed with express and malicious design', O'Brien fulminated to Turner, 'Although I am at a loss to account for any motive in my own conduct since I came to this country to which I can ascribe the evident enmity out of which that design has arisen.'[20] In fact, O'Brien represented foreign commercial interests in Montevideo that were hostile to Rosas.

O'Brien acknowledged that, on occasion, he had taken in refugees from the war, but he strenuously denied having given shelter to Rivera's troops, and claimed that he had helped members of Oribe's family.[21] To prove that he had been targeted, O'Brien pointed to the fact that neighbouring *estancias* had been spared while his property had been systematically destroyed. San Martín's prediction that Rosas would destroy O'Brien's enterprise supports O'Brien's contention that he was deliberately singled out. Recognising that the government in Montevideo needed the support of the British and French governments if it were to survive, O'Brien offered his services, and was appointed the government's unofficial representative to London and Paris.[22] He arrived in London at the end of November 1844 with a mission to convince the British and French governments that Rosas was trying to swallow up Uruguay, destroy its independence, and prevent the free exercise of commerce in the River Plate. In a letter to the Anglo-Irish diplomat Lord Ponsonby, he wrote that 'the object of … [Oribe's] invasion is spoliation, and the means by which it is endeavoured to be effected are as detestable as the object itself is vile'.[23]

O'Brien met the foreign secretary, the Earl of Aberdeen, at Downing Street on 14 December.[24] At some stage during their interview, Aberdeen must have made some positive remarks about Rosas, because, in January 1845, having 'reflected much' upon the content of their meeting, O'Brien wrote once more to Aberdeen to 'convey the precise character' of the Buenos Aires dictator in order that, 'by giving you an accurate account of the past career of Rosas, I should at the same time be performing an act of duty to your Lordship, and one of justice to those on whose behalf I plead'.[25]

O'Brien used language that had become commonplace in the propaganda war fought between the *blancos* and *colorados*. He pointed to Rosas' association with the indigenous tribes as an indication of his barbarism:

> His calling in life was that of a 'capatos' or caretaker of the property of his relatives … and this brought him into constant intercourse with the wild Indian tribes of the Pampas. He ingratiated himself greatly with these tribes: for he not only conformed himself to their habits, but he also won the favour of their caciques by presents judiciously distributed amongst them.[26]

Forging alliances with the indigenous tribes was standard practice among the royalist and patriot leaders. Indeed, O'Brien had been present for the bacchanalia that had resulted from San Martín's gift-bearing expedition in 1816 on the eve of the crossing of the Andes. Nevertheless, O'Brien was not above trying to win his argument with Aberdeen by contrasting the civilised behaviour of the metropolitan Montevideo merchant class with the barbarities of the Argentinian outback, as represented by Rosas. In another passage O'Brien wrote that Rosas had 'left the society of civilised men, and again repaired to the Indians'.[27]

This struggle between civilisation and barbarism, which was to be found in O'Brien's polemic, is a central theme of Domingo F. Sarmiento's *Facundo*, one of the most important works in the Argentinian and wider Latin American historiographical canon. It was published in 1845, and also identified Rosas and the *federales* with a regressive barbarism in opposition to European-led progress on the continent.

It was thus in the role of *unitario* propagandist that O'Brien travelled to Paris at the beginning of January 1845, meeting King Louis-Phillippe, the foreign minister, François Guizot – the guiding spirit of the French government – and the British ambassador, Lord Cowley. While the United Kingdom had tried to follow a policy of neutrality between Rosas and the Rivera government, France was more willing to confront the Argentinian dictator as it wished to prevent Rosas from controlling access to the River Paraná, the main trading route to Paraguay. The French regarded Rosas as an obstacle to French trade in South America who had to be removed.

O'Brien continued his diplomatic offensive in London, meeting Aberdeen and Charles Canning, the undersecretary at the Foreign Office, in the middle of February. He again urged the British government to intervene in the River Plate.[28] Publishing his correspondence with the government, he emphasised that what was at stake was British trade, the free navigation of South America's rivers, and 'the rights of humanity'. In the preface he wrote that war 'was carried on, not by the bravery of soldiers, but by the cowardly cruelty of assassins',[29] and claimed that the removal of Rosas would lead to Britain having 'an inexhaustible mart for the consumption of her manufactures, – giving her in return the richest productions of the globe – a communication with the finest part of this earth – with the most abundant soil, the purest climate, and the noblest position, that man could choose for colonisation, for traffic, or for health'.[30]

O'Brien made concerted efforts to bring the weight of the north of England's manufacturers' views to bear on government policy, expounding upon his dream of opening up South America to foreign trade by introducing steamships to its rivers.[31] The dispute between Rosas on one side, and the British and French governments on the other, was, ultimately, over control of these waterways connecting the continent's interior – with its rich resources and, it was hoped in Britain, expanding markets – with the Atlantic. The British and French believed that they should have unrestricted access to the rivers. Having built his regime on a heady blend of nationalism, protectionism and anti-foreign rhetoric, Rosas saw things differently. He believed that Buenos Aires should exercise sovereignty over the rivers.

On 13 November 1845 O'Brien left London for South America in good spirits. The British and French governments had finally resolved upon military action in the River Plate by instigating a joint blockade. There was also good news in relation to O'Brien's bid for compensation: the foreign secretary, Lord Aberdeen, had been sympathetic, instructing the British consul in Buenos Aires, William Gore Ouseley, to 'require the Argentine Government' to settle O'Brien's claim.[32] But the war for public opinion in Europe was far from over, and O'Brien lobbied the government in Montevideo to appoint him its private and confidential agent in London in order to counter the activities of Rosas' agents in Britain.[33] On 13 July 1846 O'Brien got his wish when he was appointed Montevideo's consul general in London.

O'Brien's campaign was met with a mixed response. His fulminations against Rosas brought him into conflict with British interests in Buenos Aires. *The Morning Chronicle* mocked his account of his imprisonment and of how he had altered a coat to make a uniform because he had wished to die like a soldier in front of the firing squad: 'As ill-luck or Rosas ordained it, he was *not* shot, and lives to mourn over his lost light-green surtout and awkwardly shaped jacket!' the *Chronicle* sneered.[34]

O'Brien and one of the leading lights of the Irish community in Buenos Aires also found themselves on opposing sides. In the mid-1840s the County Galway-born Dominican Fr Anthony Fahy was chaplain to the Irish community in Buenos Aires, which had grown considerably since the late 1820s when O'Brien had been residing in the city. Fahy had arrived in Buenos Aires on 11 January 1844. A gruff, energetic figure, he was responsible for expanding the influence of the Irish Church in Argentina, opening schools, hospitals and convents, and sending Irish priests into the Argentinian countryside to minister to the Irish farmers and labourers who had arrived in their droves over the previous two decades. He intervened directly with the archbishop of Dublin, Daniel Murray, in a bid to have him use his influence with the British government on behalf of Rosas and the *federales* in Uruguay. Fahy felt that Oribe was 'a man of stern determination, to uphold order and govern according to the established laws of the country is his greatest crime' and that 'his government was upset by French intrigue, aided by a few unscrupulous British adventurers, who had everything to gain and nothing to lose by civil war'.[35] Fahy flipped the narrative that O'Brien had presented to Aberdeen – that of the civilised *unitarios* versus the barbaric *federales* – framing the war in Uruguay as a fight between godless, foreign adventurers and Catholic traditionalists. He urged Archbishop Murray to use his influence to prevent British military involvement in the River Plate:

> My Lord, if it be possible, get some friends of the British Government to prevent an army from coming out here. Our poor Irish people will be all ruined, religion will be upset, civil war with all its frightful consequences will be ruined once more, and the government will gain nothing in the end but the malediction of every widow and orphan that will be deprived of their natural protectors. Use then, My Lord, your influence in the name of religion and humanity to prevent a recurrence of these evils which have already shocked the civilised world.[36]

In November 1846 Fahy estimated that two hundred Irish men and women had left Buenos Aires as a direct result of the Anglo-French blockade. According to the priest, most of those who had left had gone to Uruguay and the Cape of Good Hope. Writing to Lord Palmerston, Fahy said that many of the Irish who owned sheep and cattle farms in Buenos Aires province had suffered 'dreadful losses', the result of army requisitioning. He claimed that he himself had suffered grave economic setbacks during the war, which had left him 'little better than the poorest of my congregation', and he requested financial assistance from the government. He was not above a bit of blackmail to achieve his ends: 'I have laboured hard to keep my poor people faithful to their allegiance to the British government', he wrote. 'If I should be obliged through want to abandon them, they may fall into the hands of designing men who will certainly mislead them and cause a very bad feeling to exist between them and the other British subjects residing here.'[37] The government refused his request.

O'Brien made renewed efforts to persuade the British government of the merits of encouraging Irish emigrants to take up residence in the River Plate, proposing a far-reaching scheme to settle his compatriots in Uruguay. His attempts to promote emigration to South America in Ireland had been thwarted by the British government in the 1820s, but he continued to believe that such a scheme was possible. In 1846 he returned to Ireland in the middle of the Great Famine, and saw

> that an overcrowded population was suffering for want of food, when I had left a land, with the purest climate, and the richest soil in the world, where beef and mutton do not cost a halfpenny per pound, and where there are the means of feeding the whole of Ireland, and where if they were an industrious population, the finest and richest markets might be found for British manufacturers.[38]

But as long as the civil war continued in Uruguay, and his political enemies were in charge in the countryside, O'Brien was incapable of bringing his ambitious plans to fruition.

Between 1844 and 1849, O'Brien crossed the Atlantic six times. When he was not lobbying industrialists in the north of England, his time was spent in London, mixing with the great and the good at court levees and diplomatic functions. On 18 May 1848 he addressed a meeting in London of merchants, manufacturers and shipowners involved in trading with Peru and Bolivia on the subject of navigating the Andean region by steamship. He recalled how he had come up with the idea of buying and transporting the *Julia* across the Andes in the 1820s. He then proposed doing the same with a steamship. The idea was to purchase a vessel of one hundred tons (101.6 tonnes) and twenty horsepower in England and send it to the Pacific coast, where it would be disassembled and the parts transported by mule across the Andes. The steamer would be based in Puno and operate across Lake Titicaca. O'Brien estimated the capital cost at £3,500 (€4,061). Warming to his theme, he began to speak to the assembled group of severe-looking Victorian industrialists of the profits from such an enterprise. He told them that the mints at Potosí and Cuzco coined annually between five and six million dollars. The ore came from 'the gold mines of Carabaya and Zipuani, and the silver mines of Puno, Lampa and many other districts: a great proportion of this wealth would, if necessary, go by the lake to be coined at Cuzco and Potosí, and return in the same way for transport to the coast for shipment to Europe …'. He added that 'in suggesting this undertaking is the fervent desire to do permanent service to the countries of Peru and Bolivia, as also to the merchants, manufacturers, and all others interested in their trade and prosperity'.[39] This was the synthesis of O'Brien's ambitions: to open up South America to trade by way of the steamship, paving the way for the introduction of Irish settlers.

On 1 September 1848 O'Brien met the Earl of Clarendon, the Lord Lieutenant of Ireland, at the Viceregal Lodge in Dublin's Phoenix Park. In a memorial to Clarendon, dated 13 October, he wrote that he had 'secured for Irish Emigrants on the East side of the Uruguay, nearly a million of acres of the finest land in the world, a pure virgin soil abundantly supplied with wood and water, and the worst acre of which is equal to the best land in England'. He added:

> There is a home, there is welcome, there is food, there is land, there is the certainty of prosperity for the Irishman in the Oriental Republic del Uruguay. All that is required, all that is wanted to raise him from his squalid misery is the expense of transit from Ireland to Monte Video [*sic*], a steam voyage of 30 days.[40]

O'Brien spent most of that year in London, residing at 29 Upper Belgrave Place. He was short of money; his expenses came out of his own pocket. The Montevideo government was unable to recompense him. It was throwing every last peso at the continuing war, and its revenues had been squeezed by Oribe's continuing siege of the city and the Argentinian blockade. O'Brien had ploughed most of his fortune into his *estancia*. The livestock were dead and much of the farm had been destroyed. And the war meant that he was unable to return. On 22 February he lodged a claim against the Buenos Aires government with the Foreign Office for the losses he had suffered at Mataojo de Solís Grande.

In the end O'Brien's propaganda campaign failed to sway the British government. Palmerston believed that Rosas provided a better opportunity for stability in the region, and that it was the continuing defiance of the government and merchant community in Montevideo that was prolonging the crisis.[41]

Elements within the British press had also begun to criticise what they saw as O'Brien's determination to draw Britain into a lengthy war with Rosas. An editorial carried in several newspapers in Britain and in *The British Packet* questioned whether Rosas could 'possibly be such a monster of cruelty, and so utterly devoid of talent, as General O'Brien describes him to be'. It suggested that many of the atrocities reported in the Montevideo press were 'purely imaginary'.[42]

O'Brien resigned as consul general in March 1849, attributing his decision to Palmerston's rebuff.[43] The British government had decided that the cost of military intervention in the River Plate was too high, and had sought peace terms with Rosas. In November the British signed a treaty with Rosas.

Having lost his fortune and the chance of enjoying a prosperous retirement as a successful *estanciero*, O'Brien left Uruguay for the scenes of his greatest triumphs: Chile and Peru. However, he continued to attack Rosas in the press in Europe and South America. The Rosas press responded in kind. In 1849 an article in the *Dublin Review*[44] prompted a vicious war of words. Daniel O'Connell had co-founded the quarterly *Dublin Review* in London in 1836 with the barrister Michael Quin and Fr Nicholas Wiseman to represent the Catholic position to a British readership. In its edition of March 1849, the *Review* depicted the war in the River Plate as a struggle between monopolists and free-traders. The article condemned Rosas, quoting from authors hostile to his regime, including 'the high and indisputable authority of General O'Brien'.[45] It represented the Rosas regime as violently anti-Catholic, and contrasted the Jesuit missions in South America – 'that model commonwealth of which socialists dream, and communists babble, when they theorise respecting something that they, with their sordid and impure passions, could never accomplish' – with the Rosas regime. The latter was, according to the *Review*,

> despotism in its worst, most odious, most intolerant, and most sanguinary aspect, when it calls itself 'a democracy', and, in accordance with the whim, the caprices, the passions, the avarice, or the cruelty of a few – a clique, a club, or a president – pillages monasteries, confiscates public [and] appropriates private property, banishes, kills or tortures its victims, and claims an indulgence for every crime, and a reward

> for the meanest bloodiest act of vice, because perpetrated in the name of the 'The People!'.[46]

Rosas responded with fury to the article, describing it as a libel and making a formal complaint to the British government. He attacked O'Brien's character through the pages of *El Archivo Americano y Espíritu de la Prensa del Mundo*,[47] a government-sponsored publication that disseminated pro-Rosas propaganda. *El Archivo Americano* lambasted O'Brien, describing him, in January 1851, as an adventurer, a spy and a 'personal and ignoble enemy' of Rosas.[48] It reported that the government in Buenos Aires 'cannot remain indifferent before a crime so enormous, perpetrated by the press against the law of nations, in a periodical whose superintendence belongs to the Apostolic Vicar of London'. It called on the British government to disassociate itself from the *Dublin Review*. It continued:

> The libel published in the periodical that is superintended by the Apostolic Vicar of London is atrociously, infamously offensive to the Confederation ... since it represents the country in a state of barbarism, beyond the pale of the Law of Nations and of civilization, its Supreme ruler, General Rosas, as if he were an 'oppressor', a 'tyrant', an 'assassin', and guilty of 'sacrilege'...[49]

Fr Fahy also condemned the article in the *Review*, defending Rosas as an 'upright Magistrate' who had 'restored the reign of order, and the splendour of the Catholic Religion'.[50] Fahy claimed that the Irish were prospering under Rosas, and that the article had libelled the regime in Buenos Aires:

> All that is stated in the *libel* inserted in the *Dublin Review* in regard to supposed crimes and assassinations of a Mashorca society in the service of the police ... all that is said of the profanation of churches and sanctuaries, and the other suppositions of this stamp ... are but a tissue of contemptible falsehoods.[51]

In Ireland, sectarian tensions entered the debate over Rosas. In June 1852 *The Dublin University Magazine*, a periodical whose readership came from the Protestant landed class, published an article about the history of the conflict in the River Plate which mildly defended Rosas. The same issue contained a stinging criticism of Catholic Members of Parliament. *The Weekly Telegraph*, a stridently Catholic newspaper published in Dublin, responded with an article that conflated the situation in the River Plate with Irish politics:

> Place a pen in the hands of an Irish Orangeman, and we cannot be surprised to find an advocate of Rosas in him who is himself a member of *a secret society*, which has made itself known by its deeds of blood, of torture, and of cruelty – that has applied the lash to the flesh of women – that has pitchcapped men, and that has rioted in the death-agonies of its victims. The member of *the secret society* in Ireland is naturally an admirer of, and a sympathiser with, Rosas, the President of *the Buenos Ayrean secret society* – the Mashorca Club, which, as it was longer united with the supreme power in the state in which it was instituted, has surpassed in cruelty, in infamy, and in atrocity even the worst and most nefarious crimes of the Irish Orangeman in 1798.[52]

The writer of the article in *The Weekly Telegraph* criticised *The Dublin University Magazine* for failing to praise the achievements of the Irish officers who had fought during the wars of independence in South America:

> The Irish Orangeman's hero is General Miller, an *Englishman*; but there is not one word of praise for such men as General John Thomond O'Brien, for Captain O'Brien,[53] for Colonel O'Carroll,[54] for Colonel O'Leary,[55] for the desperate defence of Rancagua by O'Higgins, nor for the naval achievements of that Irishman who was called the 'Nelson of South America', Admiral Browne [*sic*].

In any event Rosas' regime was at an end. In 1851 Brazil, Paraguay, Uruguay and the Argentinian provinces of Corrientes and Entre Rios joined forces to remove the dictator from power. In 1852, realising that he risked his life by staying in Argentina, Rosas fled into exile. With the help of Robert Gore, the British chargé d'affaires in Buenos Aires, he left for England. He arrived in Plymouth on 26 April, where he was greeted with pomp and ceremony. The British government gave permission to Rosas and his family to settle in England. The former dictator of Buenos Aires rented the three-storey Rockstone House on Carlton Crescent in Southampton, one of the smartest streets in a genteel part of the city. Rosas' neighbours were army and navy officers, lawyers, bankers and merchants.[56] They would watch him riding down the street on his horse, still arrogant and aloof, even in exile.

The fact that the British had granted Rosas asylum infuriated O'Brien. For the remainder of his life he sought to convince the British public that it was sheltering a monster in its midst. But his efforts were in vain, and Rosas lived out his days – O'Brien predeceased him by sixteen years – in bourgeois respectability in the south of England, succumbing to a bout of pneumonia in 1877, aged eighty-three.

11
'Messenger of the Heroes'

O'Brien returned to Chile and Peru with little to show for the four decades he had spent in South America but a glittering record in the service of the patriot armies. In 1850 he once again attempted to make a go of the Salcedo mine, in which he still retained an interest, and tried to interest investors in Lima.[1] Lacking a steady income, he petitioned both the Chilean and Peruvian congresses for pensions. Though he was well known in both countries as San Martín's loyal aide-de-camp, it was difficult to prove his record in the war. Many of those with whom he had served in Chile and Peru were dead, and he lacked much of the documentary evidence required by the state bureaucracies to award him a pension.

In 1851, living in Santiago, O'Brien wrote to his former comrades requesting testimony from them about his services in the patriot army. It was during one of the city's frequent outbreaks of fever, and many *santiaguinos* were afraid or unable to leave their homes. Senior officers who had served alongside O'Brien, some of them writing from their sickbeds, replied that, although they were conscious of the merits of his cause, they were unable to furnish any documentary evidence.[2] Better news came from Peru. On 29 December 1851 the constituent assembly in Lima awarded O'Brien a pension based on half the salary of a cavalry lieutenant colonel, the rank he held when he embarked from Valparaíso as part of the expedition to liberate Peru.[3]

On 26 July 1852 O'Brien had to swallow his pride when petitioning the Chilean congress for the return of monies he had donated to the patriot treasury in 1818 after the Battle of Chacabuco. He had been entitled to claim a third of the 25,000 pesos (€5,802) in gold belonging to the royalist forces he had found during his pursuit of General Maroto, but, 'realising the scarcity of the country's treasury in those moments and aware that the Army could not move towards the South with resources',[4] he had given up his share. It was a noble gesture, to be regretted later. And regretted it probably was when, shortly after the achievement of independence in Chile, O'Brien found himself destitute, and had to petition the government for some monetary reward. Bernardo O'Higgins had awarded O'Brien 300 pesos (€70) rather than the 8,000 pesos (€1,934) he could have claimed when he found the royalist funds. Now, in 1852, more than three decades after the battle, O'Brien was coming cap in hand to the Chilean congress to claim the rest of the prize so eagerly given to the patriot army in 1818.

The Chilean government finally granted O'Brien a pension to add to the one he was receiving from the government in Lima. He also retained an interest in the mine at Puno. During the early 1850s O'Brien worked to improve these interests. He had financial security because of his pensions – 3,000 pesos (€517) a year, with which he was able to live with 'honour and dignity'[5] – but, perhaps, not enough to support his lifestyle. However, even though he was in his mid-sixties, he had not ceased dreaming about making his fortune from the continent's mineral resources. He had always known there were rich deposits of ore in the remote, tropical regions of eastern Peru, enough to make him a very wealthy man, but his mining career had been thwarted by war and ill health. Now, at the age of sixty-five, less well off than he had hoped and afraid of sliding into dull obscurity, he came up with new plans for an expedition into the Amazon.

The mid-nineteenth century was an energetic period in the history of Amazon exploration. In 1848 the British entomologists Henry Walter Bates and Alfred Russel Wallace set out on their celebrated expedition to the Amazon basin. Wallace returned to Britain in 1852, but Bates remained in the Amazon for eleven years, collecting 14,700 species. Bates' two-volume account of his travels in the Amazon basin, *The Naturalist on the River Amazons*, published in 1863, became a classic of natural history, and remained in print throughout the century. Wallace lost the collection he had amassed in the Amazon when the ship carrying him home to Britain caught fire. Nevertheless, he also managed to write a book about his experiences, and became a highly celebrated naturalist and proponent of the theory of natural selection.

The Amazon was not only of interest to bookish naturalists at this time. In the decades after independence, native and foreign capitalists realised there was a fortune to be made from a hitherto unimportant commodity. The rubber boom that was to transform the Amazon basin from a backwater to the centre of a global industry began in the mid-nineteenth century when Charles Goodyear developed the vulcanisation process that enabled the material to be put to important new uses. The twin inventions of the tyre and the motor car towards the end of the century led to an inexhaustible hunger for rubber and the concomitant arrival on the scene of the avaricious rubber barons. In the 1850s this was in the future, but the importance of the raw material was already being recognised, not least by O'Brien, who foresaw the developments that would turn the neglected Amazon basin into one of the most important areas of commercial growth on the continent. In 1851, in a petition to the Peruvian congress, he made a proposal to help drive trade between Europe and South America:

> Because of the meticulous and painstaking study which I have carried out into its riches, its resources, its inexhaustible mines, its productive gold washings, its delicate timbers, and, finally, the valuable commodities which exists in its forests and mountains, I have come to realise how easy it is to open South America to vast new horizons.
>
> I know the opulent valleys which the Amazon irrigates and have calculated the colossal advantages that they could bring to the Republics which border the river, most especially Peru, if all the waters of the great river brought to European markets the fabulous wealth which remains dormant because of a lack of proper exploitation.
>
> Fortunately, nobody today is ignorant that the free navigation of the Amazon is the great secret of American prosperity, which at all costs we must achieve … [*a.t.*][6]

This was a job interview. O'Brien believed that the governments of Bolivia, Peru, Ecuador, Colombia and Venezuela needed a salesman to convince Europe of the trade opportunities that would arise from the opening up of the Amazon river system. He thought that this 'sufficiently authorised person' would 'encourage [the European nations'] spirit of enterprise'. O'Brien told the Peruvian congress: 'Without boasting in any way, I believe that, more than any other, I can be that person, because of the knowledge I possess of the American nations and the friendships I count upon in the Old World.'[7]

In 1851 O'Brien secured a ten-year licence from the Peruvian government to export gutta-percha. The rubber-like material had been introduced to Europe in 1843 by William Montgomerie, and had soon become an important component in the manufacture of underwater cables. It was also used for the production of a range of goods, such as jewellery and golf balls (they were previously made from feathers encased in leather – not ideal for the wet Scottish climate). 'May God fulfil the desires and recompense the hard tasks of the illustrious adventurer, by giving to him a treasure in the soil of America which he assisted in defending with his sword', *The Waterford News* wrote of O'Brien's latest commercial ventures.[8]

In Lima, in 1853, O'Brien prepared for a new expedition to the Paucartambo valley. He was hoping for the assistance of the Peruvian government, including troops and artillery. Although he had previously established friendly relations with the indigenous tribes in the region, he was determined to use force if they did not cooperate with him.[9] Paucartambo was the valley he had explored in the 1830s when his plans to mine gold had been thwarted by the outbreak of the War of the Confederation. 'But, happily, to-day a new aurora shines for Peru, and this favourite daughter of the Sun is preparing to collect the rich treasure which, as in no other nation, are scattered in her soil', wrote *The Waterford News*.[10] Yet again, however, the outbreak of civil war was to derail O'Brien's entrepreneurial efforts in Peru. In 1854 a former Peruvian president, Ramón Castilla, led a coup that overthrew the government and plunged the country into conflict, disrupting O'Brien's exploration projects and cutting off his income from mining. In a letter to José Matías Zapiola, his former commanding officer in the mounted grenadiers, he complained of being destitute and of having lost his entire fortune because of the political situation in Peru.[11] Once again he was left to rue what might have been, and to reflect upon past glories.

Visitors to Lima may sense the city's former imperial grandeur by strolling across the Plaza de Armas. On 28 July 1821 it was here, in the shadow of the cathedral and the viceregal palace, that San Martín declared the independence of Peru, alongside sixteen fellow officers, O'Brien among them. On 28 July 1858 O'Brien once more climbed onto a platform in the Plaza de Armas. He was shielded from the elements by the viceregal crimson canopy presented to him by San Martín in 1821 in recognition of his services in the achievement of Peruvian independence. It was a bittersweet moment for O'Brien as he scanned the expectant faces waiting to hear him speak. This had been the site of his greatest triumph. Thirty-seven years later, many of his companions were dead, including San Martín, and the hopes he had entertained as a young man for a prosperous and peaceful future had not come to pass. Standing on the platform in 1858, he recalled that day in 1821 for the crowd gathered below, before adding: 'This recollection brings to mind a profound feeling: no more than three of the sixteen who climbed onto the platform accompanying San Martín that day are still alive …'. He paused, visibly moved by the memory of his dead comrades. But then his tone changed; steel replaced softness:

> I and all of America say it: were not Chile and Peru completely occupied by the Spanish when San Martín with only 3,200 men crossed the Andes, liberated Chile and established the independence of Peru? And is it not ingratitude to forget such a great hero? But no, Peru must remember and do justice to the men who established her nationhood [*a.t.*].[12]

This was not a speech couched in platitudes, there was substance, too – a direct challenge to Castilla. In 1850, during a previous term as president, Castilla had decreed that a statue of San Martín would be erected in one of the capital's principal plazas. The Peruvian congress had also passed a law to this effect. However, nearly four decades after San Martín had declared Peruvian independence in Lima, there was still no statue of him in the city, even though a statue of Simon Bolívar had been erected. 'The merits of Bolívar were great in respect of Peru, but those of San Martín were colossal [*a.t.*]', O'Brien told the crowd in the Plaza de Armas.[13]

O'Brien's rallying call in Lima that July day was the high point in a decade-long campaign to commemorate the revolutionary generation with public monuments. In Santiago O'Brien was responsible for the raising of a bronze statue to General Ramón Freire, the liberal statesman who had ousted Bernardo O'Higgins from power to become the president of Chile. O'Brien intended the statue to be the first in a series erected in honour of 'the heroes and eminent men who had given freedom, prosperity and a homeland to Chile [*a.t.*]'.[14] The monuments would line the *alameda*, the central avenue running through the heart of the city. The modern *alameda* – or Avenida Libertador Bernardo O'Higgins, as it is officially called – is a multi-lane, traffic-clogged road that splits the centre of Santiago in two. But before the advent of the motor car, the *alameda* had been a fashionable boulevard popular with the city's middle classes. It was known as the Paseo de la Cañada, after the stream that ran nearby. During the period of O'Higgins' government it was renamed the Paseo de las Delicias, or Promenade of Delights. It was where the *santiaguinos* would stroll in the evening, gossiping and flirting. In 1857 O'Brien believed that the *alameda* would rival the Champs-Elysées in Paris, and that its water features would compete with those of Versailles.[15]

Freire was a controversial figure in Chile. He was a hero of Chilean liberalism, but conservatives, including supporters of O'Higgins, regarded him as a traitor. They wondered why O'Brien had not chosen San Martín or O'Higgins to be the first hero of the revolution cast in bronze. In fact, O'Brien's initial idea had been to erect a statue to San Martín, but political considerations – not least the fact that San Martín was an Argentinian – had forced him to abandon the plan.[16] O'Brien defended his choice by insisting that he had chosen Freire because he was a soldier who had 'always drawn his sword and faced the enemy on the frontline until he had seen his country free [*a.t.*]'.[17] He believed that once the Chileans had seen Freire's statue gracing the *alameda*, they would call for further monuments to honour San Martín, O'Higgins, Carrera and Portales. Never one to pass up an opportunity to extol his own achievements, O'Brien wrote that 'for thirty years no-one had thought of statues until I had completed that of Freire's which is a beautiful and very well-made work equal to any in Europe [*a.t.*]'.[18]

O'Brien also began a project to build a monument at the site of the Battle of Chacabuco, soliciting from the Argentine government the names of all the officers who had fought there. In the hills overlooking Santiago, he built an obelisk, nearly five metres high, to commemorate Manuel Salas, the Chilean patriot who had donated the piece of land upon which O'Brien had built his cabin.

O'Brien's efforts to commemorate the revolutionary generation by building monuments and erecting plaques led Pedro Pablo Figueroa to describe him, almost half a century after his death, as an 'agent from a great age, the messenger of the heroes who demands from the free nations the gratitude of the people [*a.t.*]'.[19] O'Brien recognised this role for himself. In his own words, his raised voice was the 'echo of the tombs of the heroes of emancipation [*a.t.*]'.[20] Was it a desire to reawaken public memory from its torpor? Or was there a more selfish reason for O'Brien's civic-mindedness? The answer probably lies somewhere in between. O'Brien was a romantic, a sentimentalist, but he was also a businessman who traded on his name and past achievements, and who understood that it was important to keep himself in the public eye and firmly associated with the great names of the revolutionary generation, such as San Martín and Bolívar. It may also have been a nostalgia for his wartime career, a period that had seemed less complex. The German migrant Henrich Witt recalled O'Brien putting up bunting at a New Year's Day garden party in Lima in 1831: 'Poor O'Brien exerted himself above all in adorning the trees and tents with the Peruvian Colours red and white.'[21]

On an October day in 1858, O'Brien sat down for lunch at his small cabin in the hills overlooking Santiago de Chile. Since leaving Uruguay in 1849, he had made it his habit to spend the summers in Chile and the winters in Lima. His favourite place in Santiago, and perhaps the world, was the wooden cabin he had built on the piece of land given to him in 1826 in the hills overlooking the city. Above the narrow entrance to the cabin was written: 'O'Brien's Castle i que viva Chile!' (O'Brien's Castle and Long Live Chile!).[22] O'Brien kept a house on the Calle Monjitas in the centre of Santiago, and enjoyed socialising with friends in the city, but when he wished for tranquillity he would make his way into the hills to the modest retreat he had modelled after a ship's cabin. In the middle of the nineteenth century, the hills around El Salto were still a quiet place far from the busy streets of central Santiago. In fine weather O'Brien would sit outside reading his correspondence, occasionally glancing towards the familiar Andean passes in the distance. When it grew cold and wet, he would settle into a chair inside, surrounded by his bookcases, or shuffle through the papers proposing monuments to his fallen comrades-in-arms. If he felt like spending the night there, he would stretch himself out on a camp bed. And when he wished to entertain, there was a small table in the centre of the room and a few bottles of wine in the cupboard.

After a lifetime of frenetic activity and frequent bouts of ill-health, the seventy-two-year-old Irishman was slowing down but showed no signs of stopping. The injuries received in battle and the disappointments of a lifetime had left their mark, but there was still much of the old spark. In a natural grotto close to the cabin, he had consecrated what he called his Temple of Roses in memory of the women he had loved. He had decorated the grotto with flowers and plants, and had attached a plaque to one of the stone walls; its inscription read: 'Los Dos Amantes [The Two Lovers]. Or the true lover's hut and love amongst the roses.'[23]

O'Brien's dining companion that day in October was Benjamín Vicuña Mackenna, a twenty-seven-year-old lawyer whose enthusiasms were politics, journalism and history. Despite the age difference, Vicuña Mackenna enjoyed accompanying the 'elderly Celt' on his excursions into the breeze-filled hills. There was also a more practical reason for his friendship with O'Brien. The historian in him was eager to preserve first-hand accounts of the wars of independence. The two men made quite a contrast – the big, broad Irishman with an open face and fair hair, and the smaller, darker Chilean with expressive eyes and a slightly drooping moustache – but they had much in common, not least their Irish heritage and the experience of being imprisoned.

O'Brien had known Vicuña Mackenna's maternal grandfather, John Mackenna, the County Monaghan-born general who had counselled and fought alongside Bernardo O'Higgins. Mackenna, a hero of the Chilean revolution, had been killed in a duel in Buenos Aires. His grandson was a fiercely determined liberal who had been arrested and thrown in prison at age nineteen for his opposition to the conservative government. Vicuña Mackenna had escaped and fled into exile, travelling around Europe, including Ireland, until he was granted an amnesty and permitted to return home. He had arrived back in Chile in 1855, but now, three years later, he was once again upsetting the government, thanks to his newspaper *La Asamblea Constituyente* and its criticism of President Manuel Montt. Vicuña Mackenna was a prolific writer, publishing thousands of articles and almost two hundred books in his lifetime. In the latter part of his life – he died at fifty-four – he served as mayor of Santiago and became a respected historian, but first and foremost he was a newspaperman. Over lunch he pulled nuggets from O'Brien's memory about the war. For his part, O'Brien was interested in remembering the dead in solid form, not in the pages of dusty books; his thoughts revolved around how he would commemorate the leaders of the revolution.[24]

O'Brien and Vicuña Mackenna would take morning walks through the hills of Santiago, discussing politics, history and war. Near the monument to Salas erected by O'Brien, they would turn around and take in the views of the city. It was during these walks that Vicuña Mackenna could see that his companion was unlike many of the politicians and soldiers – some still alive, some dead – who had fought for Chile's independence. There was a naivety and innocence to the Irishman's character, which surprised the young Chilean, who might have expected the old warrior's demeanour to be wearier, worldlier.

Vicuña Mackenna believed that O'Brien built monuments and erected plaques to fill a spiritual vacuum. 'Poor, dear old O'Brien!' Vicuña Mackenna wrote after his friend's death. 'He had erected in his soul an altar to everything that is great in life, a rough altar such as those which the first men of his race erected to their gods, but which he conserved pure and intact until his last breath.'[25] The Chilean wrote that O'Brien had 'a mania for portraits'. 'We know engravings and portraits of General O'Brien in which he is depicted in his sober colonel's uniform, in his general's uniform on horseback, standing in a splendid uniform, worked in marble, captured in an engraving in battle', he continued. 'We find him everywhere, as a *copy*, suspended on some friendly wall; but the *original*, always wandering through the wide world, is almost beyond reach [*a.t.*].'[26] This passage captures the essence of a man who was obsessed with his image, and who distilled the meaning of his life from his actions during his military career but who, despite his intimate connection to the martial glories of the revolutionary era, was not able to find a way through the perilous post-independence political landscape.

That lunch in the Santiago hills was one of the last shared by O'Brien and Vicuña Mackenna in Chile. In December the Chilean government arrested Vicuña Mackenna for attending a prohibited meeting and threw him in prison. O'Brien left Chile for Europe that same month, never to return to South America. In his will, O'Brien left Vicuña Mackenna a gold ring in memory of their friendship.[27]

O'Brien embarked for Liverpool aboard the *Bogotá* in December 1858. From Liverpool he travelled to Ireland and County Wicklow, where he spent the winter, and visited his sister Catherine, who was living in Athy, County Kildare, nineteen kilometres from Baltinglass. He returned to England in the summer. Following his release from prison, Vicuña Mackenna visited O'Brien in London in August, and the two men discussed the Chilean's upcoming court case. Vicuña Mackenna and four of his fellow countrymen had been arrested in 1858 before being forcibly exiled from Chile. They were now taking a case before a court in Liverpool against the captain of the ship that had brought them to England. When O'Brien heard about the case, he insisted on being present, travelling up to Liverpool the day before the trial began. He offered to testify on behalf of the plaintiffs, but was dissuaded from doing so by Vicuña Mackenna and his companions, who feared that this course of action might lead the Chilean government to withdraw O'Brien's pension.

In old age O'Brien enjoyed the respect that came with his elevated rank in the Chilean and Peruvian armies. The Chilean and Peruvian congresses had granted him pensions, but he was by no means a rich man, and this hurt. For all that he had given on behalf of the people of South America, he felt he had never received his monetary reward. He was angry at the British government, which seemed incapable of exacting any justice for British subjects who had lost everything during the Guerra Grande. But what was worst of all, the most egregious reminder of the loss of his fortune, was the fact that the man he held most responsible for his misfortunes was living in comfort and respectability in England. In August 1859 O'Brien published *A Living Nero in England*, a polemic addressed to the mayor of Southampton, Edward Polk, condemning Rosas' presence in the town, and demanding his expulsion from the United Kingdom:

> I warn you that there is now dwelling within your bailiwick, one who is plague-spotted with crimes and cruelties; that you have in the inhabitant of Rockstone House, a man, whose atrocities as a ruler, are equal to some of the worst deeds committed by Nero, and whose

> career as the governor of Buenos Ayres, was as bloody, as pitiless, and atrocious as that of Marat, and that of Robespierre, during the brief and sanguinary 'Reign of Terror'.[28]

O'Brien intended to stir up feelings among the Irish residents of Southampton by reminding them of the tragic case of Camila O'Gorman,[29] 'a young woman of Irish descent' whose 'beauty was so remarkable as to attract universal admiration' and who had been sentenced to death for eloping with her priest lover. 'At the time that sentence of death was pronounced upon this unoffending and lovely creature', wrote O'Brien, 'she was within six weeks of becoming a mother, and her only request to the tyrant was that he might spare her life until her child was born. *The request* was *refused*. The lover, the mistress, and the unborn child were slaughtered!'[30]

In London O'Brien continued working on his compensation claim with the British government. In a letter to Lord Russell, the foreign secretary, dated 8 August 1859, in which he described the attack on Mataojo de Solís Grande as 'a preconcerted [*sic*] but unsuccessful attempt upon my life', he expressed his hope that the matter would be settled: 'My increasing years at all events forbid the hope of my being able again to visit England in order to prosecute this long deferred claim.'[31] His hopes were raised by the reply from the Foreign Office, which promised to make special mention of his case at the sitting of the commission set up by the British and French governments with the Uruguayan government in 1858 to adjudicate claims for compensation.[32]

By the year of his death, O'Brien was a well-known figure in Britain and Ireland. His name was synonymous with New World exoticism. Shipping companies hoping to attract emigrants traded on his fame. One advertisement, which appeared in *The Wexford Independent*, read:

> EMIGRATION TO BUENOS AYRES
> There is no part of the world in which Irishmen are so prosperous, acquiring fortunes so rapidly, as in Buenos Ayres. They are thriving with the good will of the people amidst whom they live, for they are as the fellow-countrymen of General O'Brien.[33]

At the end of 1860, O'Brien prepared to embark for Buenos Aires. He was determined to press the British officials working on his compensation claim. But at Lisbon he became ill and was unable to make the journey. The Irish Dominicans looked after him for months. On 16 January he wrote another letter to Lord Russell, requesting that he be given letters of introduction to the minister in Buenos Aires, Edward Thornton, and the chargé d'affaires in Montevideo, William Garrow Lettsom. He was too ill to write himself, and had to dictate the letter, but he indicated that he was still intending to travel across the Atlantic.[34] But after a few months he accepted that he was dying. In May 1861 he wrote to his 'dearest daughter', Isabel. 'I remain without the slightest hope but I am well prepared to go to heaven, since there is here an Irish priest who has confessed me and nothing, nothing is lacking in my religion.' He wrote that 'it was very sad for your father to say his last goodbye to his adored daughter', and that 'I have neither the heart nor strength to do, and nothing else remains but to ask forgiveness, and this I do on my knees before God'.[35]

The rector, Dr Patrick Russell, tended to O'Brien as he lay dying in the Irish college in Lisbon. In the last hours the patient whispered some indistinct words and made a gesture that he felt the end was close. He put his hands together and waited. He had already received the viaticum and extreme unction.[36] The end came at six in the evening of 1 June 1861.

Two days after his death, at eleven o'clock on the morning of 3 June 1861, O'Brien's remains were placed in tomb no. 1,244 in Lisbon's Prazeres cemetery. His remains lay undisturbed for thirty years, but in 1893 the Irish Dominicans sold the tomb and removed O'Brien's coffin. The remains were transferred to an urn and reinterred in another tomb, no. 3,694, in the same cemetery.

O'Brien did not live to see his compensation claim paid. He was not alone. Many of the foreign residents who had lost their fortunes during the Great War in Uruguay died in poverty. They included Maria Bruthouse, who died in hospital 'a distressed British subject',[37] and Peter Cosgrove, who passed away in a Liverpool workhouse in April 1865.[38] In 1863, two years after his death, Lettsom, who was charged with settling the claims of British subjects who had suffered losses during the Great War in the River Plate, confessed that he did not know how to proceed in relation to O'Brien's case. The mixed commission had awarded O'Brien $17,000 in bonds. O'Brien's agent in Montevideo, Dr Castellanos, who received ten per cent of the award in fees, wrote to Lettsom requesting that the remainder of the money be sent to him so he could forward it to O'Brien's children in Chile. Lettsom refused on the grounds that the power of attorney O'Brien had granted to Castellanos had lapsed upon O'Brien's death.[39] Lettsom also cast doubt on O'Brien's marriage: 'Is reported to have been married in Chile to a descendant of an Inca, by whom it is said he has left children', he wrote in 1864. 'Doubt may however be entertained as to this marriage, for had it taken place the agent here (Doctor Castellanos) would by this time have established the fact.'[40] It was only in 1865 that Charles Swinburn, the executor of O'Brien's will, having applied to the British Treasury, was granted the award for disposal to O'Brien's heirs.

Before he died, O'Brien had the comfort of knowing that he would be remembered; the thought of being forgotten had terrified him more than anything else in his final years. Dr Russell had promised him on his deathbed that a 'respectable funeral' would be organised in Lisbon, and that he would be buried 'with bricks and lime' underneath the 'monument of a high cross made of marble'.[41]

Before leaving Chile for the last time, O'Brien had attached another plaque to the wall of his cabin in El Salto in Santiago. The inscription read: 'Here rests the heart of General John O'Brien.' According to Figueroa, O'Brien had erected the plaque to signify how great his desire was for his remains be brought back to Chile.[42] Figueroa wondered whether O'Brien's wish to be buried in Chile would be fulfilled:

> As long as the Chileans do not forget to thank him for his glories, sooner or later, O'Brien's glorious remains, which rest in the crypt of the College of the Irish Dominicans in Lisbon, will be repatriated, to be placed at the side of the heroes of national independence.
>
> When one of the Navy's ships, upon which naval cadets sail the seas during voyages of instruction, ends up in Lisbon, the Government should order the repatriation of O'Brien's remains in order to bring him to his final place of rest in the pantheon of the heroes of liberty [*a.t.*].[43]

Figueroa championed the idea of repatriating the Irishman's remains to Chile. 'We wish for him this deserved glory and recompense for his services', he wrote, 'repatriating his remains which rest in the Irish monastery in Lisbon, in order to keep them in the bosom of this land which he irrigated with his blood and redeemed with his sword [*a.t.*].'[44] (In fact, his remains had been interred in the tomb owned by the Irish Dominicans in the city's Cemitério dos Prazeres, not in the Dominican monastery.)

The issue of O'Brien's final resting place was to take more than 150 years to resolve. Figueroa's prediction that his remains would be repatriated to South America was eventually proved correct – but they were not brought to Chile.

In 1935 the Argentine government requested permission to transfer O'Brien's remains to Buenos Aires. After a solemn ceremony in Lisbon, during which the Irish Dominicans handed over an urn containing his remains to government representatives, the Argentinian navy training vessel the *Presidente Sarmiento* transported O'Brien's remains across the Atlantic for the final time. In Buenos Aires the reception party included the president of the republic and members of the Cabinet. Following a requiem Mass, O'Brien's remains were interred in the city's famous Recoleta cemetery.[45]

Fifty-four years later, in 1989, the body of Juan Manuel de Rosas, O'Brien's great enemy, was also reinterred in Recoleta. The project to bring Rosas home had been long in gestation, but the political upheavals in Argentina, including the Dirty War, had intervened. It was not until the return to democracy in 1983 and the restoration of relations with the United Kingdom following the war over the Malvinas/Falkland Islands that Rosas' reburial in his homeland became viable.

O'Brien's remains lay in Recoleta, largely unnoticed, for more than eighty years, in the crypt of Pablo Riccheri, an Argentinian general, until they were reinterred, for the third time, in Mendoza on 23 January 2017. The small ceremony marked the end of a long and tortuous route from Lisbon to Mendoza. But it is fitting that O'Brien was buried with military honours at a site that figures prominently in his story and the history of the South American wars of independence, both because of the pre-eminent role he played in the liberation of Chile, and because of his efforts to ensure his comrades-in-arms' place in public memory.

Conclusion: Reputation

O'Brien consciously shaped his public image during the forty years following his participation in the wars of independence. The prolonged cultivation of his reputation as a South American military hero was essential to his postwar fortunes, and it demonstrated an acute awareness of how to use modern mass communications – such as newspapers, pamphlets and books – to shape this image. He used his fame to promote emigration schemes, silver mining, gold mining, sheep farming, alpaca farming and steamship companies. This would not have been possible if it had not been for his exemplary military-service record.

O'Brien's status as a founding member of the *granaderos a caballo*, an aide-de-camp to San Martín, an active participant at the battles of Chacabuco and Maipú, and as one of the officers present at the declaration of Peruvian independence in Lima in 1821 was crucial to his ability to pursue commercial projects in post-independence South America. He purposely played up to a well-worn image of the loyal Irish soldier that would have been familiar in the South American military circles in which he moved.[1]

All O'Brien's South American biographers gloss over his pre- and postwar careers as an agent for European capital in order to de-emphasise the role that foreign commercial interests played in the revolution. Chilean and Argentinian writers (the latter especially during the intensely nationalistic period of the 1930s and 1940s) emphasised his Irish and Gaelic origins as a means of obscuring the fact that he was a British subject and an agent of British capital.[2] O'Brien adopted the name 'Thomond' – after the historic kingdom covering modern-day Clare and Limerick ruled by the O'Brien dynasty – in order to emphasis his noble Gaelic lineage. Hence, Juan Luis Hogan opens his 1947 biographical essay on O'Brien thus:

> In Ireland, the most fertile region which the poets call the Emerald of the Sea and Green Erin, the land of the men of indomitable will and where the joy of daily living is not a myth, in the penultimate

> decade of the eighteenth century, was born Don Juan O'Brien into a comfortable family [*a.t.*].[3]

O'Brien's place in South American public memory has been defined by his connection to San Martín. Juan Estevan Guastavino wrote in the 1920s that O'Brien was 'the protagonist who presents himself to us in the shadow of "his old General [San Martín]" [*a.t.*]'.[4] O'Brien himself promoted this bond with San Martín, both for reasons of personal loyalty and material gain, and became an important source for late-nineteenth-century historiography in Argentina and Chile. Bartolomé Mitre and Benjamín Vicuña Mackenna drew heavily from O'Brien's oral accounts of the most important battles of the war in Chile: Chacabuco, Cancha Rayada and Maipú.[5] O'Brien recognised that his proximity to San Martín could only burnish his own reputation, and he thus became a willing collaborator in Mitre's project to construct a narrative of Argentinian history that attributed the achievement of independence to the actions of San Martín, to the exclusion of wider historical forces. An example of this is the burning of Osorio's correspondence, an anecdote supplied by O'Brien and which Mitre uses as evidence of San Martín's 'modest magnanimity [*magnanimidad modesta*]'.[6] O'Brien's participation in this act of national self-creation was such that his own image became entangled in the *mitrista* narrative of Argentinian history,[7] in which San Martín is depicted as single-handedly ensuring the independence of Argentina, Chile and Peru.

This inseparability from San Martín is emphasised by writers to the present day.[8] The portrayal of the bond between the two men is paternalistic: the faithful and loyal aide-de-camp and his benevolent master.[9] This characterisation serves to underplay some of the more troubling aspects of the presence of foreign-born soldiers in the patriot armies.

O'Brien's contribution to the achievement of independence continues to be celebrated in Argentina. In the 1930s the Argentine government deemed his contribution worthy enough to establish a commission to repatriate his remains from Portugal to Buenos Aires. Eighty years later his remains were reinterred at Mendoza with military honours.[10] The recent judgement of the historian Luis Miguel Glave is that O'Brien was the 'founder of not fewer than five republics: Uruguay, Argentina, Chile, Peru and Bolivia. The Irishman was a very important combatant in the attainment of Argentina and Chile's independence [*a.t.*].'[11]

In Ireland O'Brien's achievements during the South American wars of independence are less well known than those of William Brown, Francis Burdett O'Connor, Daniel Florence O'Leary and, of course, the Chilean-born

Bernardo O'Higgins. Yet he was a celebrated figure in Britain and Ireland during his lifetime, and did much to highlight the possibilities that awaited Irish emigrants and British investors in South America.

In assessing the implications of O'Brien's life and career, therefore, it is important to move away from his self-constructed image as a 'soldier and nothing more', and to place him within the context of the United Kingdom's determination to establish a commercial foothold in South America as Spanish power waned. He first travelled to the continent as part of the influx of British and Irish merchants into the ports of the Southern Cone at the beginning of the struggle for South American independence. In 1825, at the end of the wars of independence, when, as Rory Miller has written, the 'British mania for Latin America rose in crescendo',[12] O'Brien was a famed veteran, allowing him to act, often at the same time, as an agent for British commercial interests and as a diplomatic representative of South American leaders. The fact that he was, at the same time, a British subject with commercial connections to the United Kingdom, and a Catholic Irishman with a proven war record in the patriot armies and connections to the military and political establishments of the new republics, was a crucial advantage.

O'Brien's various careers outside of the military – miner, prospector, rancher – demonstrate this scramble for resources in postwar South America. His rivalry with his former comrade-in-arms William Miller underlines the rich opportunities that became available to foreign-born veterans of the wars of independence and the conflicts that arose between those vying for the patronage of the new republican governments. A proven service record in the patriot armies was the key to unlocking governmental largesse – as was the case in the northern part of the continent, where British and Irish soldiers published contesting narratives about their roles within Bolívar's campaigns. In Argentina, Chile and Peru, O'Brien fought an ongoing battle with detractors and critics to manage and protect his image as a military hero.

O'Brien's involvement in the 1820s with emigration schemes in Buenos Aires and Chile, together with contemporaneous projects in Venezuela,[13] demonstrate the dynamism of state-sponsored efforts to attract Irish emigrants to South America during the revolutionary period, but also the hostility of the British government to schemes that threatened its diplomatic efforts in Europe and the River Plate. That O'Brien was unable to implement schemes on behalf of the Chilean and Buenos Aires governments in the period 1822 to 1825 does not detract from his importance in popularising Argentina as a destination for Irish emigrants. As a respected authority on South American affairs, he promoted emigration to the River Plate in the British and Irish press throughout his postwar career, and was responsible for cultivating an image of Argentina and Uruguay as rich, fertile, welcoming places for Irish Catholics.

O'Brien's success in raising subscriptions for O'Connell's campaign for Catholic emancipation in Buenos Aires indicates the strength of political organisation among the Irish Catholic community in the city by the late 1820s. That O'Brien was regarded as one of the natural leaders of this community in the 1820s – despite his spending much of his time away from Buenos Aires – is a testament to the political and social capital he had accrued from his military career and to his own charisma. These attributes and assets enabled him to forge a brief career as a diplomat, working on behalf of the Montevideo government in the 1840s. In this role he most clearly enunciated his political thinking: representing the Rosas' protectionist regime as backward and barbaric in contrast to the civilising influences of his own liberal world view, which visualised free trade and the opening up of South America's waterways as shining a light into the continent's darkest corners. This viewpoint brought him into conflict with members of the Irish community in Buenos Aires, most notably Fr Anthony Fahy, a firm supporter of Rosas, and demonstrates the tension between the well-established Irish merchant elites and a newer generation of Irish emigrants who were more closely wedded to the conservatism of the landowning classes, and whose cultural nationalism was moulded by an Irish-born clerical leadership.

Having seen his fortune lost with the destruction of his sheep farm in Uruguay, O'Brien spent the last decade of his life seeking restitution from the Rosas government and financial recognition from the governments of Chile and Peru for the role he had played in the wars of independence. It is in this latter context that his efforts to shape the public memory of these nations should be seen. For O'Brien, whose many commercial enterprises had failed, the social and political capital he had accrued from his famed military service had to be protected. Erecting statues to the heroes of the independence era was not only a means of ensuring their ongoing importance in the narrative of national creation, it also associated him with those same luminaries in the public mind, and kept his name in the pages of the newspapers.

Ultimately, O'Brien's ability to manipulate his own image in an era during which the mass media was undergoing rapid growth was the key to his successes. His failures, mostly commercial, may be attributed to the chaotic political environment in the postwar republics and his own short-sightedness in foreseeing these challenges.

Notes

Abbreviations

AGN	Archivo General de la Nación [Argentina]
AGNP	Archivo General de la Nación, Perú
AGNU	Archivo General de la Nación, Uruguay
ANC	Archivo Nacional de Chile
BNP	Biblioteca Nacional del Perú
CSO/RP (NAI)	Chief Secretary's Office/Registered Papers
DDA	Dublin Diocesan Archives
NA	National Archives [London]
NAI	National Archives of Ireland
NLI	National Library of Ireland

Introduction

1 For more on the British and Irish soldiers who fought in the wars of independence in South America, see, among others, Matthew Brown, *Adventuring Through Spanish Colonies: Simón Bolívar, foreign mercenaries and the birth of new nations* (Liverpool: Liverpool University Press, 2006); Tim Fanning, *Paisanos: The forgotten Irish who changed the face of Latin America* (Dublin: Gill, 2016); and Eric Lambert, *Voluntarios Británicos e Irlandeses en la Gesta Bolivariana* (3 vols) (vol. 1, Caracas: Corporación Venezolana de Guayana, 1981; vols 2–3, Caracas: Ministerio de Defensa, 1993).

2 See Matthew Brown, 'Veteran Soldiers and the State', in idem, *Adventuring Through Spanish Colonies*, pp. 156–72; idem, 'How Did Rupert Hand Get out of Jail? Colombia and the Atlantic empires, 1830–1833', *History*, vol. 95, no. 317 (2010), pp. 25–43; and Tim Fanning, 'After the Revolution', in idem, *Paisanos*, pp. 195–208.

3 Karen Racine, 'A Community of Purpose: British cultural influence during the Spanish American wars for independence', in Oliver Marshall (ed.), *English-speaking Communities in Latin America* (Basingstoke: Macmillan, 2000), pp. 3–32 (p. 28).

4 See Lucy Riall, 'Garibaldi: The first celebrity', *History Today*, vol. 57, no. 8 (2007), www.historytoday.com/archive/garibaldi-first-celebrity (accessed 15 July 2019).

Chapter 1: King Cotton

1 See Andy Bielenberg and Peter M. Solar, 'The Irish Cotton Industry from the Industrial Revolution to Partition', *Irish Economic and Social History*, vol. 34, no. 1 (2007), pp. 1–28; Stuart Nisbet and John Foster, 'Protection, Inward Investment and the Early Irish Cotton Industry: The experience of William and John Orr', *Irish Economic and Social History*, vol. 35, no. 1 (2008), pp. 23–50.

2 Daniel Beaumont, 'Stratford, Edward Augustus ', in James McGuire and James Quinn (eds), *Dictionary of Irish Biography* (Cambridge: Cambridge University Press, 2009); E.I. Carlyle, revised by E.M. Johnston-Liik, 'Stratford, Edward Augustus, second earl of Aldborough', *Oxford Dictionary of National Biography*.
3 *Saunders's News-letter*, 17 February 1810.
4 Nisbet and Foster, 'Protection, Inward Investment and the Early Irish Cotton Industry', p. 33.
5 Samuel Lewis, *A Topographical Dictionary of Ireland* (2 vols), vol. 2 (London: S. Lewis & Co., 1837), p. 580.
6 Nisbet and Foster, 'Protection, Inward Investment and the Early Irish Cotton Industry', pp. 39–40.
7 The spelling of surnames was arbitrary in the late seventeenth and early eighteenth centuries. Like many Irishmen living in the Spanish empire, John Bryan added an *O* to his surname, changed the spelling to O'Brien, and began using Thomond as his middle name in order to emphasise his noble Gaelic ancestry.
8 *Saunders's News-letter*, 5 January 1785.
9 Paul Gorry, 'O'Brien's Baltinglass Origins', in Chris Lawlor and Donal McDonnell (eds), *General O'Brien: West Wicklow to South America* (Naas: West Wicklow Historical Society, 2006), p. 154.
10 See Maureen Wall, 'The Rise of a Catholic Middle Class in Eighteenth-century Ireland', *Irish Historical Studies*, vol. 11, no. 42 (1959), pp. 91–115.
11 Gorry, 'O'Brien's Baltinglass Origins', p. 147.
12 Samuel Lewis, *A Topographical Dictionary of Ireland* (2 vols), vol. 1 (London: S. Lewis & Co., 1837), p. 173.
13 Pedro Pablo Figueroa, *Vida del Jeneral Don Juan O'Brien: Héroe de la independencia Sud-Americana, Irlandés de nacimiento, Chileno de adopcion* (Santiago: Mejia, 1904), p. 28.
14 According to Sergio Garcia Váldes, a descendant of O'Brien who lives in Santiago.
15 'Su padre era un agricultor rico que tenia anexa a su propiedad una fábrica de tejidos de algodon.' Benjamín Vicuña Mackenna, *El Jeneral O'Brien* (Santiago: Universitaria, 1902), p. 10.
16 Gorry, 'O'Brien's Baltinglass Origins', p. 147.
17 See Lawrence Gittins, 'Innovations in Textile Bleaching in Britain in the Eighteenth Century', *Business History Review*, vol. 53, no. 2 (1979), pp. 194–204.
18 Gorry, 'O'Brien's Baltinglass Origins', p. 147.
19 Manuel Llorca-Jaña, 'The Organisation of British Textile Exports to the River Plate and Chile: Merchant houses in operation, *c.* 1810–59', *Business History*, vol. 53, no. 6 (2011), pp. 821–65 (p. 827).
20 Catholic Qualification Rolls, 2 May 1796, NAI.
21 Gorry, 'O'Brien's Baltinglass Origins', p. 147; Figueroa, *Vida del Jeneral Don Juan O'Brien*, p. 29.
22 Figueroa, *Vida del Jeneral Don Juan O'Brien*, p. 24.
23 Gorry, 'O'Brien's Baltinglass Origins', p. 155.
24 *Dublin Weekly Nation*, 23 January 1864.
25 Paul Gorry kindly pointed out that Mary O'Brien was listed as the mother of Anne Metcalf when the latter's marriage was registered. Marriage of John Shee and Anne Metcalf, Blanchardstown, 1 October 1862, Catholic Parish Registers, NLI.

26 Gorry, 'O'Brien's Baltinglass Origins', p. 156.
27 Landed Estates Court Rentals, 1850–1885, the Estate of Lord Aldborough, 1851, NAI, Lot 21, http://search.findmypast.ie/record?id=ire%2flec%2f4506851%2f00287&parentid=ire%2flec%2f4506851%2f00288%2f001 (accessed 2 March 2017); see also Gorry, 'O'Brien's Baltinglass Origins', pp. 144–6, 155–6.
28 Date supplied by O'Brien's descendant Salvador Valdés Morandé to Mariano Belgrano. See 'Biografia del General Juan O'Brien, 1786–1861', in Mariano Belgrano, *Repatriación de los restos del general Juan O'Brien, guerrero de la independencia Sud Americana* (Buenos Aires: Kraft, 1938), pp. 7–48 (p. 11)
29 Vicuña Mackenna, *El Jeneral O'Brien*, p. 10.
30 Ibid. pp. 10–11.
31 Benjamín Vicuña Mackenna, 'El Jeneral San Martín después de Chacabuco', *Relaciones Históricas*, vol. 1 (Santiago de Chile: Mercurio, 1877), p. 3.
32 Bartolomé Mitre wrote that 'El general O'Brien, que á pesar de su larga residencia en América, nunca pudo hablar correctamente el español ...'. Bartolomé Mitre, *Historia de San Martín y de la emancipación Sud-Americana*, vol. 2 (Buenos Aires: 1889), p. 196, n. 12.
33 The gold mines were not only of interest to financial investors in Britain and Ireland; they entered the popular culture of the late eighteenth and early nineteenth centuries. Thomas Moore composed a much-loved ballad about the Wicklow mines, and the London-based Irish playwright John O'Keeffe wrote his successful 1796 play *The Wicklow Gold Mines* about the discovery.
34 *Saunders's News-letter*, 2 October 1795.
35 Ibid. 9 October 1795.
36 For more on how the discovery of the Wicklow gold mines was represented in Irish and English popular culture, see Timothy Alborn, 'An Irish El Dorado: Recovering gold in County Wicklow', *Journal of British Studies*, vol. 50, no. 2 (2011), pp. 359–80.
37 See Ruán O'Donnell, *The Rebellion in Wicklow, 1798* (Dublin: Irish Academic Press, 1998), pp. 37–87.
38 Ibid. p. 23.
39 Ibid. pp. 66–7.
40 Ibid. pp. 96–9.
41 Anonymous letter to Edward Cooke, 7 May 1798, NAI, Rebellion Papers, 620/37/35.
42 Ibid.
43 Ibid.
44 Anonymous letter to Edward Cooke, 9 May 1798, NAI, Rebellion Papers, 620/37/43.
45 Ibid.
46 Anonymous letter to Edward Cooke, 19 May 1798, NAI, Rebellion Papers, 620/37/109.
47 Ibid.
48 O'Donnell, *The Rebellion in Wicklow*, p. 176.
49 Gorry, 'O'Brien's Baltinglass Origins', pp. 151–5.
50 Figueroa, *Vida del Jeneral Don Juan O'Brien*, p. 29.
51 Registry of Deeds, 657/437/453021, repr. in Gorry, 'O'Brien's Baltinglass Origins', p. 147.

52 Vicuña Mackenna, *El Jeneral O'Brien*, p. 10.
53 Figueroa, *Vida del Jeneral Don Juan O'Brien*, p. 29; Juan Estevan Guastavino, *Un gesto de O'Brien* (Buenos Aires: Bonarense, 1921), p. 8.
54 'Pero al pisar las calles de la capital del Plata, O'Brien oyó que se tocaban las trompetas de la Guerra, i por la primera vez se ocurrió a su espíritu de que él era un "soldado i nada mas"'. Vicuña Mackenna, *El Jeneral O'Brien*, p. 10.
55 José de San Martín to Martín Rodríguez, 24 September 1813, AGN, Granaderos a Caballo, 1812–1814, Sala X, 4/2/3.
56 Figueroa, *Vida del Jeneral Don Juan O'Brien*, p. 29.
57 'su altivez le aleja de sus jefes'. Guastavino, *Un gesto de O'Brien*, p. 8.
58 'Description of soldiers on joining the Royal Horse Artillery, 1811', NA, WO 69/5/858, 60.
59 See Manuel Llorca-Jaña, 'The Impact of Early Nineteenth-century Globalization on Foreign Trade in the Southern Cone: A study of British trade statistics', *Investigaciones de Historia Económica/Economic History Research*, no. 10 (2014), pp. 46–56 (p. 48); idem, 'The Organisation of British Textile Exports to the River Plate and Chile', pp. 821–65 (p. 825); Victor Bulmer-Thomas, 'British Trade with Latin America in the Nineteenth and Twentieth Centuries', University of London Institute of Latin America Studies, Occasional Papers no. 19 (1998), pp. 1–22.
60 Racine, 'A Community of Purpose', p. 20.
61 See LLorca-Jaña, 'Organisation of British Textile Exports', pp. 826–8.
62 'Don Diego O'Brien, natural de Irlanda, solicita carta de ciudadanía', AGN, Cartas de ciudadanía [1813–18], Sala X, 7/1/6.
63 J.J.M. Blondel (ed.), *Almanaque de comercio de la ciudad de Buenos Aires, para el año de 1830* (Buenos Aires: 1829), p. 92.
64 William and Robert Orr are mentioned among the residents of Buenos Aires in 1817 in José Antonio Wilde, *Buenos Aires desde setenta años atras* (Buenos Aires: Imprenta y Librería de Mayo, 1881), p. 89.
65 Nisbet and Foster, 'Protection, Inward Investment and the Early Irish Cotton Industry', p. 39.
66 John O'Brien to Marquess Wellesley, 30 September 1823, NAI CSO/RP/1823/1571.
67 Figueroa, *Vida del Jeneral Don Juan O'Brien*, p. 31.
68 Michael G. Mulhall, *The English in South America* (Buenos Aires: Standard, 1878), pp. 213–14.
69 Philip Ollerenshaw, 'Industry, 1820–1914', in Líam Kennedy and Philip Ollerenshaw (eds), *An Economic History of Ulster, 1820–1940* (Manchester: Manchester University Press, 1985), pp. 96–7. See also Philip Ollerenshaw, *Banking in Nineteenth-century Ireland: The Belfast banks, 1825–1914* (Manchester: Manchester University Press, 1987), p. 11.
70 See Tim Fanning, 'Merchants, Sailors, Soldiers, Spies', in idem, *Paisanos*, pp. 72–87; Andrew Graham-Yooll, *The Forgotten Colony: A history of the English-speaking communities in Argentina* (London: Hutchinson, 1981), p. 32; Patrick McKenna, 'The Formation of Hiberno-Argentine Society', in Oliver Marshall (ed.), *English-speaking Communities in Latin America* (Basingstoke: Macmillan, 2000), pp. 81–103.
71 Figueroa, *Vida del Jeneral Don Juan O'Brien*, p. 29.
72 Brown, *Adventuring Through Spanish Colonies*, p. 30.

73 Ibid. p. 16.

74 Figueroa (*Vida del Jeneral Don Juan O'Brien*, p. 30) and Guastavino (*Un gesto de O'Brien*, p. 8) write that O'Brien embarked for Rio de Janeiro in 1810. Given that he was shipwrecked off the coast of Africa, it is probable that he arrived in 1811. The evidence includes 'Un medio siglo cabal se ha cumplido desde que pisó las playas de América (1811)', in Vicuña Mackenna, *El Jeneral O'Brien*, p. 8; and a reference to having 'resided in South America for 12 years', in John O'Brien to Marquess Wellesley, 30 September 1823, NAI CSO/RP/1823/1571.

75 It is now known as Bioko, and is part of present-day Equatorial Guinea.

76 Figueroa, *Vida del Jeneral Don Juan O'Brien*, pp. 30–1.

77 Wilde, *Buenos Aires desde setenta años atras*, p. 89.

78 Figueroa, *Vida del Jeneral Don Juan O'Brien*, p. 31.

Chapter 2: The Mounted Grenadier

1 Llorca-Jaña, 'The Organisation of British Textile Exports', pp. 821–65 (pp. 825–6).

2 Fr Thomas Murray, *The Story of the Irish in Argentina* (New York: P.J. Kenedy & Sons, 1919), pp. 13–16; Graham-Yooll, *The Forgotten Colony*, p. 155.

3 Samuel Haigh, *Sketches of Buenos Ayres and Chili* (London: James Carpenter & Son, 1829), pp. 8–9.

4 Ibid.

5 Ibid. p. 133–4.

6 José de San Martín to Martín Rodríguez, 24 September 1813, AGN, Granaderos a Caballo, 1812–1814, Sala X, 4/2/3.

7 Ibid.

8 'No. 10, Regimiento de Granaderos a Cavallo [1813]', 27 September 1813, AGN, Tomás de Razon, Sala IX, 8/8/8.

9 'La vida militar (dice en la representacion citada al Congreso peruano) era poco análoga a mis ideas, pues ajitado de un espiritu romántico i enemigo decidido de la tiranía i opresion, apenas sonó el clarin de la independencia americana, cuando abandonando mis inmunidades nacionales i los intereses i afecciones de la patria i familia, resolví dedicarme a la causa de la libertad, i consagrar mi vida a la defensa de los derechos de los pueblos sudamericanos.' Vicuña Mackenna, *El Jeneral O'Brien*, p. 11.

10 For more on Brown's entrance into the war, see John De Courcy Ireland, 'William Brown at War', in idem, *The Admiral from Mayo: A life of Almirante William Brown: father of the Argentine navy* (Dublin: Edmund Burke, 1995), pp. 23–37.

11 O'Brien and Brown were not the only Irishmen in Buenos Aires seeking to join the armed forces. George Orr from Dublin arrived in the city in 1813, having also suffered during an eventful journey across the Atlantic. According to a letter he wrote to the government in Buenos Aires soliciting a commission, after being educated in Trinity College, Dublin, Orr had joined the British army in London, serving in the infantry and cavalry. Having met representatives of the Buenos Aires government in London, he had been persuaded to travel to South America and join the fight for independence. A United States privateer had attacked Orr's ship off the Brazilian coast and, 'after a battle which left some dead and many wounded', the captain of the privateer took Orr prisoner. After twelve days, having stripped him of all his possessions, including his letters of recommendation, his

letters of commission, £300 (€348) and his clothes, the crew of the privateer released Orr into the hands of a Spanish smack en route from Montevideo to the Brazilian port of Paranaguá, from where he was eventually able to make his way to Buenos Aires. George Orr to the Government of the United Provinces of the River Plate, Buenos Aires, 10 July 1813, AGN, Granaderos a Caballo, 1812–14, Sala X, 4/2/3.

12 See Brown, *Adventuring Through Spanish Colonies*, pp. 16–22.

13 'Don Diego O'Brien, natural de Irlanda, solicita carta de ciudadanía', AGN, Cartas de ciudadanía [1813–1818], Sala X, 7/1/6.

14 For the importance of 'honour' among the foreign adventurers who served in Venezuela and Colombia during the wars of independence, see 'Negotiating Honour', in Brown, *Adventuring Through Spanish Colonies*, pp. 81–109.

15 Felipe Pigna, *La voz del Gran Jefe: Vida y pensamiento de José de San Martín* (Buenos Aires: Planeta, 2014), p. 140.

16 Bartolomé Mitre, *Historia de San Martín y de la emancipación Sud-Americana*, vol. 1 (Buenos Aires: 1887), p. 158.

17 The Banda Oriental – meaning East Bank – refers to the east bank of the Uruguay River, the territory approximately corresponding to the modern state of Uruguay.

18 De Courcy Ireland, *The Admiral from Mayo*, pp. 23–37.

19 Figueroa, *Vida del Jeneral Don Juan O'Brien*, p. 32.

20 Ibid. p. 33.

21 Not to be confused with the non-commissioned rank of sergeant major.

22 'No. 45, Cedulas de retiro de las tropas veteranas y milicias del estado [1815]. A D Juan Obrien', 1 April 1815, AGN, Tomás de Razon, Sala IX, 8/9/3.

23 Figueroa, *Vida del Jeneral Don Juan O'Brien*, p. 33.

Chapter 3: The Invasion of Chile

1 'Previniendole cuide y celo sobre los medios de reprimir la deserción de sus soldados', 21 June 1815, AGN, Granaderos a Caballo [1815–1819], Sala X, 4/2/4.

2 Mitre, *Historia de San Martín y de la emancipación Sud-Americana*, vol. 1, p. 469. For a critical analysis of San Martín and the *mitrista* version of Argentinian history, see Emilio Ocampo, *La independencia Argentina: De la fábula a la historia* (Buenos Aires: Claridad, 2016), pp. 76–8.

3 Mitre, *Historia de San Martín y de la emancipación Sud-Americana*, vol. 1, p. 474.

4 Felipe Pigna, *La voz del Gran Jefe: Vida y pensamiento de José de San Martín* (Buenos Aires: Planeta, 2014), pp. 279–82.

5 'Regimiento de Granaderos a Cavallo. Lista de antiguedad de los señores oficiales de dicho regimento con expression de destinos, compañias y esquadrones a que pertenecen [1815]', AGN, Gobierno, Tomás de Razon, Sala X, 4/2/4.

6 Vicuña Mackenna, *El Jeneral O'Brien*, p. 12; Figueroa, *Vida del Jeneral Don Juan O'Brien*, pp. 35–6.

7 Those who were promoted to this rank were chosen from the most promising *tenientes* (lieutenants) and *capitanes* (captains). The *ayudante mayor* acted as a link between the staff and the squadrons, carrying out administrative functions relating to individual squadrons, but also acting as aide-de-camp to more senior staff officers.

8 José Matías Zapiola to Juan Martín de Pueyrredón, 9 September 1816, AGN, Gobierno, Granaderos a Caballo [1815–1819], Sala X, 4/2/4.
9 Damián Hudson, *Recuerdos históricos sobre la provincia de Cuyo*, vol. 1 (Buenos Aires: Juan A. Alsina, 1898), pp. 270–1; Vicuña Mackenna, *El Jeneral O'Brien*, pp. 13–14.
10 O'Brien is described as a 'bullfighter and military officer in Argentina' at the commencement of his entry in the *Dictionary of Irish Biography*. Patrick M. Geoghegan, 'O'Brien, John Thomond', in McGuire and Quinn (eds), *Dictionary of Irish Biography*, p. 53.
11 Belgrano, *Juan O'Brien*, pp. 15–16; Figueroa, *Vida del Jeneral Don Juan O'Brien*, p. 38; Guastavino, *Un gesto de O'Brien*, preface, pp. 2–3; Vicuña Mackenna, *El Jeneral O'Brien*, p. 13.
12 For more about the importance of 'honour' to foreign volunteers during the South American wars of independence, see Brown, 'Negotiating Honour', in idem, *Adventuring Through Spanish Colonies*, pp. 81–109.
13 Vicuña Mackenna, *El Jeneral O'Brien*, p. 13.
14 See José de San Martín to Juan Marrín Pueyrredón, Mendoza, 10 October 1816, AGN, Paso de los Andes y Campaña libertadora de Chile, Sala X, 4/3/9.
15 *British Packet, and Argentine News*, 31 January 1829.
16 John Miller, *Memoirs of General Miller, in the Service of the Republic of Peru* (2 vols), vol. 1 (London: Longman, Rees, Orme, Brown & Green, 1828), p. 90.
17 Ibid. pp. 94–5.
18 Ibid. pp. 96–7.
19 Vicuña Mackenna, *El Jeneral O'Brien*, p. 14; Figueroa, *Vida del Jeneral Don Juan O'Brien*, pp. 39–40.
20 Figueroa, *Vida del Jeneral Don Juan O'Brien*, pp. 40–2.
21 José de San Martín to Juan Marrín Pueyrredón, Santiago, 22 February 1817, *Archivo O'Higgins*, Ricardo Vonoso et al. (eds) (Santiago: Universitaria, 1950) vol. 7, p. 145.
22 Belgrano, *Juan O'Brien*, p. 18.
23 'estaba el jeneral San Martin en el lugar favorito de su palacio de los antiguos obispos de Santiago (que era la cocina), conversando soldadescamente con álguien i comiendo sobre parado algun bocado, porque rara vez se sentaba a la mesa, cuando, notando que pasaba el capitan O'Brien por el patio, le dió un grito de: "O'Brien!" "O'Brien!" grito tal (grito de San Martin!) que hizo jirar al último sobre su cuerpo i correr mas rápido que el relámpago.
—O'Brien! le dijo el jeneral con ese tono peculiar de San Martin, rápido, cortante, mitad del caporal que manda ¡armas al hombre! mitad del dictador que de sus propios ecos hace rayos: O'Brien! Mañana al amanecer marchamos para Buenos Aires.
—Para Buenos Aires, señor! contestó casi balbuceando i palideciendo el bravo celta, que tenia ya mas de un requiebro a cuestas i mas de una conquista comenzada entre el cauce del Mapocho i el del Zanjon de la Aguada. [...]
—Sí, señor! A Buenos Aires, por Mendoza. Mañana al aclarar!
—¿I llevaremos *carga*, señor? agregó el sorprendido galan que habria querido tener cien almofrejs [*sic*] para atajar el paso al vencedor de los Andes.
—Carga! repuso San Martin, entre riéndose i enfadado. Se ha figurado Ud. que voi a meterme fraile para viajar con petacas ... Vaya! Déjese Ud. de *santiaguinadas*.

En lo montado!' Benjamín Vicuña Mackenna, 'El Jeneral San Martín después de Chacabuco', *Relaciones Históricas*, vol. 1 (Santiago de Chile: Mercurio, 1877), pp. 4–5.

24 Ibid. pp. 7–9.
25 Ibid. pp. 9–10.
26 Ibid. pp. 11–12.
27 Ibid. p. 29.
28 John O'Brien, 'A Journal in Peru and Others', ANC, Fondo Benjamín Vicuña Mackenna, Archivos Varios, 926, F.49r; Figueroa, *Vida del Jeneral Don Juan O'Brien*, pp. 48–9.
29 O'Brien, 'A Journal in Peru and Others', F.49r.
30 Miller, *Memoirs of General Miller*, vol. 1, p. 172.
31 Ibid. F.50v–51r, pp. 171–2.
32 O'Brien, 'A Journal in Peru and Others', F.49r.
33 All subjects of the United Kingdom, including the Irish, were referred to as *ingleses*. The literal translation of *inglés,* or its plural, *ingleses*, is 'English'. However, *inglés* was commonly used in Spain and Latin America in reference to both the British and Irish.
34 O'Brien, 'A Journal in Peru and Others', F.53r, F.56r.
35 Vicuña Mackenna, 'El Jeneral San Martín después de Chacabuco', p. 3.
36 Ibid. p. 5.
37 Vicuña Mackenna, *El Jeneral O'Brien*, p. 13.
38 Guastavino, *Un gesto de O'Brien*, p. 5.
39 O'Brien, 'A Journal in Peru and Others', F.51r.
40 Figueroa, *Vida del Jeneral Don Juan O'Brien*, p. 42.
41 The merchant Samuel Haigh estimated that there were two English residents in Valparaíso in 1817, compared with two thousand in 1828. Haigh, *Sketches of Buenos Ayres and Chili*, p. 176.
42 Miller, *Memoirs of General Miller*, vol. 1, p. 202.
43 Haigh, *Sketches of Buenos Ayres and Chili*, p. vii.
44 He is also recorded as Santiago O'Brien – Santiago and Diego are both translations of James. John O'Brien was known in Spanish as Juan O'Brien.
45 Murray, *The Story of the Irish in Argentina*, p. 41.
46 'Don Diego O'Brien, natural de Irlanda, solicita carta de ciudadanía', AGN, Cartas de ciudadanía [1813–1818], Sala X, 7/1/6.
47 Figueroa, *Vida del Jeneral Don Juan O'Brien*, p. 49.
48 César Famin, *Historia de Chile* (Barcelona: Guarda Nacional, 1839), p. 63.
49 Figueroa, *Vida del Jeneral Don Juan O'Brien*, p. 52.
50 Diego Barros Arana, *Historia de Chile,* vol. 11 (Santiago: Cervantes, 1890), p. 459.
51 Ibid. p. 460.
52 'que San Martín se halló durante esta batalla á una gran distancia de su ejército, tendido en el suelo, y tan ébrio, que no dió la menor disposicion.' José de la Riva-Agüero [P. Pruvonena], *Memorias y documentos para la historia de la independencia del Perú, y causas del mal éxito que tenido ésta* (Paris: Garnier Hermanos, 1858), p. 97.
53 'que pasa una gran parte del dia en dormir su borrachera.' Ibid.
54 'Entonces notó que San Martín estaba totalmente ébrio; como lo habia estado

anteriormente en Cancharayada, y que él, esto, es O'Brien, regresó inmediatamente al campo de batalla y tomando el nombre de San Martín mandó por sí mismo, cargar á la caballeria, con lo que se logró la Victoria. Que la respuesta que dió San Martín al comandante O'Brien fué presentarle una botella de ron, y decirle: "*Toma, bébela en mi nombre.*"' Ibid. p. 98.

55 Ulrich Muecke (ed.), *The Diary of Heinrich Witt* (Leiden: Brill, 2016), p. 243.

56 Both medals awarded to O'Brien by the Chilean government for his heroism at Chacabuco and Maipú are housed in the Museo de Carmen de Maipú in Santiago. They were donated by one of O'Brien's descendants.

57 'en ningunos hombros estarán mejor que en los de Usted por lo que me tomo la confianza de remitirselos para que los use en mi nombre'. José de San Martín to John O'Brien, Santiago, 21 April 1820, AGN, Documentos Varios, Sala VII, Legajo 9.

58 Ibid.

59 Figueroa, *Vida del Jeneral Don Juan O'Brien*, p. 54.

60 'En seguida pidió que hiciesen una fogata á sus pies, y quemó todos aquellos testimonios acusadores, que convertidos en cenizas se llevó el viento del generoso olvido. Al consumar este acto, hallábase sentado en una tosca silla de madera, que fué en tal occasión el trono de la magnanimidad modesta del que, al trabajar por la libertad de un continente, perdonaba ante su conciencia á los que habían dudado de su genio. Fué único testigo de esta escena, su fiel ayudante de campo, á quien ordenó imperiosamente guardara silencio sobre lo que había visto ó podido leer.' Mitre, *Historia de San Martín y de la emancipación Sud-Americana*, vol. 2, p. 247.

61 See ibid. p. 247 n. 21.

62 José de San Martín to the minister of war, 26 June 1818, AGN, Ejército de los Andes, enero-junio 1818, Sala X, 4/2/10.

63 'La solicitud que hace al Sargento Mayor del Regimiento de Granaderos a Caballo Don Juan O'Brien', AGN, Granaderos a Caballo [1815–1819], Sala X, 4/2/4.

Chapter 4: The Liberation of Peru

1 Figueroa, *Vida del Jeneral Don Juan O'Brien*, p. 55.

2 Miller, *Memoirs of General Miller*, vol. 1, p. 266.

3 Ibid. pp. 267–70.

4 Figueroa, *Vida del Jeneral Don Juan O'Brien*, pp. 55–6.

5 Miller, *Memoirs of General Miller*, vol. 1, p. 331.

6 Figueroa, *Vida del Jeneral Don Juan O'Brien*, p. 57.

7 Ibid. p. 58.

8 Eduardo Torres Arancivia, *Corte de virreyes: El entorno del poder en el Perú en el siglo xvii* (Lima: Pontificia Universidad Católica del Peru, 2006), p. 106.

9 Basil Hall, *Extracts from a Journal, Written on the coasts of Chili, Peru, and Mexico, in the Years 1820, 1821, 1822* (2 vols), vol. 1 (Edinburgh: Archibald Constable & Co., 1824), p. 260.

10 Miller, *Memoirs of General Miller*, vol. 1, p. 337.

11 Ibid.

12 Ibid.

13 Ibid.

14 Ibid. p. 378.
15 Ibid.
16 Ibid. p. 379.
17 *El Argos de Buenos Aires*, 3 April 1822.

Chapter 5: The Emigrant's Dream

1 See Patrick McKenna, 'Nineteenth Century Irish Emigration to, and Settlement in, Argentina', MA thesis, National University of Ireland, Maynooth, 1994, pp. 87–8; Pat Nally, 'Los Irlandeses en la Argentina', *Familia: Ulster Genealogical Review*, no. 8 (1992), pp. 69–77; Edmundo Murray, 'John Thomond O'Brien', in James P. Byrne, Philip Coleman and Jason King (eds), *Ireland and the Americas: Culture, politics, and history: a multidisciplinary encyclopedia*, vol. 1 (Santa Barbara: ABC-Clio, 2008), pp. 690–1; Murray, *The Story of the Irish in Argentina*, p. 53; Patrick Speight, *Irish-Argentine Identity in an Age of Political Challenge and Change, 1875–1983* (Oxford: Peter Lang, 2019), pp. 42–7; James M. Ussher, *Father Fahy: A biography of Anthony Dominic Fahy, O.P., Irish missionary in Argentina (1805–1871)* (Buenos Aires: 1951), pp. 37–8.
2 Speight, *Irish-Argentine Identity*, pp. 42–7.
3 See McKenna, 'Nineteenth Century Irish Emigration to, and Settlement in, Argentina', p. 85.
4 *British Packet, and Argentine News*, 31 January 1829.
5 Ibid.
6 For more about Fields, see Guillermo Furlong, *Tomás Fields S.J. y su 'Carta al Prepósito General'* (Buenos Aires: Casa Pardo: 1971); Patrick M. Geoghegan, 'Field (Fehily), Thomas (1546/9–1625)', in McGuire and Quinn (eds), *Dictionary of Irish Biography*; Aubrey Gwynn, *Father Thomas Fields, SJ: A pioneer of the Church in Paraguay* (Dublin: Irish Messenger, 1924); Edmund Hogan, 'Father Thomas Filde', in idem, *Distinguished Irishmen of the Sixteenth Century* (London: Burns & Oates, 1894); and Robert McGeagh, 'Thomas Fields and the Precursors of the Guaraní *Reducciones*', *Colonial Latin American Historical Review* (1993), pp. 35–55.
7 See Aubrey Gwynn, 'Early Irish Emigration to the West Indies', *Studies*, vol. 71, no. 18 (1929), pp. 377–93; idem, 'Documents relating to the Irish in the West Indies', *Analecta Hibernica*, no. 4 (1932), pp. 139–286; Joyce Lorimer (ed.), *English and Irish Settlement on the River Amazon 1550–1646* (London: The Hakluyt Society, 1989); and Thomas G. Mathews, 'Memorial autobiográfico de Bernardo O'Brien', *Caribbean Studies*, vol. 10, no. 1 (1970), pp. 89–106.
8 See Ricardo Donoso, *El Marqués de Osorno: Don Ambrosio O'Higgins, 1720–1801* (Santiago: Universidad de Chile, 1941), pp. 367–73.
9 See Fanning, *Paisanos*, p. 75.
10 Ibid. pp. 209–21.
11 Laura Izarra, *Narrativas de la diaspora irlandesa bajo la Cruz del Sur* (Buenos Aires: Corregidor, 2010), p. 77.
12 Oliver Marshall, *English, Irish and Irish-American Pioneer Settlers in Nineteenth-century Brazil* (Oxford: Centre for Brazilian Studies, University of Oxford, 2005), p. 7.
13 Fanning, *Paisanos*, p. 143.

14 John O'Brien to the Earl of Clarendon, Dublin, 13 October 1848, NA, FO 51/60.
15 Ibid.
16 'Copy of contract between John O'Brien and the government of Buenos Aires for an emigration scheme [3 June 1822]', AGN, Gobierno, Asuntos Civiles y Militares, Sala X, 13/6/7.
17 According to Thomas Murray, Belgrano, now an expensive *barrio* in Buenos Aires, was to be the Irish emigrants' new home. Murray, *The Story of the Irish in Argentina*, p. 53.
18 Curiously, O'Brien wrote in 1848 that he intended 'to locate them on the Uruguay, in the Banda Oriental'. John O'Brien to the Earl of Clarendon, Dublin, 13 October 1848, NA, FO 51/60.
19 Ibid.
20 John O'Brien to Bernardo O'Higgins, London, April 1823, Fondo Benjamín Vicuña Mackenna, ANC, 359, 52.
21 John O'Brien to Marquess Wellesley, Dublin, 30 September 1823, NAI, CSO/RP/1823/1571.
22 Ibid.
23 See Fanning, *Paisanos*, pp. 141–61.
24 *Morning Post*, 24 August 1822.
25 John O'Brien to Marquess Wellesley, Dublin, 30 September 1823, NAI, CSO/RP/1823/1571.
26 John O'Brien to Bernardino Rivadavia, Dublin, 4 January 1824, AGN, Gobierno, Sala X, 14/4/4.
27 'estan pronto á embarcar 200 hombres jovens honrados y virtuosos, escogidos, la flor de Irelanda [*sic*]'. Ibid.
28 Ibid.
29 Ibid.
30 In September 1819 O'Higgins had attempted to induce General Alexander Hore of the Spanish army to release two hundred, mostly Irish, patriot soldiers captured in Portobello in present-day Panama in exchange for royalists taken prisoner during the Battles of Chacabuco and Maipú. Hore was a Dublin-born Catholic, and O'Higgins made his appeal on the basis of their common ancestry, but he received no response. Bernard O'Higgins to Sir John Doyle, Montalbán, 1 September 1828, *Archivo O'Higgins* (Santiago: Academia Chilena de la Historia, 1980), vol. 32, pp. 216–17.
31 Senado Conservador, sesion 416 de 11 de enero de 1822, pp. 459–60.
32 Bernardo O'Higgins to Sir John Doyle, Montalbán, 1 September 1828, repr. in Patricio Estellé Méndez, 'Epistolario de Don Bernardo O'Higgins con autoridades y corresponsales ingleses, 1817–1831', *Historia*, no. 11 (1972–73), pp. 399–458 (pp. 447–8).
33 Antonio José de Irisarri to Bernardo O'Higgins, Paris, 31 December 1822, *Archivo O'Higgins* (Santiago: Universitaria, 1947), vol. 3, pp. 389–90.
34 Antonio José de Irisarri to Bernardo O'Higgins, London. 3 March 1823, *Archivo O'Higgins* (Santiago: Universitaria, 1948), vol. 4, pp. 33–4.
35 John O'Brien to Bernardo O'Higgins, London, April 1823, Fondo Benjamín Vicuña Mackenna, ANC, 359, 52.
36 Ibid.
37 Ibid.

38 John O'Brien to Bernardo O'Higgins, Liverpool, 6 May 1823, Fondo Benjamín Vicuña Mackenna, ANC, 359, 54.
39 See Klaus Gallo, 'Rivadavia and the British Attitude Towards Recognition', in idem, *Great Britain and Argentina: From invasion to recognition, 1806–26* (Basingstoke: Palgrave, 2001), pp. 115–36.
40 John O'Brien to the Earl of Clarendon, Dublin, 13 October 1848, NA, FO 51/60.
41 Henry Goulburn to John O'Brien, 6 October 1823, repr. in John O'Brien to the Earl of Clarendon, Dublin, 13 October 1848, NA, FO 51/60.
42 *Morning Post*, 10 September 1824.
43 *El Argos de Buenos Ayres*, 19 January 1825.
44 'de regresar a este pais por quien ha hecho tantos sacrificios, con el objeto de continuar la Carrera de las armas en que ha insumido lo mas florido de sus años'. 'Petition of John O'Brien to the Government of Buenos Aires', 1 February 1825, AGN, Gobierno, Asuntos Civiles y Militares, Sala X, 13/6/7.
45 'los recomendables y distinguidos servicios'. Ibid.
46 McKenna, 'Nineteenth Century Irish Emigration to, and Settlement in, Argentina', p. 82.
47 Patrick McKenna, 'Irish Emigration to Argentina: A different model', in Andy Bielenberg (ed.), *The Irish Diaspora* (Harlow: Longman, 2000), p. 201.
48 Nally, 'Los Irlandeses en la Argentina', p. 69.
49 McKenna himself cites evidence that the first emigrants from Streamstown, County Westmeath were living in Argentina well before the late 1820s, giving the example of Thomas Murray from Streamstown, a British army veteran who had fought in the English Invasions of the River Plate in 1806–07 and remained in Buenos Aires. McKenna, 'Nineteenth Century Irish Emigration to, and Settlement in, Argentina', p. 199.
50 'I did not my Lord, again return to this Country until something more than two years ago …'. John O'Brien to the Earl of Clarendon, Dublin, 13 October 1848, NA, FO 51/60.
51 Ussher, *Father Fahy*, pp. 37–8.

Chapter 6: Laykakota

1 Vicuña Mackenna, *El Jeneral O'Brien*, p. 17; Figueroa, *Vida del Jeneral Don Juan O'Brien*, p. 66.
2 'O'Brien, por su parte, mantuvo siempre un culto en su Corazon por los dos grandes guerreros de nuestro hemisferio, a los que comparaba siempre entre sí, dando su preferencia a San Martin. Decia de Bolívar que era el Napoleon de la América i de San Martin, para hacer mas grande su elojio, decia que era el Wellington de sus guerras.' Vicuña Mackenna, *El Jeneral O'Brien*, pp. 17–18.
3 *British Packet, and Argentine News*, 29 November 1834; Figueroa, *Vida del Jeneral Don Juan O'Brien*, p. 66.
4 *British Packet, and Argentine News*, 29 November 1834. See also Luis Miguel Glave, *La república instalada: Formación nacional y prensa en el Cuzco, 1825–1939*, online edn (Lima: Institut français d'etudes andines, 2004), ch. 4, para. 76 (n. pag.).
5 See Henri Favre, 'Bolívar y los Indios', *Histórica*, vol. 10, no. 1 (1986), pp. 1–18.

6 A term used to describe those of mixed European and indigenous extraction.
7 'Extract of a Letter from Arica, Dated 20th September, 1825', *Morning Chronicle*, 11 April 1826.
8 Captain Joseph Andrews, *Journey from Buenos Ayres Through the Provinces of Cordova, Tucuman, and Salta, to Potosi, Thence by the Deserts of Caranja to Arica, and Subsequently, to Santiago de Chili and Coquimbo, Undertaken on Behalf of the Chilian and Peruvian Mining Association, in the Years 1825–26* (2 vols), vol. 1 (London: John Murray, 1827), p. vi.
9 Ibid. p. 85.
10 R.A. Humphreys, *Liberation in South America, 1806–1827: The career of James Paroissien* (London: Athlone Press, 1952), pp. 145–6.
11 John Miller, *Memoirs of General Miller, in the Service of the Republic of Peru* (2 vols), vol. 2 (London: Longman, Rees, Orme, Brown & Green, 1829), p. 289.
12 The Irish officer Francis Burdett O'Connor, who was born near Bandon in County Cork, mentions that Crawley was from close to his birthplace. See Francis Burdett O'Connor, *Independencia Americana: Recuerdos de Francisco Burdett O'Connor, coronel del ejército, libertador de Colombia y general de division de los del Perú y del Bolivia*, ed. Tomás O'Connor d'Arlach (Madrid: Ayacucho, 1915), p. 334.
13 'Nota del Prefecto del departamento de Puno al ministerio de Hacienda acompañándole una nota del Administrador del Tesoro del departamento con el certificado de la primera entrega de 500 pesos que hizo el general O'Brien por concepto de canon de la mina Salcedo', 21 July 1849, Biblioteca Nacional del Perú, Colección General, código: 2000008457.
14 *El Peruano*, 29 July 1843.
15 O'Connor, *Independencia Americana*, p. 334.
16 In 1848 O'Brien claimed to have been resident in Puno for the best part of a decade. Although he spent much of this period (1826–1836) travelling across Europe and South America, his principal residence was in Peru. John O'Brien, *Steam Navigation in the Andes, Sixteen Thousand Feet Above the Level of the Sea: General O'Brien's address to British merchants, manufacturers and ship-owners interested in the trade and welfare of Peru and Bolivia* (London: 1848), p. 1, NA, FO 51/60.
17 See Muecke (ed.), *The Diary of Heinrich Witt*, p. 121.
18 For more on Begg, see Cristina Mazzeo de Vivó, 'Comerciantes en conflicto. La independencia en el Perú y la transformación de la elite mercantile 1780–1830', *Anuario del Instituto de Historia Argentina*, no. 11 (2011); Susanna Bryant Dakin, *The Lives of William Hartnell* (Stanford: Stanford University Press, 1949).
19 O'Brien, *Steam Navigation in the Andes*.
20 Page never got to see the results of his handiwork. While walking with the British consul, Thomas Crompton, through the Peruvian town of Arequipa, a balcony containing fourteen people collapsed, crushing him to death. He died before the ship was launched.
21 *Caledonian Mercury*, 1 April 1844.
22 Loosely based on the life of Carlos Fermín Fitzcarrald, a nineteenth-century Peruvian rubber baron of Irish ancestry, the film centres on Brian Sweeney Fitzgerald's attempts to build an opera house in the middle of the rainforest. In order to fund the project he enters the rubber business. Prevented from sailing upriver to his rubber farm by a series of rapids, Fitzgerald (played by Klaus Kinski)

decides instead to steam up a parallel river. He then orders an army of Indians to drag his battered steamship over a steep hill in the middle of the jungle to the river near his rubber farm, from where he can sail downriver towards the Atlantic. The director of the film, Werner Herzog, has throughout his career been attracted to the quixotic. One of his earlier films, *Aguirre, the Wrath of God* (1972), reimagined the Basque conquistador Lope de Aguirre's expedition in search of El Dorado. Aguirre is also played by the combustive Kinski, to manic effect, as a type of demonic Teuton transplanted from Bayreuth to the Amazonian rainforest. Neither Fitzgerald nor Aguirre can permit mere geography to get in the way of their obsessions. O'Brien lacked the singlemindedness of one of Herzog's obsessives, but he, too, spent much of his life chasing nebulous dreams in the rainforest.

23 O'Brien, *Steam Navigation in the Andes*, p. 3.
24 Figueroa, *Vida del Jeneral Don Juan O'Brien*, p. 68.
25 Ibid.
26 *British Packet, and Argentine News*, 30 July 1831.
27 Ibid.
28 John O'Brien to John Thomas, Valparaíso, 6 September 1826, Fondo Benjamín Vicuña Mackenna, ANC, 359, 57.
29 Figueroa, *Vida del Jeneral Don Juan O'Brien*, p. 69.
30 J.P. Robertson and W.P. Robertson, *Letters on South America; Comprising travels on the banks of the Paraná and Rio de la Plata* (3 vols), vol. 1 (London: John Murray, 1843), p. 254.
31 *British Packet, and Argentine News*, 15 September 1827.
32 See D.C.M. Platt, 'Foreign Finance in Argentina for the First Half-century of Independence', *Journal of Latin America Studies*, vol. 15, no. 1 (1983), pp. 23–47.

Chapter 7: The Irish Community in Buenos Aires

1 *British Packet, and Argentine News*, 20 September 1828.
2 Ibid. 7 February 1829.
3 Ibid.
4 Ibid. 31 January 1829.
5 In a letter to the archbishop of Dublin, Dr Murray, the Irish chaplain in Buenos Aires, Fr Patrick O'Gorman, wrote: 'There are about four hundred foreign Catholics. Those only of note are Admiral Brown, Colonel O'Brien and Dr Oughan …'. Fr Patrick O'Gorman to Dr Murray, 24 April 1831, DDA, Murray Papers, 33/13/3.
6 Murray, *The Story of the Irish in Argentina*, pp. 54–5.
7 *British Packet, and Argentine News*, 30 March 1830.
8 John Oughan to Dr Murray, Buenos Aires, 12 June 1828, DDA, Murray Papers, 33/13/1.
9 Ibid.
10 See Marshall, *English, Irish and Irish-American Pioneer Settlers*, p. 67.
11 John Oughan to Dr Murray, Buenos Aires, 12 June 1828, DDA, Murray Papers, 33/13/1.
12 Ibid.
13 Ibid.

14 Patrick Moran to Dr Murray, Buenos Aires, 22 February 1829, DDA, Murray Papers, 33/13/2.
15 Ibid.
16 *British Packet, and Argentine News*, 14 February 1829.
17 Ibid. 28 February 1829.
18 Ibid.
19 Ibid.
20 Ibid. 7 March 1829.
21 *Dublin Morning Register*, 7 July 1829.
22 *British Packet, and Argentine News*, 4 July 1829.
23 Ibid. 5 September 1829.

Chapter 8: El Dorado

1 *Morning Chronicle*, 28 July 1828.
2 'The Cornish in Latin America: Gongo Soco', University of Exeter Projects, https://projects.exeter.ac.uk/cornishlatin/gongosoco.htm (accessed 28 April 2017).
3 Marshall C. Eakin, *British Enterprise in Brazil: The St John d'el Rey Mining Company and the Morro Velho gold mine 1830–1960* (Durham, North Carolina: Duke University Press, 1989), p. 18; Imperial Brazilian Mining Association, *Reports of the Directors Addressed to the Share-holders* (London: 1826), pp. 3–36.
4 *Durham County Advertiser*, 8 June 1849.
5 Figueroa, *Vida del Jeneral Don Juan O'Brien*, p. 77.
6 Belgrano, *Juan O'Brien*, p. 33.
7 John O'Brien, 'Quien haya alguna vez visto la profusion de oro que ostentan los palacios i templos del Rio Janeiro, en su macisa bajilla i adornos, de este precioso metal, no podrá facilmente olvidarse de ello, ni dejara de suscitarsele el natural deseo de saber como haya podido reunirse en algun privilejiado una tal magnificencia orifera, que raya en lo fabuloso'. 'Representación Presentada por el Jeneral O'Brien al Supremo Gobierno de Perú, Comunicándole su Proyecto de Esploración de los Valles Oríferos de la Amazonia', in Figueroa, *Vida del Jeneral Don Juan O'Brien*, p. 80.
8 *British Packet, and Argentine News*, 11 May 1833.
9 For the Victorian obsession with collecting animal specimens, see Ann C. Colley, *Wild Animal Skins in Victorian Britain: Zoos, collections, portraits, and maps* (Farnham: Ashgate, 2014).
10 Helen Cowie, *Conquering Nature in Spain and its empire, 1750–1850* (Manchester: Manchester University Press, 2011), pp. 151–2.
11 Ibid. p. 151.
12 *Glasgow Herald*, 27 December 1822.
13 *Belfast Commercial Chronicle*, 14 September 1835.
14 For more about Derby's collections, see Colley, *Wild Animal Skins in Victorian Britain*, pp. 74–8. For O'Brien's contact with Derby, see William Walton, *The Alpaca: Its naturalization in the British Isles considered a national benefit, and as an object of immediate utility to the farmer and manufacturer* (New York: 1845), p. 5.
15 *Bell's Life in London and Sporting Chronicle*, 27 April 1928; *Atlas*, 27 April 1928; *Nottingham Review and General Advertiser for the Midland Counties*, 2 May 1828.
16 Helen Cowie, *Llama* (London: Reaktion, 2017), loc. 1,031 (Kindle ebook).
17 Walton, *The Alpaca*, p. 27.

18 Cowie, *Llama*, loc. 1211 (Kindle ebook).
19 Ibid. loc. 1189 (Kindle ebook).
20 William Danson, *Alpaca, the Original Peruvian Sheep, before the Spaniards Invaded South America, for Naturalisation in Other Countries* (Liverpool: Rourke, 1852), pp. 13–15. See also Helen Cowie, 'From the Andes to the Outback: Acclimatising alpacas in the British Empire', *Journal of Imperial and Commonwealth History*, vol. 45, no. 4 (2017), pp. 551–79.
21 *Leeds Intelligencer*, 12 April 1845.
22 *British Packet, and Argentine News*, 11 May 1833.
23 Ibid. 29 November 1834.
24 Paul Lawrence Farber, 'The Development of Taxidermy and the History of Ornithology', *Isis*, vol. 68, no. 4 (1977), pp. 550–66.
25 Cowie, *Conquering Nature in Spain*, p. 163.
26 *British Packet, and Argentine News*, 29 November 1834.
27 Ibid.
28 Ibid.
29 For more, see Richard Chase Smith, 'Liberal Ideology and Indigenous Communities in Post-independence Peru', *Journal of International Affairs*, vol. 36, no. 1 (1982), pp. 73–82 (pp. 78–80).
30 O'Brien was correct about the reserves in the Madre de Dios region. Gold is plentiful, but its existence has been a mixed blessing to the local communities. In recent years tens of thousands of illegal miners have eked out a living in this remote part of the Amazon. The environmental consequences have been devastating, especially the contamination of the river system with mercury, with which the miners separate the ore. And violence, addiction and sexual exploitation are rife in the villages and towns where the miners congregate.
31 General William Miller, 'Notice of a Journey to the Northward and Also to the Eastward of Cuzco, and Among the Chunchos Indians', *Journal of the Royal Geographical Society of London*, no. 6 (1836), pp. 174–86 (p. 179).
32 O'Brien, 'Representación Presentada por el Jeneral O'Brien', in Figueroa, *Vida del Jeneral Don Juan O'Brien*, p. 80.
33 *British Packet, and Argentine News*, 29 November 1834.
34 Contained in Julián Bovo de Revello, *Brillante Porvenir del Cuzco* (Cuzco: 1848), pp. 15–16.
35 Glave, *La república instalada*, ch. 4, para. 83 (n. pag.).
36 Miller, 'Notice of a Journey to the Northward and Also to the Eastward of Cuzco …', p. 174.
37 Miller, *Memoirs of General Miller*, vol. 2, p. 237.
38 'El Coronel D. Juan O'Brien a sus antiguos compañeros de armas argentinos, chilenos y peruanos', repr. in José María Blanco, *Diario del viaje del presidente Orbegoso al sur del Peru*, vol. ii, ed. Felix Denegri Luna (Lima: Instituto Riva-Agüero, 1974), p. 179.
39 Glave, *La república instalada*, ch. 4, para. 89 (n. pag.); *British Packet, and Argentine News*, 27 June 1835.
40 *British Packet, and Argentine News*, 27 June 1835.
41 The following footnote in Miller's memoirs probably riled a number of officers, not least O'Brien: 'It is remarkable that Lieutenant-Colonel Miller was the only field-officer who sailed with the expeditionary army from Valparaíso, who was

also present at the great final victory of Ayachucho. Thus it was his singular fortune to have been the first patriot officer to land on the coast (1819), and to have heard the first and last shots fired during the Peruvian war of independence. Of nearly five thousand that sailed from Valparaíso in 1820, not more than ten officers and ninety privates continued in active service in Peru.' Miller, *Memoirs of General Miller*, vol. 1, p. 265.

42 'infortunado *sansculote*, plaga en la sociedad, picaro embustero, demente aventurero'. Glave, *La república instalada*, ch. 4, para. 100 (n. pag.).

43 'era poco elocuente con las hazañas ajenas y laudatorio en extremo, al punto de la exageración, con las propias, lo que bien merecía la ira del irlandés y la comprensión de Orbegoso, que no impidío el acto'. Ibid. ch. 4, para. 98 (n. pag.).

44 'I tal es la abundancia del precioso metal en esa privilejiada rejion, i tal fué mi conviccion de la facilidad de estraerlo, con la necesaria proteccion de las armas, que yo no trepidé entónces en proponer al Presidente Gamarra, que el Gobierno enviase sin demora una espedicion militar i minera, para ocupar aquellos valles, que siendo tan cercanos al populoso pais del Cuzco, i tan pocos i débiles los indios que alli habitan, no demandaria su conquista mas que un esfuerzo …'. O'Brien, 'Representación Presentada por el Jeneral O'Brien', repr. in Figueroa, *Vida del Jeneral Don Juan O'Brien*, pp. 80–1.

45 El Presidente Gamarra al Jeneral O'Brien, Cuzco, 17 July 1835, repr. in Figueroa, *Vida del Jeneral Don Juan O'Brien*, p. 84.

46 Peru–Bolivian Confederation, *Colección de documentos y de sucesos notables en las campañas de la pacificación del Perú* (Lima: Aranda, 1837), p. 45.

47 *British Packet, and Argentine News*, 9 January 1836.

48 Ibid.

49 Ibid.

50 John O'Brien to Manuel de la Cruz Méndez, Santiago de Chile, 4 March 1836, BNP, Correspondencia Particular.

51 W.G. Lettsom to Earl Russell, Montevideo, 16 June 1863, NA, FO 97/291.

52 Murray, *The Story of the Irish in Argentina*, p. 44.

53 'Cuatro documentos, sobre reconocimiento y entrega de la urna conteniendo sus restos mortales', AGN, Polícia, Sala X, 33/3/3.

Chapter 9: The Restorer of the Laws

1 General John Thomond O'Brien, *Monte-Video, Buenos Ayres, and the River Plate: Correspondence with the British government relative to the war between Buenos Ayres and Monte-Video, and the free navigation of the River Plate. With an appendix, detailing some of the acts committed by Rosas, governor of Buenos Ayres* (London: Reynell & Wright, 1845), p. 36.

2 Ibid.

3 *Manifiesto de las razones que legitiman la declaración de guerra contra el gobierno del General D. Andrés Santa Cruz, titulado presidente de la Confederación Perú-Boliviana* (Buenos Aires: 1837).

4 John Lynch, *Argentine Caudillo: Juan Manuel de Rosas* (Lanham, MD: SR Books, 2001) (digital edition), ch. 1, paras 2–3 (n. pag.).

5 Ibid. ch. 2, paras 25–7 (n. pag.).

6 Ibid. ch. 1, para. 6 (n. pag.).

7 Ibid. ch. 1, para. 18 (n. pag.).
8 Ibid. ch. 3, para. 22 (n. pag.).
9 Ibid. ch. 6, para. 12 (n. pag.).
10 John Henry Mandeville to John Fox-Strangways, Buenos Aires, 14 July 1837, NA, FO 6/58.
11 O'Brien, *Monte-Video, Buenos Ayres, and the River Plate*, p. 37.
12 John Henry Mandeville to Lord Palmerston, Buenos Aires, 12 July 1837, NA, FO 6/58.
13 See Emilio Ocampo, 'Rosas y Alvear: Una relación turbulenta y poco conocida', https://entrelafabulaylahistoria.tumblr.com/post/23606644803/rosas-y-alvear-una-relación-turbulenta-y-poco (accessed 1 November 2016).
14 John Henry Mandeville to John Fox-Strangways, Buenos Aires, 14 July 1837, NA, FO 6/58.
15 Ibid.
16 Antonio Zinny, *Historia de los gobernadores de las provincias argentinas desde 1810 hasta la fecha*, vol. 1 (Buenos Aires: 1879), p. 161.
17 O'Brien, *Monte-Video, Buenos Ayres, and the River Plate*, p. 37.
18 Maxine Hanon, 'Mandeville, John Henry', *Oxford Dictionary of National Biography*.
19 John Henry Mandeville to John Fox-Strangways, Buenos Aires, 14 July 1837, NA, FO 6/58.
20 John Henry Mandeville to Viscount Palmerston, Buenos Aires, 15 August 1837, NA, FO 6/58.
21 O'Brien, *Monte-Video, Buenos Ayres, and the River Plate*, p. 38.
22 Ibid.
23 Ibid. p. 39.
24 Ibid. p. 40.
25 *Waterford Chronicle*, 1 October 1845.
26 John Henry Mandeville to Viscount Palmerston, Buenos Aires, 15 August 1837, NA, FO 6/58.
27 O'Brien, *Monte-Video, Buenos Ayres, and the River Plate*, p. 41.
28 Ibid.
29 Ibid. p. 42.
30 Ibid.; see also Zinny, *Historia de los gobernadores de las provincias argentinas*, p. 161.
31 O'Brien, *Monte-Video, Buenos Ayres, and the River Plate*, p. 42.
32 Ibid.
33 John Henry Mandeville to Viscount Palmerston, Buenos Aires, 15 August 1837, NA, FO 6/58.
34 Ibid.
35 John Henry Mandeville to Viscount Palmerston, Buenos Aires, 3 March 1838, NA, FO 6/63.
36 O'Brien, *Monte-Video, Buenos Ayres, and the River Plate*, p. 43; Zinny, *Historia de los gobernadores de las provincias argentinas*, p. 162; José de San Martín to Bernardo O'Higgins, Paris, 3 December 1837 in José de San Martín, *Su correspondencia (1823–1850)* (Madrid: América, 1919), p. 75.
37 John Henry Mandeville to Viscount Palmerston, Buenos Aires, 12 January 1838, NA, FO 6/63.
38 Felipe Arana to the interim chief of police, Buenos Aires, 24 December 1837, AGN, Policía, Sala X, 33/3/3.

39 O'Brien, *Monte-Video, Buenos Ayres, and the River Plate*, p. 44.
40 Ibid.
41 Ibid. p. 37.
42 John Henry Mandeville to Viscount Palmerston, Buenos Aires, 3 March 1838, 3 March, NA, FO 6/63.
43 A racist reference to the fact that Santa Cruz was of mixed indigenous and Spanish heritage.
44 John O'Brien to Bernardo O'Higgins, Baltinglass, 20 July 1838, Fondo Benjamín Vicuña Mackenna, ANC, 359, 65.
45 Ibid.
46 Figueroa, *Vida del Jeneral Don Juan O'Brien*, p. 89.
47 See Ramón Sotomayor Valdés, *Historia de Chile bajo el gobierno del General Don Joaquín Prieto*, vol. 3 (Santiago: Universitaria, 1980), p. 431; Figueroa, *Vida del Jeneral Don Juan O'Brien*, p. 91.
48 Figueroa, *Vida del Jeneral Don Juan O'Brien*, p. 91.
49 O'Brien, *Monte-Video, Buenos Ayres, and the River Plate*, p. 36.

Chapter 10: The Great War

1 *Waterford Chronicle*, 1 October 1845.
2 *Dublin Evening Post*, 25 December 1838.
3 *Freeman's Journal*, 20 December 1838.
4 *Dublin Evening Post*, 25 December 1838.
5 John O'Brien to Bernardo O'Higgins, Baltinglass, 20 July 1838, Fondo Benjamín Vicuña Mackenna, ANC, 359, 65.
6 Ibid.
7 *Cork Examiner*, 11 February 1842.
8 Leslie Bethell (ed.), *The Cambridge History of Latin America (c. 1870–1930)*, vol. 4 (Cambridge: Cambridge University Press, 1986), p. 10.
9 Deposition of John O'Brien, Montevideo, 7 August 1846, NA, FO 97/51.
10 Bridget O'Neill to John Henry Mandeville, Buenos Aires, 30 December 1839, NA, FO 97/48.
11 Bridget O'Neill to John Henry Mandeville, Buenos Aires, 5 January 1840, NA, FO 97/48.
12 Confusingly, Rosas was allied with the *blancos* in Uruguay, even though his own political followers in Argentina wore red and the militia he created in 1819 was known as the '*Colorados del Monte*'.
13 José de San Martín to William Miller, Paris, 25 February 1843, in San Martín, *Su correspondencia (1823–1850)*, p. 118.
14 Deposition of Patrick O'Donoghue, Montevideo, 30 March 1844, NA, FO 97/50.
15 John O'Brien to Ángel Pacheco, Buceo, 24 February 1844, AGN, Museo Histórico Nacional, Legajo 61.
16 John O'Brien to Adophus Turner [copy], Montevideo, 5 July 1844, NA, FO 97/50.
17 Deposition of Edward Connell, 19 June 1844, NA, FO 97/50.
18 Commodore John Purvis to John O'Brien, HMS *Alfred*, off Montevideo, 23 February 1844, NA, FO 97/50.

19 John O'Brien to Adolphus Turner [copy], Montevideo, 5 July 1844, NA, FO 97/50.
20 Ibid.
21 Ibid.
22 Santiago Vasquez to the Earl of Aberdeen, 25 July 1844, NA, FO 51/32.
23 O'Brien, *Monte-Video, Buenos Ayres, and the River Plate*, p. 11.
24 *London Evening Standard*, 16 December 1844.
25 John O'Brien to the Earl of Aberdeen, London, 13 January 1845, NA, FO 6/110.
26 Ibid.
27 Ibid.
28 John O'Brien to the Earl of Aberdeen, London, 15 April 1845, NA, FO 51/39.
29 O'Brien, *Monte-Video, Buenos Ayres, and the River Plate*, p. 5.
30 Ibid. p. 6.
31 'Petition to the Lords and Commons for the free navigation of the River Plate to Paraguay, signed by nearly all the bankers, merchants and manufacturers of Great Britain and Ireland', NA, FO 6/111.
32 Charles Canning to John O'Brien, Foreign Office, 7 January 1846, NA, FO 97/51.
33 John O'Brien to Francisco Magariños, Montevideo, 19 April 1846, AGNU, Caja 1717, Carpeta 14.
34 *Morning Chronicle*, 7 September 1846.
35 Fr Anthony Fahy to Dr Daniel Murray, Montevideo, 12 September 1846, DDA, Murray Papers, 33/13/6.
36 Ibid.
37 Fr Anthony Fahy to Lord Palmerston, Buenos Aires, 20 November 1846, NA, FO 6/126/143.
38 John O'Brien to the Earl of Clarendon, Dublin, 13 October 1848, NA, FO 51/60.
39 O'Brien, *Steam Navigation in the Andes*.
40 John O'Brien to the Earl of Clarendon, Dublin, 13 October 1848, NA, FO 51/60.
41 Lord Palmerston to John O'Brien, Foreign Office, 13 November 1848, NA, FO 51/60.
42 *British Packet, and Argentine News*, 10 February 1849; *Manchester Courier and Lancashire General Advertiser*, 3 January 1849.
43 *Manchester Times*, 22 May 1849.
44 Despite its name, the *Dublin Review* was published in London.
45 *Dublin Review*, March 1849, p. 41.
46 Ibid. p. 35.
47 Translated as *The American Archive and Spirit of the World Press*.
48 *Archivo Americano y Espíritu de la Prensa del Mundo*, 8 January 1851, pp. 1–2.
49 Ibid. 7 September 1850, p. 57.
50 *La Gaceta Mercantil*, 7 November 1849, in *Archivo Americano y Espíritu de la Prensa del Mundo*, 21 September 1850, p. 183.
51 Ibid.
52 *Weekly Telegraph*, 12 June 1852.
53 George O'Brien was a former Royal Navy officer who enlisted in the Chilean navy. He was killed at Callao in 1818 during an attempt to 'cut out' the *Esmeralda*.
54 Charles O'Carroll was a veteran of the British army, enlisting in the patriot

army in 1818. He was taken prisoner by royalist forces in the south of Chile, and executed in 1820.

55 Daniel Florence O'Leary enlisted in the regiments raised in Britain and Ireland in 1817, which fought in the north of South America. He fought in Venezuela, Colombia, Ecuador and Peru. He was one of Bolívar's aides-de-camp, and rose to become a general.

56 AGK Leonard, 'Carlton Crescent: Southampton's most spectacular regency development', *Journal of Southampton Local History Forum*, no. 17 (2010), pp. 33–45.

Chapter 11: 'Messenger of the Heroes'

1 Muecke (ed.), *The Diary of Heinrich Witt*, p. 420.

2 'Contestaciones de varios jenerales', repr. in Figueroa, *Vida del Jeneral Don Juan O'Brien*, pp. 108–11.

3 'Resolución expedida por el Congreso de la República del Perú, reconociendo medio sueldo a Dn. Juan O'Brien, por sus servicios prestados en la guerra de la independencia', Lima, 29 December 1851, BNP, D2081.

4 'El Jeneral don Juan O'Brien al Soberano Congreso', repr. in Figueroa, *Vida del Jeneral Don Juan O'Brien*, p. 111.

5 John O'Brien to José Matías Zapiola, Valparaíso, 20 May 1858, AGN, Museo Histórico Nacional, Legajo 28.

6 'Un studio prolijo i concienzudo como el que yo he [hecho] de sus riquezas, de sus elementos de produccion, de sus inagotables minas, de sus fecundos lavaderos de oro, de sus esquisitas maderas, i en fin de los valiosos artículos que viven en el seno de sus bosques i montañas, me ha dado a conocer cuán fácil es abrir a la América del Sur vastos horizontes de vida.

'Yo conozco los opulentos valles que riega el Amazonas i he calculado las ventajas colosales que reportarian bajo todos aspectos a sus Repúblicas ribereñas, i mui en especial al Perú, si sobre las aguas del gran rio condujeran a los mercados de Europa las fabulosas riquezas que conservan muertas, por career de conveniente esplotacion.

'Por fortuna, nadie ignora hoi que la libre navegacion del Amazonas es el gran secreto de la prosperidad Americana, que a todo trances debemos realizar ...'. Figueroa, 'El Jeneral O'Brien a la Asamblea Constituyente del Perú', in idem, *Vida del Jeneral Don Juan O'Brien*, pp. 100–1.

7 Ibid. p. 101.

8 *Waterford News*, 1 July 1853.

9 *Daily Alta California*, 27 June 1853.

10 *Waterford News*, 1 July 1853.

11 John O'Brien to José Matías Zapiola, Valparaíso, 20 May 1858, AGN, Museo Histórico Nacional, Legajo 28.

12 'Este recuerdo me trae a la memoria un sentimiento profundo, ya no existen mas que tres de los diez i seis que subimos ese dia al tablado acompañando a San Martin ... Digalo yo i toda la América: no estaban Chile i el Perú ocupados completamente por los españoles cuando San Martin con solo 3,200 hombres pasó los Andes, libertó a Chile i fundó la independencia del Perú? ¿I no es una ingratidud olvidar a tan grande héroe? ¿Pero nó, el Perú sabe recordar i hacer justicia a los hombres que fundaron su nacionalidad.' Figueroa, 'El Jeneral O'Brien

en el aniversario del Perú, 28 de Julio de 1858', in idem, *Vida del Jeneral Don Juan O'Brien*, p. 119.

13 'Los méritos de Bolívar fueron grandes respect al Perú, pero los de San Martin fueron colosales …'. Ibid. p. 120.

14 'promover Estatuas de los Heroes y hombres Emenientos [*sic*] q[e] ha dado la libertad, prosperidad y Patria a Chile.' 'Papel escrito por el General O'Brien sobre la estatua de Freire', 20 August 1853, ANC, Archivo Fernández Larrain, vol. 46, p. 71.

15 Ibid.

16 John O'Brien to José Matías Zapiola, Valparaíso, 20 May 1858, AGN, Museo Histórico Nacional, Legajo 28.

17 '<u>siempre</u> un buenos espada y su pecho al frente del enemigo hasta ha visto su patrio Libre'. 'Papel escrito por el General O'Brien sobre la estatua de Freire', 20 August 1853, ANC, Archivo Fernández Larrain, vol. 46, p. 71.

18 'en triente años nadie pensaba en estatuas hasta yo concluyo aquella de Freire que es obra hermosa y muy completa igual a ninguno en Europa … [*sic*]'. John O'Brien to José Matías Zapiola, Valparaíso, 20 May 1858, AGN, Museo Histórico Nacional, Legajo 28.

19 'Es el verdadero ajente de una época grandiose, el mensajero de los heroes que reclama a las naciones libres la gratitud de las nacionalidades.' Figueroa, *Vida del Jeneral Don Juan O'Brien*, pp. 121–2.

20 'Por esto es que mi voz al elevarse sirviendo de eco a las tumbas de los heroes de la emancipacion …'. Figueroa, *Vida del Jeneral Don Juan O'Brien*, p. 120.

21 Muecke (ed.), *The Diary of Heinrich Witt*, p. 285.

22 Vicuña Mackenna, *De Valparaíso a Santiago* (Santiago: Mercurio, 1877), p. 301.

23 Ibid. p. 302.

24 See Vicuña Mackenna, *El Jeneral O'Brien*, pp. 22–3.

25 Vicuña Mackenna, *De Valparaíso a Chile*, p. 302.

26 'Rara dificultad del escritor al tratarse de un hombre que tuvo la mania de los retratos! … Conocemos láminas i efijies del jeneral O'Brien que le representan en su sobrio traje de coronel, de uniforme de jeneral i a caballo, de pié en gran uniforme, tallado en mármol, grabado en láminas de batallas. En todas partes le encontramos, como *copia*, suspendido a algun hospitalario muro; pero al *original*, vagando siempre por el ancho mundo, es casi imposible darle alcance.' Vicuña Mackenna, *El Jeneral O'Brien*, p. 9.

27 Vicuña Mackenna, 'El Jeneral San Martín después de Chacabuco', p. 7.

28 John Thomond O'Brien, *A Living Nero in England* (London: 1859), Fondo Benjamín Vicuña Mackenna, ANC, 359.

29 See Fanning, *Paisanos*, pp. 214–15.

30 O'Brien, *A Living Nero in England*, Fondo Benjamín Vicuña Mackenna, ANC, 359.

31 John O'Brien to Lord Russell, London, 8 August 1859, NA, FO 97/51.

32 Foreign Office to John O'Brien, 17 August 1859, NA, FO 97/51.

33 *Wexford Independent*, 24 July 1861.

34 John O'Brien to Lord Russell, Lisbon, 16 January 1861, NA, FO 97/51.

35 Vicuña Mackenna, *El Jeneral O'Brien*, pp. 25–6.

36 Figueroa, *Vida del Jeneral Don Juan O'Brien*, p. 137.

37 *Dublin Daily Express*, 27 December 1864.

38 H.R. Reynolds to G.A. Hamilton, Treasury Chambers, 24 August 1865, NA, FO 97/291.
39 William Garrow Lettsom to Lord Russell, Montevideo, 16 June 1863, NA, FO 97/291.
40 'A List of British claimants under the Mixed Commission, whose awards in bonds have not yet been applied for', Montevideo, 29 October 1864, NA, FO 97/291.
41 Vicuña Mackenna, *El Jeneral O'Brien*, p. 26.
42 Figueroa, *Vida del Jeneral Don Juan O'Brien*, p. 75.
43 'Si la gratitud de los chilenos no se olvida de sus glorias, repatriará, mas tarde o mas temprano, las gloriosas cenizas de O'Brien que descansan en la cripta del Convento Irlandes Dominicano de Lisboa, para ser colocadas al lado de los heroes de la independencia nacional.

'Cuando alguno de los buques de la Armada, que recorrea los mares en viaje de instruccion de cadetes navales, recale en Lisbona, ordene el Gobierno la repatriacion de las cenizas de O'Brien para darles su lugar de reposo eterno en el panteon de los héroes de la libertad.' Ibid. p. 76.
44 'Desearíamos para él esta merecida gloria i recompense de sus servicios, repatriando sus cenizas que descansan en la cripta del convento irlandes de Lisboa, para guardarlas en el seno de esta tierra que regó con su sangria i que redimió con su espada.' Ibid. p. 21.
45 See Fanning, *Paisanos*, pp. 224–9.

Conclusion

1 Vicuña Mackenna uses O'Brien's quote 'I am a soldier and nothing more' as the epigraph to his thirty-page biographical sketch of the Irishman: 'Yo soi un soldado i nada más.' Vicuña Mackenna, *El Jeneral O'Brien*, p. 7.
2 On the title page of Figueroa's biography, O'Brien is described as 'irlandés de nacimiento, chileno de adopción'. Figueroa, *Vida del Jeneral Don Juan O'Brien*, p. 1. He later traces O'Brien's ancestry to Brian Boru, p. 25. However, he also includes English and Scottish soldiers in a list of foreigners who fought for South American independence, pp. 10–11.
3 'En Irlanda, la comarca fertilísima a la que los poetas llamaran Esmeralda de los mares y Verde Erín, la tierra de los hombres de voluntad indomable y donde la alegría del cuotidiano vivir no es un mito, allá por la penultima década del siglo XVIII, proveniente de familia de desahogada posición, nacía don Juan O'Brien.' Juan Luis Hogan, 'Juan O'Brien: Camarada de San Martín', *San Martín: Revista del Instituto Nacional Sanmartiniano*, vol. 5, no. 17 (1947), pp. 119–23.
4 'se nos presenta a la sombre "de su viejo General".' Guastavino, *Un gesto de O'Brien*, p. 7.
5 For references to Mitre's conversations with O'Brien, see Mitre, *Historia de San Martín*, vol. 2, p. 19 n. 15, p. 170 n. 28, p. 247 n. 21, p. 254 n. 26.
6 Mitre, *Historia de San Martín*, vol. 2, p. 247.
7 A reading of Argentine history based on the political thought and writings of Bartolomé Mitre.
8 'Peleó luego en Maipo y siempre estuvo al lado de San Martín, de quien no se separó hasta 1822.' Glave, *La república instalada*, ch. 4, para. 74 (n. pag.).

9 Vicuña Mackenna gives the best example: 'San Martín tenia una especie de afecto paternal por sue decan favorito; i en verdad, hubo en la naturaleza de éste, hasta en sus últimos años, algo de ese candor i de esa espontaneidad de la infancia que reviste todos los actos de la vida de un simpatico atractivo.' Vicuña Mackenna, *El Jeneral O'Brien*, p. 17. Hogan similarly describes a strong emotional bond: 'O'Brien está frente a San Martín, gobernadora de Cuyo. Los ojos plenos de suave bondad, pero donde la mirada del guerrero semeja la penetrante y aguda del águila, parecen sondear hasta el fondo mismo del pensamiento, escudriñando los abismos de sus sentimientos.' Hogan, 'Juan O'Brien', p. 120. Figueroa describes the bond as follows: 'O'Brien podia ostentar como su mayor título de guerrero el noble afecto del jeneral San Martín, que en nadie puso jamas su cariño fuera de la libertad de América i que al bravo celta le acordó todo el sentimiento de estimación de su pecho de bronce.' Figueroa, *Vida del Jeneral Don Juan O'Brien*, pp. 36–7.

10 During the ceremony, the historian Horacio Fórmica described O'Brien as 'un guerrero de la Independencia, irlandés, tozudo, empecinado y peleador. Que acompañó y luchó con San Martín. Hoy el general descansa en paz.' Anon., 'Los restos de O'Brien descansan en Plumerillo', *Los Andes*, 24 January 2017, http://www.losandes.com.ar/article/los-restos-de-o-brien-ya-estan-en-mendoza (accessed 9 February 2017).

11 'O'Brien fue fundador nada menos que de cinco repúblicas: Uruguay, Argentina, Chile, Perú y Bolivia. El irlandés fue un combatiente importantísimo en la consecución de la independencia de Argentina y Chile.' Glave, *La república instalada*, ch. 4, para. 73 (n. pag.).

12 Rory Miller, *Britain and Latin America in the Nineteenth and Twentieth Centuries* (Harlow: Longman, 1993), p. 2.

13 See Brown, *Adventuring Through Spanish Colonies*, pp. 19–20; Fanning, *Paisanos*, pp. 209–11.

Bibliography

PRIMARY SOURCES

Archives

Archivo General de la Nación, Buenos Aires
Asuntos Civiles y Militares
Cartas de ciudadanía
Ejército de los Andes
Fondo Ignacio Nuñez
Granaderos a Caballo
Museo Histórico Nacional
Polícia
Tomás de Razon

Archivo General de la Nación, Uruguay
Colección General
Correspondencia Particular

Archivo Nacional de Chile, Santiago
Archivos Varios
Fondo Benjamín Vicuña Mackenna

Biblioteca Nacional del Perú
Relaciones Exteriores: Caja 1717, Carpeta 14

Dublin Diocesan Archives
Murray Papers 33/13/1

National Archives, Kew [London]
British Claims, Buenos Aires: FO 97/48–51
Consular Records, Buenos Aires: FO 6/58–9, 63–4, 110–11, 114, 128, 139–41, 158, 162
Foreign Office Consular Records, Montevideo: FO 51/26–62; FO 507/1–3
Mixed Commission of Claims, Montevideo: FO 97/50–1, 291

National Archives of Ireland, Dublin
Catholic Qualification Rolls
Chief Secretary's Office: CSO/RP/1823/1571
Landed Estates Court Rentals, 1850–1885
Rebellion Papers: RP 620/37

Parliamentary records

Sessions of the Cámara de Diputados, Chile
Sessions of the Cámara de Senadores, Chile
Sessions of the Senado Conservador, Chile

Books, articles and pamphlets

Andrews, Captain Joseph, *Journey from Buenos Ayres, Through the Provinces of Cordova, Tucuman, and Salta, to Potosi, Thence by the Deserts of Caranja to Arica, and Subsequently, to Santiago de Chili and Coquimbo, Undertaken on Behalf of the Chilian and Peruvian Mining Association, in the Years 1825–26* (2 vols) (London: John Murray, 1827)

Anon., *Colección de documentos y de sucesos notables en las campañas de la pacificación del Perú* (Lima: Eusebio Aranda, 1837)

Beaumont, J.A.B., *Travels in Buenos Ayres and the Adjacent Provinces of the Rio de la Plata. With observations, intended for the use of persons who contemplate emigrating to that country: or, embarking capital in its affairs* (London: James Ridgway, 1828)

Blanco, José María, *Diario del viaje del presidente Orbegoso al sur del Peru*, vol. 2, ed. Felix Denegri Luna (Lima: Instituto Riva-Agüero, 1974)

Blondel, J.J.M. (ed.), *Almanaque de comercio de la ciudad de Buenos Aires, para el año de 1830* (Buenos Aires: 1829)

Bovo de Revello, Julián, *Brillante Porvenir del Cuzco* (Cuzco: 1848)

Caldcleugh, Alexander, *Travels in South America, During the Years 1819–20–21; Containing an account of the present state of Brazil, Buenos Ayres, and Chile* (2 vols) (London: John Murray, 1825)

Danson, William, *Alpaca, the Original Peruvian Sheep, Before the Spaniards Invaded South America, for Naturalisation in Other Countries* (Liverpool: Rourke, 1852)

Donoso, Ricardo, et al. (eds), *Archivo de Don Bernardo O'Higgins* (vol. 3, Santiago: Universitaria, 1947; vol. 4, Santiago: Universitaria, 1948; vol. 7, Santiago: Universitaria, 1950; vol. 31, Santiago: Academia Chilena de la Historica, 1980)

Doyle, John, *Speech of Gen. Sir John Doyle, Bart. G.C.B. President of the First Anniversary Meeting of the Society for Improving the Condition and Increasing the Comforts of the Irish Peasantry* (London: Philanthropic Society, 1823)

Fraser, Robert, *General View of the Agriculture, Mineralogy, Present State and Circumstances of County Wicklow, with Observations on the Means of Their Improvement* (Dublin: Graisberry & Campbell, 1801)

Graham, Maria, *Journal of a Residence in Chile During the year 1822, and a Voyage from Chile to Brazil in 1823* (London: Longman, Hurst, Rees, Orme, Brown & Green, 1824)

Haigh, Samuel, *Sketches of Buenos Ayres and Chili* (London: James Carpenter & Son, 1829); repr. as *Sketches of Buenos Ayres, Chile, and Peru* (London: Effingham Wilson, 1831)

Hall, Basil, *Extracts from a Journal, Written on the Coasts of Chili, Peru, and Mexico, in the Years 1820, 1821, 1822* (2 vols) (Edinburgh: Archibald Constable & Co., 1824)

Lewis, Samuel, *A Topographical Dictionary of Ireland* (2 vols) (London: S. Lewis & Co., 1837)

Miers, John, *Travels in Chile and La Plata, Including Accounts Respecting the Geography,*

Geology, Statistics, Government, Finances, Agriculture, Manners and Customs, and the Mining Operations in Chile. Collected during a residence of several years in these countries (2 vols) (London: Baldwin, Cradock & Joy, 1826)

Miller, John, *Memoirs of General Miller, in the Service of the Republic of Peru* (2 vols) (vol. 1, London: Longman, Rees, Orme, Brown & Green, 1828; vol. 2, London: Longman, Rees, Orme, Brown & Green, 1829)

___, 'Notice of a Journey to the Northward and Also to the Eastward of Cuzco, and Among the Cunchos Indians', *Journal of the Royal Geographical Society of London*, no. 6 (1836)

Muecke, Ulrich (ed.), *The Diary of Heinrich Witt* (Leiden: Brill, 2016)

O'Brien, John Thomond, *A Living Nero in England* (London: 1859)

___, *Monte-Video, Buenos Ayres, and the River Plate: Correspondence with the British government relative to the war between Buenos Ayres and Monte-Video, and the free navigation of the River Plate. With an appendix, detailing some of the acts committed by Rosas, governor of Buenos Ayres* (London: Reynell & Wright, 1845)

___, *Steam Navigation in the Andes, Sixteen Thousand Feet Above the Level of the Sea: General O'Brien's address to British merchants, manufacturers and ship-owners interested in the trade and welfare of Peru and Bolivia* (London, 18 May 1848)

O'Connor, Francis Burdett, *Independencia Americana: Recuerdos de Francisco Burdett O'Connor, coronel del ejército, libertador de Colombia y general de división de los del Perú y del Bolivia*, ed. Tomás O'Connor d'Arlach (Madrid: Ayacucho, 1915)

Paroissien, James, 'James Paroissien's Notes on the Liberating Expedition to Peru', ed. Robin A. Humphreys, *Hispanic American Historical Review*, vol. 31, no. 2 (1951)

Proctor, Robert, *Narrative of a Journey Across the Cordillera of the Andes, and of a Residence in Lima, and Other Parts of Peru, in the Years 1823 and 1825* (London: Constable & Co., 1825)

Riva-Agüero, José de la [P. Pruvonena], *Memorias y documentos para la historia de la independencia del Perú, y causas del mal éxito que tenido ésta* (Paris: Garnier Hermanos, 1858)

Robertson, J.P. and W.P. Robertson, *Letters on South America; Comprising travels on the banks of the Paraná and Rio de la Plata* (3 vols) (London: John Murray, 1843)

Rosas, Juan Manuel de and Felipe Arana *Manifiesto de las razones que legitiman la declaración de guerra contra el gobierno del General D. Andrés Santa Cruz, titulado presidente de la Confederación Perú-Boliviana* (Buenos Aires: 1837)

San Martín, José de, *Su correspondencia (1823–1850)* (Madrid: América, 1919)

Temple, Edmond, *Travels in Various Parts of Peru, Including a Year's Residence in Potosi* (2 vols) (London: Henry Colburn & Richard Bentley, 1830)

Ussher, James M., *Father Fahy: A biography of Anthony Dominic Fahy, O.P., Irish missionary in Argentina (1805–1871)* (Buenos Aires: 1951)

Walton, William, *The Alpaca: Its naturalization in the British Isles considered a national benefit, and as an object of immediate utility to the farmer and manufacturer* (New York: 1845)

Newspapers and periodicals

Argentina

Los Andes

El Archivo Americano y Espíritu de la Prensa del Mundo

El Argos de Buenos Ayres

The British Packet, and Argentine News
El Censor
La Gaceta Mercantil

Britain
Caledonian Mercury
Dublin Review [published in London]
Dundee, Perth and Cupar Advertiser
Glasgow Herald
Leeds Intelligencer
London Evening Standard
Manchester Courier and Lancashire General Advertiser
Manchester Times
Morning Chronicle
Morning Post

Chile
El Argos de Chile

Ireland
Belfast Commercial Chronicle
Cork Examiner
Dublin Daily Express
Dublin Evening Post
Dublin Morning Register
Dublin University Magazine
Dublin Weekly Nation
Freeman's Journal
Saunders's News-letter
Southern Reporter and Cork Commercial Courier
Waterford Chronicle
Waterford News
Weekly Telegraph
Wexford Independent

Peru
El Peruano
Gaceta de Lima

United States
Daily Alta California

Uruguay
Gaceta de Montevideo

SECONDARY SOURCES

Articles

Alborn, Timothy, 'An Irish El Dorado: Recovering gold in County Wicklow', *Journal of British Studies*, vol. 50, no. 2 (2011)

Bielenberg, Andy and Peter M. Solar, 'The Irish Cotton Industry from the Industrial Revolution to Partition', *Irish Economic and Social History*, vol. 34, no. 1 (2007)

Brown, Matthew, 'How Did Rupert Hand Get out of Jail? Colombia and the Atlantic empires, 1830–1833', *History*, vol. 95, no. 317 (2010)

Bulmer-Thomas, Victor, 'British Trade with Latin America in the Nineteenth and Twentieth Centuries', University of London Institute of Latin America Studies, Occasional Papers no. 19 (1998)

Chase Smith, Richard, 'Liberal Ideology and Indigenous Communities in Post-independence Peru', *Journal of International Affairs*, vol. 36, no. 1 (1982)

Cowie, Helen, 'From the Andes to the Outback: Acclimatising alpacas in the British Empire', *Journal of Imperial and Commonwealth History*, vol. 45, no. 4 (2017)

Delaney, Robert W., 'General Miller and the Confederación Perú-Boliviana', *Americas*, vol. 18, no. 3 (1962)

Estellé Méndez, Patricio, 'Epistolario de Don Bernardo O'Higgins con autoridades y corresponsales ingleses, 1817–1831', *Historia*, no. 11 (1972–73)

Farber, Paul Lawrence, 'The Development of Taxidermy and the History of Ornithology', *Isis*, vol. 68, no. 4 (1977)

Favre, Henri, 'Bolívar y los Indios', *Histórica*, vol. 10, no. 1 (1986)

Gittins, Lawrence, 'Innovations in Textile Bleaching in Britain in the Eighteenth Century', *Business History Review*, vol. 53, no. 2 (1979)

Gorry, Paul, 'O'Brien's Baltinglass Origins', in Chris Lawlor and Donal McDonnell (eds), *General O'Brien: West Wicklow to South America* (Naas: West Wicklow Historical Society, 2006)

Hasson Camhi, Moises, 'Viaje y migración de los Blest en los albores de la independencia', *Irish Migration Studies in Latin America*, vol. 7, no. 3 (2010)

Hogan, Juan Luis, 'Juan O'Brien: Camarada de San Martín', *San Martín: Revista del Instituto Nacional Sanmartiniano*, vol. 5, no. 17 (1947)

Leonard, A.G.K., 'Carlton Crescent: Southampton's most spectacular regency development', *Journal of Southampton Local History Forum*, no. 17 (2010)

Llorca-Jaña, Manuel, 'The Impact of Early Nineteenth-century Globalization on Foreign Trade in the Southern Cone: A study of British trade statistics', *Investigaciones de Historia Económica/Economic History Research*, no. 10 (2014)

___, 'The Organisation of British Textile Exports to the River Plate and Chile: Merchant houses in operation, *c.* 1810–59', *Business History*, vol. 53, no. 6 (2011)

Longfield, Ada K., 'Linen and Cotton Printing at Stratford-on-Slaney, County Wicklow', *Journal of the Royal Society of Antiquaries of Ireland*, vol. 75, no. 1 (1945)

Mazzeo de Vivó, Cristina, 'Comerciantes en conflicto. La independencia en el Perú y la transformación de la elite mercantile 1780–1830', *Anuario del Instituto de Historia Argentina*, no. 11 (2011)

McKenna, Patrick, 'The Formation of Hiberno-Argentine Society', in Oliver Marshall (ed.), *English-speaking Communities in Latin America* (Basingstoke: Macmillan, 2000)

___, 'Irish Emigration to Argentina: A different model', in Andy Bielenberg (ed.), *The Irish Diaspora* (Harlow: Longman, 2000)
Murray, Edmundo, 'The Irish "Ingleses" in Nineteenth-century Buenos Aires', *History Ireland,* vol. 16, no. 4 (2008), http://www.historyireland.com/20th-century-contemporary-history/the-irish-ingleses-in-nineteenth-century-buenos-aires (accessed 28 February 2017)
Murray, Edmundo, 'John Thomond O'Brien', in James P. Byrne, Philip Coleman and Jason King (eds), *Ireland and the Americas: Culture, politics, and history: a multidisciplinary encyclopedia*, vol. 1 (Santa Barbara, CA: ABC-Clio, 2008)
Nally, Pat, 'Los Irlandeses en la Argentina', *Familia: Ulster Genealogical Review*, no. 8 (1992)
Nisbet, Stuart and John Foster, 'Protection, Inward Investment and the Early Irish Cotton Industry: The experience of William and John Orr', *Irish Economic and Social History*, vol. 35, no. 1 (2008)
Ocampo, Emilio, 'Rosas y Alvear: Una relación turbulenta y poco conocida', https://entrelafabulaylahistoria.tumblr.com/post/23606644803/rosas-y-alvear-una-relación-turbulenta-y-poco (accessed 1 November 2016)
Platt, D.C.M., 'Foreign Finance in Argentina for the First Half-century of Independence', *Journal of Latin America Studies*, vol. 15, no. 1 (1983)
Racine, Karen, 'A Community of Purpose: British cultural influence during the Spanish American wars for independence', in Oliver Marshall (ed.), *English-speaking Communities in Latin America* (Basingstoke: Macmillan, 2000)
Reynolds, Keld J., 'The Lautaro Lodges', *Americas*, vol. 24, no. 1 (1967)
Riall, Lucy, 'Garibaldi: The first celebrity', *History Today*, vol. 57, no. 8 (2007), www.historytoday.com/archive/garibaldi-first-celebrity (accessed 15 July 2019)
Vines, Gail, 'The Hunt for the Wicklow Gold', *New Scientist*, vol. 193, no. 2,588 (2007)
Wall, Maureen, 'The Rise of a Catholic Middle Class in Eighteenth-century Ireland', *Irish Historical Studies*, vol. 11, no. 42 (1959)

Books

Arana, Diego Barros, *Historia de Chile*, vol. 11 (Santiago: Cervantes, 1890)
Bagshawe, William H.G., *The Bagshawes of Ford: A biographical pedigree* (London: Mitchell & Hughes, 1886)
Belgrano, Mariano, *Repatriación de los restos del general Juan O'Brien, guerrero de la independencia Sud Americana* (Buenos Aires: Kraft, 1938)
Bethell, Leslie (ed.), *The Cambridge History of Latin America (*c. *1870–1930)*, vol. 4 (Cambridge: Cambridge University Press, 1986)
Brake, Laurel and Marysa Demoor (eds), *Dictionary of Nineteenth-century Journalism* (Ghent: Academia Press, 2009)
Brown, Matthew, *Adventuring Through Spanish Colonies: Simón Bolívar, foreign mercenaries and the birth of new nations* (Liverpool: Liverpool University Press, 2006)
Bryant Dakin, Susanna, *The Lives of William Hartnell* (Stanford: Stanford University Press, 1949)
Chavasse, Claude, *The Story of Baltinglass: A history of the parishes of Baltinglass, Ballynure and Rathbran in County Wicklow* (Kilkenny: Kilkenny Journal, 1970)
Colley, Ann C., *Wild Animal Skins in Victorian Britain: Zoos, collections, portraits, and maps* (Farnham: Ashgate, 2014)

Cowie, Helen, *Conquering Nature in Spain and its Empire, 1750–1850* (Manchester: Manchester University Press, 2011)

___, *Exhibiting Animals in Nineteenth-century Britain: Empathy, education, entertainment* (Basingstoke: Palgrave Macmillan, 2014)

___, *Llama* (London: Reaktion, 2017)

De Courcy Ireland, John, *The Admiral from Mayo: A life of Almirante William Brown: father of the Argentine navy* (Dublin: Edmund Burke, 1995)

Díaz-Trechuelo, Lourdes, *Bolívar, Miranda, O'Higgins, S. Martín: Cuatro vidas cruzadas* (Madrid: Encuentro, 1999)

Eakin, Marshall C., *British Enterprise in Brazil: The St John d'el Rey Mining Company and the Morro Velho gold mine, 1830–1960* (Durham, NC: Duke University Press, 1989)

Espejo, General Gerónimo, *El paso de los Andes: Crónica histórica de las operaciones del ejercito de los Andes para la restaración de Chile en 1817* (Buenos Aires: Imprenta de Mayo, 1882)

Famin, César, *Historia de Chile* (Barcelona: Guarda Nacional, 1839)

Fanning, Tim, *Paisanos: The forgotten Irish who changed the face of Latin America* (Dublin: Gill, 2016)

Figueroa, Pedro Pablo, *Vida del Jeneral Don Juan O'Brien: Héroe de la independencia Sud-Americana, Irlandés de nacimiento, Chileno de adopción* (Santiago: Mejia, 1904)

Gallo, Klaus, *Great Britain and Argentina: From invasion to recognition, 1806–26* (Basingstoke: Palgrave, 2001)

Glave, Luis Miguel, *La república instalada: Formación nacional y prensa en el Cuzco 1825–1939* (Lima: Institut français d'études andines, 2004) (digital edition)

Graham-Yooll, Andrew, *The Forgotten Colony: A history of the English-speaking communities in Argentina* (London: Hutchinson, 1981)

___, *Imperial Skirmishes: War and gunboat diplomacy in Latin America* (Oxford: Signal Books, 2002)

Guastavino, Juan Estevan, *Un gesto de O'Brien* (Buenos Aires: Bonarense, 1921)

Hudson, Damián, *Recuerdos históricos sobre la provincia de Cuyo*, vol. 1 (Buenos Aires: Juan A. Alsina, 1898)

Hudson, Thomas, N., *Brothers in Arms: Generals Paroissien and O'Brien* (Buenos Aires: Dunken, 2005)

Humphreys, R.A., *Liberation in South America 1806–1827: The career of James Paroissien* (London: Athlone Press, 1952)

Izarra, Laura, *Narrativas de la diaspora irlandesa bajo la Cruz del Sur* (Buenos Aires: Corregidor, 2010)

Johnson, Lyman L. (ed.), *Death, Dismemberment, and Memory: Body politics in Latin America* (Albuquerque: University of New Mexico Press, 2004)

Kennedy, Líam, and Philip Ollerenshaw (eds), *An Economic History of Ulster, 1820–1940* (Manchester: Manchester University Press, 1985)

Lambert, Eric, *Voluntarios Británicos e Irlandeses en la Gesta Bolivariana* (3 vols) (vol. 1, Caracas: Corporación Venezolana de Guayana, 1981; vols 2–3, Caracas: Ministerio de Defensa, 1993)

Lanctot, Brendan, *Beyond Civilization and Barbarism: Culture and politics in postrevolutionary Argentina* (Lewisburg, Pennsylvania: Bucknell University Press, 2014)

Lawlor, Chris, *In Search of Michael Dwyer* (Naas: Leinster Leader, 2003)

___ and Donal McDonnell (eds), *General O'Brien: West Wicklow to South America* (Naas: West Wicklow Historical Society, 2006)

Lynch, John, *Argentine Caudillo* (Lanham, MD: SR Books, 2001) (digital edition)
___, *The Spanish American Revolutions, 1808–1826* (New York: Norton, 1973)
Marshall, Oliver, *English, Irish and Irish-American Pioneer Settlers in Nineteenth-century Brazil* (Oxford: Centre for Brazilian Studies, University of Oxford, 2005)
___, (ed.), *English-speaking Communities in Latin America* (Basingstoke: Macmillan, 2000)
Miller, Rory, *Britain and Latin America in the Nineteenth and Twentieth Centuries* (Harlow: Longman, 1993)
Mitre, Bartolomé, *Historia de San Martín y de la emancipación Sud-Americana* (2 vols) (vol. 1, Buenos Aires: 1887; vol. 2, Buenos Aires: Félix Lajouane, 1889)
Mulhall, Michael G., *The English in South America* (Buenos Aires: Standard, 1878)
Murray, Fr Thomas, *The Story of the Irish in Argentina* (New York: P.J. Kenedy & Sons, 1919)
Ocampo, Emilio, *La independencia Argentina: De la fábula a la historia* (Buenos Aires: Claridad, 2016)
O'Connor, Francis Burdett, *Independencia Americana: Recuerdos de Francisco Burdett O'Connor, coronel del ejército, libertador de Colombia y general de division de los del Perú y del Bolivia*, ed. Tomás O'Connor d'Arlach (Madrid: Ayacucho, 1915)
O'Donnell, Ruán, *Aftermath: Post-rebellion insurgency in Wicklow, 1799–1803* (Dublin: Irish Academic Press, 2000)
___, *The Rebellion in Wicklow, 1798* (Dublin: Irish Academic Press, 1998)
Ollerenshaw, Philip, *Banking in Nineteenth-century Ireland: The Belfast banks, 1825–1914* (Manchester: Manchester University Press, 1987)
___, 'Industry, 1820–1914', in Líam Kennedy and Philip Ollerenshaw (eds), *An Economic History of Ulster, 1820–1940* (Manchester: Manchester University Press, 1985)
Pigna, Felipe, *La voz del Gran Jefe: Vida y pensamiento de José de San Martín* (Buenos Aires: Planeta, 2014)
Ruggeri, Paula (ed.), *Archivo americano y espíritu de la prensa del mundo: Primera serie 1843–1847* (Buenos Aires: Biblioteca Nacional, 2009)
Sotomayor Valdés, Ramón, *Historia de Chile bajo el gobierno del General Don Joaquín Prieto*, vol. 3 (Santiago: Universitaria, 1980)
Speight, Patrick, *Irish-Argentine Identity in an Age of Political Challenge and Change, 1875–1983* (Oxford: Peter Lang, 2019)
Torres Arancivia, Eduardo, *Corte de virreyes: El entorno del poder en el Perú en el siglo xvii* (Lima: Pontificia Universidad Católica del Peru, 2006)
Vicuña Mackenna, Benjamín, *Al Galope* (Santiago: Gutenberg, 1885)
___, *De Valparaiso a Santiago* (Santiago: Mercurio, 1877)
___, *El Jeneral O'Brien* (Santiago: Universitaria, 1902)
___, 'El Jeneral San Martín después de Chacabuco', *Relaciones Históricas*, vol. 1 (Santiago de Chile: Mercurio, 1877)
___, *El ostracismo del Jeneral D. Bernardo O'Higgins* (Santiago: Mercurio, 1860)
Wilde, José Antonio, *Buenos Aires desde setenta años atras* (Buenos Aires: Imprenta y Librería de Mayo, 1881)
Zinny, Antonio, *Historia de los gobernadores de las provincias argentinas desde 1810 hasta la fecha*, vol. 1 (Buenos Aires: 1879)

Academic theses

Delaney, Robert W., 'The Latin American Career of General William Miller', PhD thesis, University of New Mexico, 1955

LLorca-Jaña, Manuel, 'British Textile Exports to the Southern Cone During the First Half of the Nineteenth Century: Growth, structure and the marketing chain', PhD thesis, University of Leicester, 2009

McKenna, Patrick, 'Nineteenth Century Irish Emigration to, and Settlement in, Argentina', MA thesis, Maynooth University, 1994

Reber, Vera Blinn, 'British Mercantile Houses in Buenos Aires, 1810–1880', PhD thesis, University of Wisconsin, 1972

Online sources

McGuire, James and James Quinn (eds), *Dictionary of Irish Biography* (Cambridge: Cambridge University Press, 2009)

Oxford Dictionary of National Biography (Oxford: Oxford University Press)

Index